TEENS PARENTING

Also by Jeanne Warren Lindsay:

Pregnant Too Soon: Adoption Is an Option

Parenting Preschoolers:
Curriculum Help and Study Guides
(Teacher's Guide)

Parenting Preschoolers:
Study Guides for Child Care Books
(Student Manual)

They'll Read If It Matters:
Study Guides for Books About Pregnancy and Parenting

You'll Read If It Matters:
A Student Manual

TEENS PARENTING

THE CHALLENGE OF
BABIES AND TODDLERS

By Jeanne Warren Lindsay
Illustrated by Pam Patterson Morford

Morning Glory Press
Buena Park, California

MORNING GLORY PRESS
6595 San Haroldo Way   Buena Park, CA 90620
Telephone (714) 828-1998

To the Young Parents
Who Share So Generously on These Pages
Their Views on Childrearing.

Contents

A Teacher's Guide and a Student Study Guide are available for
Teens Parenting. The non-consumable Student Guide contains study
questions, suggested writing assignments, and student projects for
each chapter. The Teacher's Guide includes the study questions with
suggested responses, quizes covering the information in the book,
additional curriculum suggestions, an extensive annotated bibliography
of parenting books, and a section titled "The Fine Art of Teaching
Parenting."

Foreword

Child by child we build the future—that of our Nation, our Society, our communities, our families and ourselves. As our children become physically, emotionally and intellectually strong, so is the strength of our future assured.

Parents stand, then, as guardians of the quality of future life for all of us, as they give daily direction to the growth and development of their children. In turn, as parents are better enabled to undertake and perform the responsibilities involved in their role as parents, the level of life quality is enhanced.

Many have expressed concern, as we are here concerned, with the ability of young parents to meet adequately the challenges of parenting. It is important to point out that many of the characteristics desired in parents need not be related to age: love, affection, concern, compassion, communication and physical stamina—to cite a few. Being younger, and greatly concerned with one's own development and need for independence, may interfere with the proper direction of these qualities toward one's child—but it need not. In fact, being older, if one is overly concerned with the accumulation of life's frustrations, may make it even more difficult to share these qualities with others.

In the areas of knowledge and skill, however, the younger parent is at a distinct disadvantage because of fewer opportunities for training and experience, whether in formal or informal situations. That is precisely why we engage in parenthood education. We need to over-

11

come our knowledge and skill deficiencies by benefiting from the experience of our peers and members of older generations, as well as from the special expertise of professionals whose talents are devoted to particular areas of parental concern.

In reading *Teens Parenting: The Challenge of Babies and Toddlers,* you will benefit from the experience and training of many others. Attention is focused on those topics of pregnancy, childbearing and childrearing identified as important by young parents and professionals who work with them. Specific problems confronting every new parent, but of special concern to young parents, are presented from a balanced view toward current thinking as to how these problems can best be solved.

Much of the discussion herein is in the words of young parents themselves. Their problems are real, expressed as they perceive them. Their solutions are real, too, whether derived from intuition, family interaction, education, or their own practical experience. It is important to keep in mind that, by and large, you are here presented with the "good answers" which selected young parents have given: problem solutions which they will use for their children's life-long benefit.

Somewhere, in a discard pile, are another set of answers to the problems facing young parents—"poor answers" offered by those young parents whose intuition, training and experience have not benefited by the type of careful guidance which, in this instance, Jeanne Lindsay has provided in *Teens Parenting: The Challenge of Babies and Toddlers.* The parenting inadequacies of these young parents will also have a life-long effect—on their children, on our children, and on a lessened quality of future life for us all.

Most young parents want to be good parents. Most young parents can be good parents if they will apply time and energy toward learning the knowledge and building the skills needed for success in the task. Many of us who first became parents while teenagers know that the opportunities of life need not be diminished by early parenting, if we, with those who care for us, strive to overcome the additional challenges which early parenting brings.

November, 1980   Stanley Kruger, Director
                   Parent/Early Childhood and Special Programs
                   U.S. Department of Education
                   Washington, D.C.

Preface

One-fifth of the babies born in the United States each year have teenage mothers. One-third of all first-born children are delivered to women in their teens.

Books about parenting are generally written for older parents. Most parenting books assume father is at home with mother and baby, and that he is earning enough money to support his family. Grandparents come to visit, but the nuclear family of mother, father, and children forms a separate household.

High school textbooks usually follow the same theme. They appear to be written as if the young reader may expect to have a baby several years down the road. The need for day care may be mentioned, but usually within the context of Mother getting a job. Seldom mentioned is the importance of Mother continuing her education.

About 90 percent of all women in the United States bear children. If one-third of these women deliver their first child during their teen years, then three out of every ten high school girls will have a baby before they are 20. About one-third of these young mothers will not be married when their child is born. Of those who marry, many will soon be divorced.

A large majority of these young mothers live with their parents during pregnancy and for some time after the baby is born. Many who move out, either because of marriage or to live on their own, return later to live with their parents.

A teenage mother's life is quite different from the lives of her non-pregnant, non-parent peers. It may also be quite different from the young families who delay childbearing until both parents have completed their education and are able to form their own household.

I have worked with about 350 pregnant teenagers during the past nine years. About five percent of these young women have relinquished their babies for adoption. The others are rearing their children themselves. Because our school district provides an Infant Center to care for their babies, many of these young mothers continue attending school on our campus after they deliver.

They often discuss the ramifications of living with their own parents while they are parents themselves. For example, how do you handle Grandma giving candy to your child when you'd rather she didn't have junk food? How do you child-proof your home when it's really your parents' house or apartment? It gets even more complicated when you must also cope with brothers and sisters.

If you're 16 and you have a child, you know you need your parents' help desperately. You have to "get along" if you don't have money or even the legal right to move out. You may also realize it is a real advantage to have the emotional and, sometimes, financial support of extended family living. But it isn't easy, either for the young parent(s) or for the baby's grandparents.

Excellent materials written especially for pregnant adolescents have recently been published. Care of the newborn is usually discussed along with prenatal care information. Very little has been written, however, for teenagers who are parenting toddlers.

Infants grow up quickly. The 15-year-old who delivered last week will soon be the 17-year-old mother of an active, into-everything, exploring two-year-old. The changes in her life will be even more drastic than those brought about by early pregnancy.

As I worked with young mothers, I looked for the "right" parenting book. I read publishers' catalogs, browsed in book stores and conference exhibit rooms, and talked with other teachers. I was disappointed with most textbooks for the reasons outlined above and for an additional reason—most are written at a high school reading level. I wanted a book which could be used by young women who don't like to read as well as by those who do. Of course I wanted a book written at an adult level. I also wanted a book which discussed single parenthood, living in a three-generation household, and the importance of young parents continuing their education.

Needless to say, I never found the book I wanted.

So I contacted the real experts, the young mothers themselves, and this time I got results. First, I sent a questionnaire to about 200 students and former students. What did they think should be included in a book about parenting? Would they be willing to help produce such a book?

The response was gratifying. Sure enough, three-generation living, financial problems, single parenting, and education-career planning were considered especially important topics. Many young mothers agreed to be interviewed for the book. Others who had moved out of the area sent letters sharing their ideas and experiences.

I decided to limit the book to the first two years of the child's life. I thought the most accurate picture of young mothers' lives would come from discussion of their current situations. Therefore, most of the 61 mothers selected for intensive interviewing had a child less than two years old at the time of our discussion. Two-thirds of the group were mothers of first-born children two years old or younger. Of the others, about half had a second child not yet two. I interviewed these "older" mothers in order to be able to discuss typical life styles of teenage parents several years after their first child was born. Age at first delivery for those interviewed ranged from 13 to 18.

I wish young fathers could have been more involved in this book. A few were present during the interviews, but only eleven of the 61 mothers were married at the time I talked with them. Certainly no effort was made to exclude married mothers. The weighting toward single parents is simply because single mothers are more apt to stay in school than are married teenagers. Because I was looking for "experts," I deliberately favored women who, because they stayed in school, had been enrolled in our parenting class and had utilized the Infant Center for child care.

More detailed information about the young women who were interviewed is given in the Appendix.

The results of the interviews were exciting. Only a few of the young mothers had big problems and seemed discouraged. The overwhelming majority were coping remarkably well with their parenting role and with the other areas of their lives. I took verbatim notes of most of the interviews, and was often astonished at the wisdom and maturity shown by these young people.

At first, I meant to write a book strictly for teenage parents because such a book was not available. I now feel, however, that *Teens Parenting* is a good text for use with non-parent teenagers as well. I think that learning about parenting through the words of other teenagers will make the subject appear extremely relevant to young students. I hope so.

I have another reason for suggesting this book be used as a text with non-parent teenagers. Although most of the young mothers on these pages are coping well with motherhood, I think their stories of the constant responsibilities and sheer hard work involved in rearing a child may encourage teenagers not yet pregnant to delay childbearing until they are older.

Parenting at 15, or even 17, is an extremely difficult task. In fact, parenting at any age is quite a challenge for most of us. I hope this book will help young people, non-parents as well as parents, understand a little better the world of babies and toddlers. I hope it will show them ways of dealing with their children, now and/or in the future, in a loving, caring, teaching manner.

January, 1981

Acknowledgments

Sally McCullough, head teacher, Tracy Infant Center, and Jean Brunelli, Infant Center nurse, shared with me a great deal of their thinking about parenting. In fact, back in the beginning, I suggested that "we" write a book about teenage parenting. Each assured me she was eager to help, but did not want to write the book. Each then proceded to be a marvelous source of information, ideas, suggestions, and support. I appreciate them both tremendously.

My very special consultants for *Teens Parenting,* of course, were the young mothers who shared their ideas on parenting. I am especially grateful to the 61 young women who allowed me to interview them for this book. A detailed description of these young people is included in the Appendix. Their quotes, I feel, are the most important part of each chapter. Although their comments do not reveal their identities, these young parents gave me permission to list their names here.

Thank you, each one of you, for your help in producing "our" book: Alayna Binchi, Alicia Pacheco, Ana Flores, Angel Lucero, Angela Jones, Annette McLaughlin, Ardell Klumper, Barbara Parker, Carol Aragon, Cathy Thuss, Cathy Veloz, Cheri Rutherford Grace, Cindy Quier, Connie Freeman, Connie Neely, Cora Camargo, Darlene Brassell, Dayna Prutch, Debbie Kissling, Debbie Lorberter, Donna Burns, Donna Piascik, Doris Boozer, Emelda Martinez, Estela Mendoza, Eve Tow, Jackie Jacks, Joyce Shelby, Karen Kester, Karina Bergslien, Kathy Moore, Laureen Carey, Lauri Bonsor, Lawanna Neal, Linda Cruz Torres, Lisa Adams, Lisa Bebereia, Lisa Gonzalez,

Lorena Flores, Lori Judd, Lupe Cano, Marcella Climaco, Michele
Priebes, Michelle Viberos, Nancy Harlow, Patty Salley, Paula
Schmidt, Pilar Perez, Priscilla Villaescusa, Renee Whitfield, Ruth
Vander Plas, Sandra Solaryano, Sandy Lawson Ledesma, Sandy
Romito, Susan Davis, Terry Ruiz, Vanessa Parham, Vergie Pensader,
Traci Thompson, Yvonne Jones, and Zena Camerena.

Vera Casey greatly influenced my thinking concerning school age
parents and their parenting capabilities. Vera founded the Berkeley
Parent-Child Education Center and directed it until a few months
before her death from cancer in September, 1980. I had hoped Vera
could provide direct guidance for this book, and I'm sad that she was
not able to do so. She was a remarkable, lovely, caring woman who
made a difference in the lives of many school age parents.

Stanley Kruger, U.S. Office of Education, provided encouragement
and a fine Foreword. Pat Nolcox, director of the Locke High School
Infant Center, read the manuscript, tested part of it in her classroom,
and offered helpful suggestions. Chuck Ramirez, Supervising Worker
for Children's Services, County of Los Angeles, and Don Teague,
Tracy High School English teacher, also checked the completed
manuscript. Each made constructive suggestions. Jim Mead, director
of For Kids Sake, Brea, California, helped with the discipline, toilet
training, and community resource sections. Corrine Ray, Administrator, Los Angeles Poison Control Center, approved the child-
proofing chapter.

Mary Crowley, Barbara Pettingall, and Stephanie Bruner work with
me in the Teen Mother Program. They have been very supportive of
this entire project from student interviews to the pre-publication "trial
run" use of the manuscript in our class.

Most of all, of course, I appreciate Bob and Erin. It takes a lot of
tolerance and love to put up with a wife/mother while she's writing a
book. They handled the experience quite well.

January, 1981   Jeanne Lindsay

Introduction

Parenting a child is both difficult and rewarding. It is probably the most important task many of us will ever perform.

Yet many of us stumble into parenthood almost on impulse, often accidentally. Seldom do we do much advance study in order to learn the arts and the skills necessary for the job. We get pregnant, give birth—and start parenting.

Every child is different. Every parent is different. Mix a child with one or two parents, and you will have a unique, one-of-a-kind mixture every time, a family unit which will never be duplicated.

Because each child and each parent is different, parenting can never become an exact science complete with how-to-do-it rules for each situation. But we do have some commonly accepted standards for raising children. Most of us would agree that a child needs a lot of love and caring from his/her parents. A child needs respect, needs to be treated as a person who matters. A child needs to learn self control, how to cope with the culture in which s/he lives.

This book is a parenting guide especially designed for teenage parents. A major part of it are the comments and parenting suggestions from young people who are "practicing" parents, teenagers who have children of their own.

Some of you reading this book may already be parents. Others will be before you are twenty. One-third of all first-born babies delivered in the United States each year are born to teenage mothers.

But the so-called "teenage pregnancy epidemic" is not discussed

19

here. Teenage parenting is. Many of the young parents quoted in the following pages say they would rather have waited a few years before becoming parents. But they are parents now, and they want to be "good" parents.

> *I never wanted kids until I was about 24 years old. I wanted to be able to walk into a bar by myself before I had a baby. I wanted to have fun like everyone else, like people should, but, well, you know, I have a baby now.*
>
> *It's hard because sometimes I'll think back and say, "What happened to all my plans I made?" Well, it's just that they didn't work out, they didn't even happen. But I still love my baby as much as I would if I were 24 and wanted to have children. (Bev, 17 - Jay, 8 months)*

Whether the young parents on these pages "should" have gotten pregnant and had babies when they did is irrelevant. What matters is that they are working hard at being good parents, and that they are willing to share their stories of young parenthood.

Incidentally, these young people probably are *not* typical of teenage parents across the country. Eighty percent of all teenagers who give birth before 18 never finish high school. Most of the young people quoted here, however, have either finished high school or are in the process of doing so.

Many of them have received AFDC (Aid to Families with Dependent Children) for awhile, but the great majority are, or soon will be, self-supporting.

These young parents live in a school district which provides an Infant Center where their babies are cared for while they attend school. Each young mother works in the Center with her baby for one period each day. Included in their school schedule is a parenting class.

Many of these young mothers may have fallen into parenthood accidentally, but it is no accident that most of them are good parents. They've had help along the way from their families and their community, and, most important, they work hard at their parenting job.

You will meet many of these young parents in the following chapters. Some of them are married, some are single. Whatever their marital status, they are more apt to have money problems than are older parents. They are more likely to be living with their own parents because of their age and/or lack of money.

These young people represent many different situations, but they are alike in attempting to do the best parenting job possible for their children.

Names of the parents and their children and a few personal details have been changed in order to hide their true identities. Parents' and children's ages have not been changed. Their comments are real, and quotes are almost always in the exact words used by the young parent.

This book is written to you. You may be a single parent coping with or without extended family help. You may be one of two people who are parenting together. Or you may not be a parent.

Many teenagers practice parenting skills when they baby-sit someone else's baby. When you take care of a baby or child, even if it's only for a few hours in the evening, you need to know *how*. You'll do a better job if you know what to expect from your young charge, how best to deal with a child of his/her age.

Even if you are never the birth mother or father of a child, you probably will be "parenting" at various times throughout your life. Babies and children are an important part of our culture—after all, we all started out that way!

Chapter One

Parenting Starts with Pregnancy

This book is about parenting. Parenting for most people starts with pregnancy. Some adopt a child, others are foster parents, and many of us take care of other people's children temporarily. Good "parenting" is important in all of these situations.

But the overwhelming majority of parents start their parenting through the process of pregnancy. What happens to the mother during pregnancy has a great deal to do with what happens to the baby. If she sees her doctor regularly, eats the "right" foods, and avoids alcohol, tobacco, and drugs, she is being a "good" parent long before she can hold her baby in her arms.

As important as pregnancy is to the whole parenting picture, this book is not going to give a detailed description of how pregnancy occurs, the development of the baby before birth, or the process of labor and delivery. These topics are well covered in many other books including books and pamphlets written especially for pregnant teenagers. (See "For More Information" at the end of this chapter.)

The importance of early prenatal medical care, good nutrition throughout pregnancy, and the high risks of smoking, drinking, and using drugs while pregnant will be discussed, however, even though these topics are also covered in many other places.

It is these topics *that matter to the baby.* Whether his mother knows what he looks like three months after conception may be important to her, but it's not to the baby. But what his mother is eating three months after conception (and all through pregnancy) is extremely important to that baby.

A detailed study of the reproductive organs and the process of conception may be interesting to the mother, but the fetus doesn't care whether or not she has this information. (The baby is called an embryo during the first two or three months after conception, a fetus during the rest of the pregnancy.) He is vitally interested, however, in whether or not his mother is getting *early* and regular prenatal care—that she sees her doctor throughout pregnancy.

It also makes a great deal of difference to the baby whether or not his mother takes drugs, smokes, or drinks alcohol while he's living in her uterus.

These topics—prenatal care, nutrition, and dangers of drugs, alcohol, and smoking—will be covered briefly in this chapter *because they matter to the baby.*

Of course, they also matter to the mother. The woman who produces a healthy baby is much more apt to be healthy herself. She will surely have an easier, happier pregnancy if she takes good care of herself.

Baby can be most damaged, in fact, during the first two months after conception. Many women don't see a doctor and may not even know they are pregnant during this time.

SEE THE DOCTOR EARLY!

If you have a friend who thinks she is pregnant, strongly encourage her to see a doctor right away. Is she scared? Doesn't know what to do? Then perhaps you can help her find a clinic where she can get a pregnancy test.

Trying to pretend she isn't pregnant won't help anyone. Yet many young women, shocked at the idea of having conceived, ignore the whole thing—sometimes for several months.

Getting her pregnancy verified early is important for several reasons.

First, a lot of girls who don't want to be pregnant go through the agony of thinking they are, when, in fact, they aren't. If she isn't pregnant, she might as well find out. Then, if she doesn't want to be pregnant, she can do something about seeing that she doesn't conceive accidentally.

Second, she has more options if her pregnancy is verified early. If she considers having an abortion, she needs to make her decision as soon as possible. An abortion performed very early in pregnancy, preferably during the first twelve weeks after conception, is easier on the woman both physically and mentally than is a later abortion. Seldom will a clinic or a doctor perform an abortion on a person who is more than twenty weeks pregnant.

For six months I didn't show, I didn't gain weight, and I just didn't think about it. I blocked it out of my mind. Then all of a sudden, I had a sonogram done, and I was 26 weeks pregnant. Of course that was too far along to do anything except keep it. I didn't really realize I couldn't have an abortion until the counselor said, "Well, it's too late now." (Lucia, 16 - placed her baby for adoption)

Third—and perhaps the most important reason for an early pregnancy test—is the need for early and regular prenatal care throughout pregnancy. If your friend is pregnant, she needs to see her doctor right away.

Early prenatal care is essential for baby's as well as mother's health. Many of the problems teenagers face during pregnancy are the result of these young women not seeing their doctors until late in their pregnancies. Anyone who thinks she might be pregnant should be under a doctor's care at least by the time she is three months pregnant.

The doctor will check her carefully for any problems which might interfere with a healthy pregnancy. S/he will probably prescribe prenatal vitamins and recommend the kinds of foods she should be eating.

MEDICAL EXPENSES OF PREGNANCY

Important as it is, medical care during pregnancy and delivery is very expensive. A pregnant teenager may qualify for medical care under her family's health plan. Or she and/or her baby's father may have health insurance through her/his work.

In some states, if she doesn't have health insurance, she may be eligible for Medicaid. If she is, she can get prenatal medical care at no charge to her or to her parents. To find out if this is available where you live, call your local welfare department.

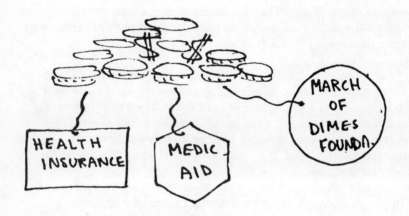

Some areas have prenatal health clinics where women can get prenatal checkups at no charge—or they may be charged according to their income.

The March of Dimes Birth Defects Foundation is concerned about the poor outcome of many teenage pregnancies. They know that teenagers who do not get early medical care are more apt to have serious health problems themselves during pregnancy. They also know that babies born to teenage mothers may be born too soon and be smaller than average. Premature, too-small babies are more likely to have physical and mental handicaps than are bigger, full-term babies.

For these reasons, the March of Dimes Foundation wants to help pregnant teenagers get good prenatal care. If you don't know where to go or how to pay for such care, contact your local March of Dimes office. They may be able to help you.

The important point is—when you are pregnant, no matter how old you are, see your doctor quickly and regularly.

NUTRITION DURING PREGNANCY

"Inside My Mom" is a sound filmstrip produced by the March of Dimes. The hero of the filmstrip is a cartoon fetus who is concerned about his mother's diet. At one point he comments, "If she doesn't start eating better, I'm getting out of here before I'm supposed to." His point is that babies of poorly nourished mothers are apt to be born too early.

The little fetus continues to talk about his mother's eating habits. "Oh good! She's finally getting me something to eat," he exclaims. But in the next scene, his mother is buying from a junk food machine.

The little fetus moans, "Oh no! Just a candy bar. Doesn't she know I need real food?"

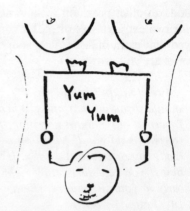

Before long, however, his mother's doctor convinces her that she should eat healthy foods so she will have a healthy baby. She starts eating foods from the Basic Four food groups, and the little fetus is delighted.

A generation ago, doctors wanted pregnant women to limit their weight gain, often to less than 20 pounds. We know now this limit wasn't healthy for the baby. Now most doctors suggest a weight gain between 24 and 35 pounds. If the mother is 17 or younger and still growing, she will need to gain more weight.

So often pregnant teenagers think that if they gain much weight, they'll not be able to get back into their jeans and bikinis. If they were eating a lot of junk food before pregnancy (as too many "normal" teenagers seem to do), they may continue this way of eating. If she has French fries and a coke for a snack very often, a pregnant 16-year-old either won't have any appetite for the nutritious foods she needs—or her weight will shoot up far higher than she or her doctor wants. Gaining 50 to 60 pounds during those nine months certainly isn't healthy either.

> *This time I'm not going to overeat. I'm going to watch my weight, eat good, but not gain too much. Last time I went from 115 to 180 pounds. I'm still ten pounds away from my normal weight—and I'm pregnant again! (Eileen, 18 - Jackie, 17 months)*

The solution is to eat the good food mother and baby need—and not much else. During pregnancy, a woman should have daily at least four servings of fruits and vegetables (preferably more), four servings of bread and cereals, four glasses of milk (more if she's under 18), and three servings of foods from the meat group.

If she eats all of these foods and cuts out most of the cokes, candy, French fries, and chocolate cake, she won't gain too much weight. She should have a healthy pregnancy and a healthy baby—and she should be able to get back into that bikini not too long after her baby is born.

Remember, if you are under 18 and pregnant, you need all the good

foods an older pregnant woman needs
plus two extra glasses of milk. You
need that extra milk because your
bones are still growing.

> *I really didn't know you
> should drink all that milk. When
> I learned more about nutrition, I
> started to eat good. Nutrition is
> really important to the baby. It's
> best if you can start eating right
> early in your pregnancy. (Beth,
> 18 - Patty, 3 weeks)*

Eating enough protein foods is especially important for pregnant
women. Babies whose mothers eat plenty of protein have more brain
cells than do babies whose mothers do not eat at least three servings
of protein foods each day during pregnancy. More brain cells mean a
smarter baby!

Protein foods include all kinds of meat, fish, and poultry. Peanut
butter, refried beans with cheese, baked beans, and eggs are also high
in protein. The milk you drink provides a lot of protein.

During pregnancy, even if you are eating a very good diet, your
doctor will want you to take prenatal vitamins with iron. Don't pick
out your own brand, however. Be safe—take only what the doctor
recommends.

SMOKING / ALCOHOL / DRUGS = CHILD ABUSE

We think of child abuse as damage done to an infant or child, not
to a fetus. But when we consider the real danger to the fetus if the
mother smokes (including pot), uses drugs, or drinks liquor, it appears
that these activities are also a form of child abuse.

Do you smoke? If you are pregnant—or when you become
pregnant—you could do your child a big favor by stopping. Each time
you smoke, your baby has a hard time "breathing" inside you. A
fetus doesn't breathe as we do, of course, but when his mother
smokes, he gets less oxygen. Recent research shows that the fetus may
even be in distress when his mother is in a smoke-filled room.

> *I smoked a lot the first four months I was pregnant. I was hor-
> ribly upset. Inside I knew I was pregnant by two months, but I*

wouldn't admit it, even to myself, for another two months. So I was always nervous and had to have cigarettes. I'd smoke one to 1½ packs a day trying to convince myself I wasn't pregnant. I was just a basketcase, crying and smoking, crying and smoking.

I went to the doctor when I was 4½ months pregnant. When I finally accepted the fact I was pregnant, I cut back on my smoking. Then in my last month I got this real hangup about smoking—even though I hadn't seen Karl yet. I suddenly wanted to do this for him (or her—I didn't know which yet). So I just quit. Then I couldn't stand someone else smoking—it almost made me sick.

I'm still not smoking. I feel I should do everything I can to influence Karl not to smoke. If I get upset and want to smoke, I get a coke or a glass of water or sometimes a carrot or a toothpick—anything but a cigarette. I know if I smoke even one, I'll start again. So I simply can't have that first one. (Kimberly 17 - Karl, 2 months)

Mothers who smoke are far more likely to have a premature and/or small birthweight baby. This fact has been shown over and over with large research projects such as the one reported recently by the U.S. Attorney General. In our school last year, we researched this question. Thirty-nine babies were born to students in our special program for pregnant teenagers. Four of the babies weighed less than six pounds. The mothers of three of those tiny babies smoked during pregnancy, a far higher percentage of smokers than occurred in the class as a whole.

As soon as I found out I was pregnant, I quit smoking because they say you can have a premature baby. I didn't want to take any chances. It's only nine months not to smoke, and you might as well not risk it. After all, it's another life inside you. I did the same thing with drinking. (Cheryl, 16 - Racquelle, 2 months)

Taking drugs during pregnancy is real child abuse. Don't take any unless your doctor prescribes them.

Most of us know not to take "hard" drugs during pregnancy. Babies born to heroin addict mothers are likely to be pathetic little

creatures who go through withdrawal after birth. These tiny babies experience the same kind of agony an adult experiences who, after
becoming addicted to heroin, goes off it cold turkey.

But did you know that drugs sold "over the counter" can also be a
problem to a fetus? The right dose for mother generally means baby is
getting a huge overdose.

Many drugs have been shown to be harmful to the fetus, so many
that March of Dimes literature stresses, "Take no drugs, not even a
nose spray, aspirin, or Tums, unless your doctor prescribes it." And
your doctor will undoubtedly agree with the March of Dimes.

FETAL ALCOHOL SYNDROME (FAS)

*I was into pot pretty bad and into alcohol. Once after I was
one or two months pregnant, I got mad at Jim, so I got drunk,
and I was scared. But Orlando's OK, and now I'm going to stay
clear of it all. He's fine in every way, but I don't want to be
afraid next time. I know that drinking or smoking dope is not going to help matters. It'll make it worse. (Holly, 17 - Orlando, 5
months)*

If you're pregnant, think before you drink—then *don't!* Fetal
Alcohol Syndrome (FAS) is a condition affecting babies whose
mothers drank a lot during pregnancy. We don't know how much "a
lot" is. We only know that alcohol can cause a pattern of physical
and mental defects in the fetus.

An FAS baby may be abnormally small at birth, especially in head
size. Unlike most small newborns, the FAS baby never catches up in
growth. Most of these youngsters have small brains resulting in mild
to severe mental retardation. They are often jittery and have behavior
problems. Almost half of the FAS babies have heart defects which
may require surgery.

The worst thing for a pregnant woman to do is to go on a binge.
Lots of drinking at once is especially risky for the fetus.

"To be safe, forget about drinking throughout pregnancy,"
cautions Anita Gallegos, Assistant Executive Director of the March of
Dimes in Los Angeles. "This is one birth defect the mother alone can
prevent."

*Friends would say, "Oh, just a little (liquor) won't hurt." But
I didn't. I was always trying to think back to those first two or
three months, wondering if I had done a lot of things that would*

harm her. I worried that my baby might not be all right. Smoking is bad enough, but drugs and alcohol—I don't see how anybody could do that during pregnancy. (Beth)

PREPARED CHILDBIRTH

Prepared childbirth means just what it says—preparing for childbirth.

Prepared childbirth classes usually consist of a series of meetings for parents-to-be. Purpose of the meetings is to help the parents understand the processes of labor and delivery. The mother and father, or the mother and another helping person, prepare themselves for the birth of the child.

Mothers and fathers who are prepared will understand what is going on during labor and delivery. They will know how to work with the contractions and the baby in order to get the baby born as comfortably and safely as possible.

Prepared childbirth was a help because I knew what was going to happen, and it didn't scare me so much. It helped a lot with the breathing. Without it, I think I would have panicked. (Vicki, 17 - Deanna, 3 weeks)

Prepared childbirth helped me a lot. It teaches you to concentrate on something so you won't scream. Women (in the hospital) who hadn't had preparation were screaming and screaming, taking out IV's, taking out the fetal monitor, screaming at their husbands—it sounded like a mental hospital, not a delivery ward. (Theresa, 16 - Nick, 6 months)

If/When you are pregnant, check into the prepared childbirth classes in your area. You will be expected to take someone with you to your classes so that s/he can "coach" you during labor. Usually this person is the father of the baby. But if your baby's father either isn't around or he doesn't want to be involved in labor and delivery, ask someone else. Your mother, friend, even your father might make an excellent coach.

The coach plays an important role in prepared childbirth. S/he knows what is going on in your labor, and will be able to coach (tell you what to do) so you can cope better with the whole process. Most hospitals now allow the coach to go into the delivery room with the mother.

Prepared childbirth does not mean any one "method." Any one of several different methods may be used. Neither does prepared childbirth (sometimes called "natural" childbirth) mean you must endure whatever happens without the help of anesthesia. With adequate preparation, however, many women find they need very little help from drugs during labor and delivery.

There are three especially important reasons for taking a prepared childbirth class during pregnancy, according to Mary Crowley, prepared childbirth teacher. First, the class will help you conquer the fear of labor and delivery that you may have.

Second, you will learn about your body and what happens throughout pregnancy and delivery.

Third, you will be able to share your childbirth experience with someone else—the person you choose to be your coach.

"You'll also find you aren't out there all by yourself being pregnant," Ms. Crowley commented. "You'll meet other parents-to-be, and this is one place you can ask *all* your questions about childbirth."

Prepared childbirth will help you understand what's going on when you're going through labor and delivery. My mom will be my coach. I feel better about it now because I understand what will be happening to me when my baby is born. My sister can't believe I know so much about pregnancy. She thinks I'm an expert. (Marlene, 8 months pregnant)

FOR MORE INFORMATION

Good parenting starts with a healthy pregnancy. To learn more about pregnancy and prenatal care, check some of the following resources, most of them written especially for teenagers.

Barr, Linda, and Catherine Monserrat. *Teenage Pregnancy: A New Beginning.* 1978. Albuquerque: New Futures, Inc.

Koschnick, Kay (ed.) *Having a Baby.* 1975. Syracuse, NY: New Readers Press, Laubach Literacy, Inc.

Lindsay, Jeanne Warren. *Pregnant Too Soon: Adoption Is an Option.* 1980. St. Paul: EMC Corporation.

March of Dimes Birth Defects Foundation. "Preparenthood Education Program" (PEP). 1978. White Plains, NY.

U.S. Department of Health, Education, and Welfare. *Prenatal Care.* 1973. Washington, D.C.

Chapter Two
Those First Two Months

Labor is called labor because it's such hard work for the mother. But it's also hard on baby. A just-born baby doesn't look at all like the charming little person in the diaper commercials. Instead, she's apt to seem forlorn and careworn.

When I first saw Patty, I thought, "Golly, was that inside me for nine months?" She didn't look very pretty— too white and awfully tiny. But the doctor said her color would come soon, and it did. (Beth, 18 - Patty, 3 weeks)

Nearly every mother, father, and grandparent, however, will swear she is the most beautiful baby ever born!

It was instant love . . . but still it was hard to believe Dennis was here, that what was inside of me was now a little baby. I thought

*he was cute. What I liked best was his little neck—he didn't have
any! (Andrea, 16 - Dennis, 2½ months)*

WHAT DOES SHE LOOK LIKE?

Most babies look pretty messy after delivery until the nurse cleans
them up. Often a baby's head becomes molded during labor and
delivery. Instead of looking round like most people's heads, hers
seems longer than it should. Sometimes there are bumps and lumps on
her head, too.

*I thought Dennis was ugly. He had a big lump on his head
right in front, but it was down the next day. (Ted, 19, Dennis'
father)*

At birth, the bones in baby's head are soft enough to change shape
slightly in order to go through the birth canal. Within a few days,
baby's head will become round. If her mother is in labor a long time,
baby's head is more apt to undergo molding.

Regardless of their ethnic origin, most babies are fairly red when
they're born, sometimes even purplish looking. By the time she goes
home from the hospital, her skin will look better. When she cries, her
skin may turn red and blotchy. This, too, is normal.

Black babies' skin is often lighter at birth than it will be later. The
skin at the tip of the ear is a good indication of the baby's permanent
color.

*When Racquelle came out, I said, "She's all purple!" Her head
was shaped a little funny because they used forceps. She was all
messy. They held her up and let me kiss her. I almost started crying—it's a real good feeling you get. (Cheryl, 16 - Racquelle, 2
months)*

Babies have a "soft spot," actually more than one, on the top of
their heads. This also helps make it possible for the head to be molded
during birth with no damage to the brain.

Some people are afraid of the soft spot. They think baby might be
injured if the soft spot is touched. However, this spot is covered with
a tough membrane which gives plenty of protection.

The skull doesn't close over the soft spot for about 18 months. During that time, it's important to wash the baby's head thoroughly to
prevent cradle cap. Cradle cap is a scaliness similar to heavy dandruff

which sometimes develops on a baby's head. When you give your baby a shampoo, just massage her head with your finger tips as you would your own. Touching the soft spot is not going to hurt it.

If cradle cap does develop, the best way to treat it is with cotton balls dipped in baby oil. Rub the scalp gently with the oil-soaked cotton until the scales loosen enough to be washed away.

Newborn babies have a couple of inches of umbilical cord still attached to their navels. This cord turns black and usually drops off within a week. Most doctors suggest that baby not be put in water until after the cord drops off. Sometimes the area bleeds a little those first few days. It can be cleaned gently with cotton dipped in alcohol.

Some babies' belly buttons stick out more than usual. In the past, people often put snug binders on their babies—pieces of cloth wrapped firmly around the baby's middle. Sometimes people put tape over the navel, or even taped a penny or other flat item over it. They thought this would keep it from sticking out. Actually, it won't help, and it could cause irritation.

If baby's belly button sticks out, it sticks out. That's all right. This condition usually disappears sometime during childhood. If it sticks out a lot, however, ask your doctor to check for umbilical hernia.

A new baby is not quiet, even when she's not crying. She will hiccup, startle, and shake because her nervous system is still immature. This is not a problem. Sometimes, however, a young mother needs reassurance:

> *Once I got scared because Nick started shaking and making weird sounds after I fed him. It was 1 A.M., and I woke Paul up. He said Nick had the hiccups, so I relaxed. (Theresa, 16 - Nick, 6 months)*

Baby's bowel movements are worth watching. If color, texture, and odor are normal, the number doesn't matter much. A breastfed baby will usually have a BM every time she nurses.

The first bowel movement a baby has after birth is called meconium. Meconium is a greenish-black sticky substance which fills the intestines of babies before they are born. Almost all babies pass meconium during the first day, sometimes for three or four days. Ted, a young father, advised, "Don't get upset by the black poops—that freaked me out!"

All babies lose a few ounces during the first two or three days after birth. This is perfectly normal. Baby will gain it all back within a few days.

Sometimes parents worry about their newborn's eyes. They seem hazy, and sometimes even appear to be crossed. The baby can't focus well yet because nerve connections between her brain and eye muscles aren't complete. Her vision and control will develop gradually, and soon her eyes will stay put.

At birth, most babies' eyes are dark blue or gray. Their eyes will gradually change to their permanent coloring. Some dark-skinned infants are born with dark brown eyes.

Babies, both boys and girls, sometimes have swollen breasts for a few days after delivery. This is caused by the hormones in the mother's body. Sometimes the baby's breasts will contain a little milk—called witch's milk in some cultures. This is normal and will go away within a few days.

Don't squeeze out the milk because that would make more milk form. If there are red lines radiating out from the nipples, call your doctor. Probably an infection has started.

Newborn boys often have very large testicles. In fact, both boys and girls have oversized genitals which appear swollen and red at birth. These are also caused by the mother's hormones. They will become smaller within a couple of weeks.

Girl babies sometimes have a slight amount of bleeding from the vagina for two or three days after delivery. This, too, is caused by mother's hormones. It is nothing to worry about. In fact, if it happens, it will probably be while baby is still in the hospital.

Baby may have birthmarks. Some of these will disappear in time. "Strawberry" marks and dark moles, however, generally stay on baby for life. These marks tend to run in families, and you can do nothing to make them go away. If a strawberry mark has little heads on it from time to time, don't squeeze them.

If the baby becomes too warm, she may develop miliaria. These are little white heads on the surface of the skin, usually on the nose and cheeks. To prevent them, don't overdress your baby. Babies need about the same amount of clothing that you need. This does *not* mean wrapping her in a warm blanket on a hot summer day!

Some boy babies are circumcised soon after birth. This is an operation in which the loose folds of skin at the end of the penis are cut off by the doctor. It heals within a few days. It helps to place gauze strips smeared with vaseline on the penis. If you see any fresh bleeding, tell your doctor.

Before a baby boy can be circumcised, parents must sign a consent form. Before delivery, parents should decide, if they have a boy, whether or not they want him to be circumcised.

Some people feel it is easier to clean a circumcised penis. Others say it is an unnecessary operation. Sometimes deciding whether or not to have a son circumcised depends on the family's ethnic and/or cultural background.

Some parents decide to circumcise or not to circumcise depending on whether the father has had this operation. They think their son might be more comfortable if he "matched" his father. Others think it is important for their son to look like the other boys around him. If most boys are being circumcised, he will be, too.

WHAT DOES A NEW BABY DO?

If you know something about your baby's development, you'll find him more interesting. And if you think he's interesting, you'll give him more attention. If you give him more attention, he'll respond more to you. A beautiful circle to enter!

Of course all babies are different. Even at birth, your baby will look different than other babies in the hospital nursery. He may cry a lot, or he may be quiet much of the time. Most babies sleep a lot the first weeks, but yours may stay awake several hours a day. Accept him as he is and love him.

A newborn human is far more helpless than is a new kitten, colt, or other baby animal. He depends completely on his parents or other caregivers for survival.

But he is able to lift his head off the bed for a few seconds when he is lying on his stomach—long enough to keep him from smothering in a soft mattress. In fact, a baby can't smother by lying face down in a bed with no pillows. When he needs air, he can turn his head enough to get it.

Babies usually respond to sounds at birth. He will startle at a loud noise, perhaps cry.

He can hear rather well. Of course he doesn't understand your words, but he likes the sound of your loving voice. After all, during the last few months before birth, he was "hearing" your voice, or at least feeling the rhythm of it, while he was in your uterus. Now it's important to talk and sing to him. Loud sharp noises and angry voices will

upset him, but he loves your gentle voice.

> *When I changed Sonja's diaper, I always talked to her and*
> *played with her. I'd talk to her when I fed her, too. She always*
> *liked that. (Julie, 16 - Sonja, 7 months)*

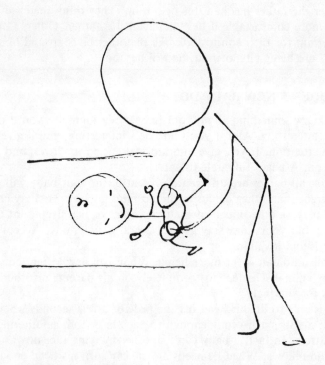

He can't see well when he's born. The world probably looks hazy to
him. He can see objects best which are about nine inches from his
eyes. When he's breastfeeding, this is about the distance between his
and his mother's eyes.

Sometime between birth and six weeks of age, most babies can
begin to follow an object for a short distance with their eyes.

You can "test" this ability with your baby. Use a big brightly
colored object. A piece of red cardboard at least five inches across is
fine. Choose a time when he is awake and comfortable. Hold the
cardboard about 12 inches from his eyes. Move it slowly from one
side to the other. Do his eyes follow? For how long?

At first, he may show interest for only a few seconds. By the time
he is two or three months old, he may watch the item as it moves all
the way from one side of his head to the other.

His favorite "object" is your face. He may look at you occasionally almost from birth. And sometime between birth and about two months of age, he will smile at you.

Experts used to insist that if a new baby looked like he was smiling, it was "only gas." But as Jean Brunelli, our Infant Center nurse, says, "Who ever smiled because they had gas?"

Since your newborn is most interested in looking at faces, make him a "face" for his crib. The simplest way is to draw colorful features on a paper plate. Attach the plate to the side of the crib about ten inches from his head. Choose the side of the crib toward which he most often looks.

Baby's behavior at birth is mostly reflex action. Reflex action means he responds to something without having to learn to do so. Rooting and sucking are reflex actions. While a newborn usually needs some help in finding the nipple, he generally knows how to suck once he gets there.

Another reflex action exhibited by a newborn baby is the "walking" reflex. If you hold him upright with his feet just touching a firm surface, he will take "steps." He will actually place one foot after another while you support his weight. This lasts only a week or so. Then if you hold him upright, he will simply sag rather than making walking movements.

Baby's hands are almost always clenched into fists during the first month or two. This, too, is a reflex action. If you put your finger in his fist and pull back gently, you'll find surprising strength in that little fist.

But the main thing you may notice about your newborn is his sleepiness. During his first days of life "outside," he will probably be alert only about three minutes per hour on the average. He will be even less alert at night (you hope). This "alert" time is in addition to the time baby spends crying because he is hungry, wet, generally uncomfortable, or lonely, and the time he spends eating.

WHAT DOES SHE WANT OUT OF LIFE?

Comfort is the most important thing to a newborn. She is a very sensitive little creature.

Your newborn will probably startle and cry at any sudden change. If there is a loud noise or if her bassinet is jolted, she may cry. If you lift her suddenly from her bed, she may cry.

She will feel more secure if you put your hands carefully under her, then wait a second or two before you lift her. She'll then have time to

adjust to being moved. Of course you *always* provide head support
for a young baby when you are lifting or holding her.

> *That first month was not what I expected. I thought taking
> care of Chandra would be easy, but it was hard. When she cried,
> I thought I could just pick her up and she'd go to sleep right
> away. But she didn't.*
> *It was more work than I expected. I had to fix her milk,
> change her diapers—I didn't think she'd be wet all the time. She
> had to be changed constantly. I'd be watching TV, and I'd hear
> her crying. I'd get kind of mad because I didn't want to move.*
> *(Maria, 18 - Chandra, 6 weeks)*

Comfort first of all means having her needs met. Letting her "cry it
out" makes sense only when you can't do anything to help her feel
better. Even then, most babies prefer to be held in their misery.

Nearly every baby loves to be touched, held, and cuddled. They
have a way of snuggling into your arms that makes both you and
baby feel good. When baby is fussy, holding her upright with her
head near your shoulder may quiet her.

Most parents, if they "let themselves go," love holding their baby.
Touch her, love her. Above all, don't worry about spoiling her in
these early months.

Most experienced mothers and other child development experts
agree that babies under six months of age don't cry because they're
spoiled. We're sure of this because we know babies don't develop a
memory until late in the first year.

"But if I pick her up when she cries, won't she think she can get
whatever she wants by crying?" This old idea simply isn't true. Yes,
she'll cry when she needs something, and she will learn something
from the parent who answers her cries. She'll learn a basic sense of
trust in her world. And that sense of trust is the most important thing
she can learn during her first months.

> *I talked to my great-grandmother before she died (before I was
> pregnant), and she said, "I never let any of my babies cry.
> Whenever a baby cries, it has a need, even if it's just to be held."
> So that was stuck in my head.*
> *So when Sonja was little, if she cried, I fed her. If she cried
> and wanted to be picked up, I picked her up. My mom would tell
> me I would spoil her. She was eating every two hours until she
> was about 2½ months old. (Julie)*

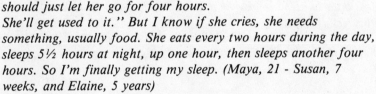

Sometimes Paul will lie there for a long time after he eats. He just looks around. He really gets upset only when he's wet. He hates lying on his back—he cries and screams and hollers. The hospital told me to put him on his side, but that didn't make too much sense. He would roll right back over on his back, and then he would cry more.

We feed him when he cries. He wakes up every three or four hours, sometimes in 2½ hours. My mom thinks I should feed him every time he moves. (Deanna, 16 - Paul, 3 weeks)

Susan is always hungry, even more than Elaine was. I feed her whenever she wants. Some people tell me, "You should just let her go for four hours. She'll get used to it." But I know if she cries, she needs something, usually food. She eats every two hours during the day, sleeps 5½ hours at night, up one hour, then sleeps another four hours. So I'm finally getting my sleep. (Maya, 21 - Susan, 7 weeks, and Elaine, 5 years)

By the way, research shows that babies who are picked up often during their first months cry *less* at one year of age than do the children who weren't picked up when, as infants, they cried.

So hold your baby. Pick her up when she cries. Feed her if she's hungry. (See Chapter Three, "Breast or Bottle Feeding?") Change her if she's wet or messy. Keep her clean, dry, warm (but not too warm), and fed.

When Chandra gets uncomfortable, she just cries and cries and I don't know what to do. My mom works so she's not here during the day to advise me. (Maria)

If she's not hungry, perhaps she is uncomfortable for some other reason. Does she need changing? Was she burped enough at her last feeding? Is she too warm? Too cold?

If nothing seems to work, perhaps she is lonely. Have you ever thought about what it must be like to be able to do nothing except lie in a bassinet by yourself? For nine months, you've been carried securely in your mother's uterus, then suddenly you're outside. And you're expected to sleep by yourself with no human contact. Quite a change!

Perhaps she simply wants to be held. Do you have a rocking chair? Use it! A rocking cradle is also nice for a baby. Sing to her as you rock her.

> *I love rocking Stevie. The one thing my mother insisted on buying before he was born was that rocking chair, and now I know why. (Alison, 18 - Stevie, 2½ months)*

If money for baby things is limited, your baby would undoubtedly rather you'd buy a cheap unpainted or used crib *and* a rocking chair, rather than just a fancy crib.

> *Babies like to be held close. Our friend, when her baby cries, sets him way out on her knees and bounces him up and down. He just cries harder because he doesn't like it. Poor little baby, I feel so sorry for him.*
> *When Stevie cries, we pick him up and hold him close and love him. I think that's pretty important instead of sticking him out there on your knees. (Alison)*

As baby grows older, she probably won't need as much holding and rocking as she did at first.

> *Racquelle is seven weeks old now. She looks more like a little girl, and she's a lot bigger than when she was born. I'll lay a blanket down, and she'll lie there now—I don't have to hold her all the time. At first I was holding her constantly. We don't have a rocking chair so I'd sit on the couch and rock back and forth.*
> *When she cries, I pat her on her back trying to make her burp, or I put her on my legs and pat her back. She just gets this way once in awhile when I feed her. (Cheryl)*

Babies need a lot of sucking. Breastfed babies can probably suck more while eating than bottle-fed babies. If the milk in the bottle is gone, it's gone. But the breast keeps producing a dribble of milk. A baby who needs lots of sucking can get it there.

Lots of babies, however, whether breastfed or bottle-fed, need still

more sucking. Your baby may
find her fist soon after birth.
(Many babies suck their thumbs
while still in mother's womb!)

If she seems to want more
sucking, offer her a pacifier.
Even if the neighbors frown,
giving your baby a pacifier is
fine.

You can throw it away as
soon as she doesn't seem to
need the extra sucking—
probably before the end of
the first year.

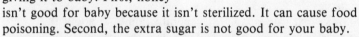

Don't ever dip a pacifier in
honey or anything else before
giving it to baby. First, honey
isn't good for baby because it isn't sterilized. It can cause food
poisoning. Second, the extra sugar is not good for your baby.

Just don't substitute the pacifier for the attention, food, or diaper
changes she wants and needs when she's crying.

Riding in the car is soothing to some babies. However, to be safe in
case of an accident, she should ride in a good car seat instead of in
your arms. See Chapter Eight for car seat suggestions.

*When we have Carol in the car, she's asleep the minute Mario
turns on the motor. When the motor stops, she wakes up and
cries. (Kristyn, 17 - Carol, 2½ months)*

Sometimes swaddling helps a fussy baby. This practice of wrapping
baby tightly in a blanket is common in many cultures. After being
somewhat cramped before birth, baby may feel more secure if she is
wrapped snugly.

To swaddle a baby, center her on the blanket with her head just
over one edge. Pick up an upper corner of the blanket and bring it
down diagonally over her shoulder. Her elbow will be inside, but one
hand should be free. Tuck the corner under baby's knees.

Pull up the other side of the blanket and fold it snugly over baby.
Lift her a little so you can put the edge of the blanket under her.

You'll have a snugly wrapped baby, and you may have a more con-
tented baby. In fact, some infants will sleep better if they are swad-
dled as they are put to bed.

Incidentally, when Stevie is asleep, we let him sleep. A lot of people don't realize this. I've seen friends wake their babies up just because they have company. I think it's important to pick him up when he cries. Or if he's awake and not crying and you want to pick him up, fine. But not when he's sleeping. It's just as important to let him sleep as it is to pick him up when he cries. (Alison)

BABIES AND COLIC

Some babies cry and cry, and it seems impossible to comfort them. Such a baby may have colic. If he does, he may seem to have a stomach ache and have attacks of crying nearly every evening.

His face may suddenly become red; he'll frown, draw up his legs, and scream loudly. When you pick him up and try to comfort him, he keeps screaming, perhaps for 15 to 20 minutes.

Just as he is about to fall asleep, he may start screaming again. He may pass some gas.

No one knows what causes colic. It generally comes at about the same time every day. During the rest of the day, the colicky baby will probably be happy, alert, eat well, and gain weight.

If your baby seems to have colic, check with your doctor to be assured nothing else is wrong. Then make sure he isn't hungry, wet, cold, or lonely. During an attack of colic, holding him on his stomach across your knees may comfort him.

The good news about colic is that baby will grow out of it by the time he is about three months old. In the meantime, he will be harder to live with because of his colic. Comfort him as best you can, and look forward to the time his colic ends.

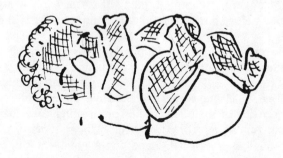

PEACEFUL HOME IS NEEDED

In addition to simple comfort, baby prefers a generally peaceful home. If her parents argue a lot, she will sense it. She may become as upset as they are. One young mother described her first month home with her baby. She lived with the baby's father, and their relationship was not going well.

The baby cried a great deal which proved to be the breaking point in his parents' relationship. Kimberly was so tired from caring for little Karl that she had no time left for Tom. She also resented the fact that he refused to help her take care of their baby. Tom, in turn, felt left out and generally unhappy.

One night they had another terrible argument. Kimberly decided to take Karl and move back with her mother.

> *I stayed there with Tom for two more days, but we weren't speaking. Karl was upset the whole time. In fact, he cried a lot from the day we came home from the hospital.*
>
> *But as soon as we moved in with my mother, he started sleeping through the night. He's been an entirely different baby— instead of crying all the time, he's smiling at us now. I know all that arguing was hard on him. I'm glad I finally found the courage to leave. (Kimberly, 17 - Karl, 2 months)*

Jeanne, mother of two-month-old Eric, explained:

> *Your home life has a lot to do with a child. If I'm tense, he is, too. If a lot of yelling goes on, it bothers the baby.*
>
> *Sometimes Mike and I fight, but we don't in front of the baby. It's really bad to do that because he can feel the tension, and it's not good for him. You would think a two-month-old baby wouldn't know, but they do. If they hear you fighting, it's bad. (Jeanne, 16 - Eric, 2 months)*

BATHING YOUR NEWBORN

We know baby wants to be comfortable. To be comfortable, she needs to be kept clean.

Until baby's navel cord drops off, she shouldn't be put in water. Just give her a "sponge" bath—lay her on a towel in a warm room and wash her with a soapy washcloth. Then rinse her off thoroughly and dry her. Sometimes young mothers worry about that first "real" bath.

*My mother gave Orlando his first bath. She offered for me to
do it, but I let her the first two times. I was totally scared when I
first bathed him. Then I would cry because he cried. I think he
didn't like to be naked. But now he loves it. He even holds on to
the sides. I use a little plastic bathtub. (Holly, 17 - Orlando, 5
months)*

Not all babies like baths, but some love them. By the time they are
four or five months old and can sit up with your support, they usually
begin to enjoy bathtime.

Wash her head and face first. Don't use soap on her face, but you
probably should wash her hair with plain soap at least once a week.
After you have washed and dried her face, use your hand to lather the
rest of her body with plain soap, or wash her without using any soap.
Soap really isn't necessary. Wash the baby's genitals just as you do
the rest of her body. Rinse her thoroughly, wrap her in a towel, and
pat her dry. Be sure you talk to her the entire time.

*Racquelle's first bath was clumsy—I didn't know how to hold
her. I took her down to my sister's house for the first time. I
used her sink, but it was easier at home using the little plastic
bathtub we have. (Cheryl)*

Often mother prefers to bathe baby in the sink. It's a comfortable
height, and she doesn't have to lift the tub to empty the water.

If you live in a family home with a lot of different people, however,
using the sink may interfere with their routine. If you do wash baby in
the sink, be very thorough about cleaning it before and after her bath.

One mother referred to the first bath as "trying to hold on to a wet
seal." She continued:

*A lot of girls are scared to hold the baby because he's too slip-
pery. He's little, but he's a person too, and you shouldn't be
afraid of holding him.*

*Gary likes his bath now—he laughs a little when I wash his hair
with warm water. But he cries when I take him out because he's
cold. (Leica, 18 - Gary, 3½ months)*

Even though some infants find bathtime relaxing and soothing, a lot
of tiny babies don't like their bath. Sometimes when you put her in
the water, she may shiver. If you have a tiny baby who shivers, leave
her shirt on while you bathe her. Don't prolong it. And there's

nothing wrong with using a washcloth to wash her while she lies on the towel.

Don't try to clean any body opening (nose, ears, navel), with cotton-tipped sticks. Anything you can't clean with a corner of a washcloth doesn't need cleaning. You don't need to use cream, lotion, or powder on baby's body either. In fact, some of these products may irritate her skin. Clean babies smell good without the help of these items.

Always test the water to be sure it isn't too hot. Stick your elbow in it. It's more sensitive to temperature than your hands are. If the water feels OK to your elbow, it's all right for baby.

NEVER leave baby alone in her bath.

THE DIAPER QUESTION

Almost anyone in the United States who has ever had a baby must have had a visit from a diaper service salesperson! They'll talk about how much more sanitary their diapers are than any you could wash yourself. (If you use a diaper disinfectant, you can have the same results.) They will talk about the economy—"Only a few dollars per week."

To confuse you further, disposable diapers seem to be used "by everyone." They're easy to use, and may sometimes be considered simply another necessary expense of baby care.

A young mother defended her use of disposable diapers:

> But you don't have to have stinky diaper pails, and you don't have wet babies. They're always clean and fresh when you pick them up. And you don't have all that urine smell in the house. I hardly ever have to change a sheet on Wayne's bed.
>
> Then you don't have that eternal washing, drying, folding, running completely out. And what if you don't have a drier? All the soap, all the bleach. And all that going into the bathroom and there's a diaper soaking in the toilet.
>
> I agree with disposable diapers completely. They are more expensive, but they're worth every penny. You can find specials on them, and when you do, buy them. You know you'll be using them. Coupons help, too. (Erin, 23 - Wayne, 9 months, and Kelton, 7 years)

But it is still possible—and very respectable!—to buy cloth diapers and wash them yourself. You will spend a lot less money.

Before you wash diapers, you should pre-soak them. Fill your washer with warm water. Add one cup white vinegar, but no soap. Put the diapers in the washer and let it run through the cycle. Then wash the diapers, using hot water and a mild detergent.

I use cloth diapers. I don't like disposables. Robin gets rashes from paper and not from cloth diapers. If you rinse them out, they don't stink. I put them in the washer before I leave for school, and put them in the dryer when I get home. I fold them after she goes to sleep.

She stands there in her crib and watches me as I put them in the washer. She laughs at me as if she's saying, "I did it, now you have to clean it up." I separate her other clothes just like I do mine, and wash them once a week. (Melinda, 15 - Robin, 9 months)

I've never used paper diapers. We have a washer and dryer, so it isn't that big a deal. If you were a kid, which would you rather wear? It seems to me I would prefer cloth instead of paper. We got some free disposables in the mail, and I put them on Todd. He kept taking them off. (Jill, 18 - Todd, 16 months)

Before you decide whether to use a diaper service, disposables, or diapers you wash yourself, figure out the comparative cost in *your* area. In Los Angeles in 1980, the following comparison was made:

Average cost of four dozen diapers was about $40. Three loads per week in a laundromat cost $2.25 plus soap and disinfectant. Home laundry should cost less. Thus the first year's diapers plus laundry would total about $155.

Diaper service costs about $28 per month, a total of $336 per year.

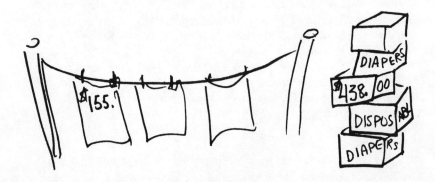

Well-known ("big name") brands of disposable diapers are usually the most expensive. One of the *cheaper* brands (mail order catalog) cost $12.29 for 172 diapers, about 7¢ each. As baby grows bigger, she needs bigger diapers. According to the same catalog, diapers for a toddler cost about 13¢ each.

Most babies need to be changed ten to twelve times each day, sometimes more often at first. At this rate, a year's supply would cost about $438 (12 diapers per day at an average cost of 10¢ each). Remember—some brands are even more expensive.

I was using _____ (big name brand), but now I'm going to the cheapest kind. I decided on disposable diapers out of laziness and because of the smell of having the diapers in the house. And I didn't want the mess of cleaning them out in the toilet. Disposables are a lot more convenient, but they're pretty expensive.

I use cloth diapers when Jay goes to sleep, disposables the rest of the time. I think the cloth is more comfortable when he's sleeping. (Bev, 17 - Jay, 8 months)

I like to use cloth diapers just to save money. Sometimes I buy one of those big boxes of 48 disposable diapers for $5.75, and Sonja goes through it in two to four days. I'd rather save that money to buy me a pair of pants or something for Sonja. (Julie)

It is, indeed, easier to use either disposable diapers or diapers from a commercial service. If you have plenty of money, take your pick.

But if you can't buy everything you want, remember that any money spent on disposable diapers can't be spent on clothes, entertainment, or anything else you'd like to have.

Most of us would find an extra $283 quite welcome at the end of the year—and that's the difference in cost between using disposable diapers or the wash-your-own kind. If you have good laundry facilities, washing diapers isn't hard. And you can always fold them while you watch television.

DEALING WITH DIAPER RASH

During her first month of life, a baby should not wear plastic pants for more than very short periods of time. Her bed can be protected with waterproof pads. So can people's laps—including your own.

When baby starts sleeping ten to twelve hours at night (such luxury!), put two diapers on her. If she still wets an enormous amount—her clothing and bedding are drenched—you can triple-diaper, using a combination of cloth and disposable diapers.

Change the baby often. Wash her with clean water when you change her. The main cause of diaper rash is the ammonia in the urine coming in contact with air. If she gets a rash, it is even more important to wash her thoroughly each time you change her.

You can put cornstarch or baby powder on her bottom after you take off her wet diaper, but it isn't necessary. If you use baby powder, don't shake it directly on baby. Instead, put a little in your hand first, then pat it on the baby. Baby powder shaken in the air can hurt baby's lungs.

There are both prescription and non-prescription remedies for diaper rash. You can get these either as powder or ointment. During the day the powder is better because, each time you change her, you can wash it off without irritating the rash. At night, however, when baby will sleep longer, use the ointment. It will give longer protection.

If baby has a bad diaper rash, let her go without a diaper as much as possible. During her nap you can protect the bed with waterproof sheeting so that she doesn't have to wear a diaper. The air on the rash will help clear it up.

Louise, 19, mother of five-month-old Mark, described her fight with a serious diaper rash:

> *It started all over from below Mark's belly button all the way to the back, and it scared me. It seemed to appear overnight*

*when he was about three months old. It would start to bleed if
you barely touched it.*

*When he was messy or wet, I washed him very gently. Every
time I changed him, I put him in the sink and washed him really
good. He loved that.*

*But that wasn't working—washing him and putting powder on
him each time. I also tried several kinds of non-prescription
medicines, but they didn't do it. Then the nurse called the doctor,
and they wanted to see him right away. They prescribed an ointment, and it started clearing up. But it took two tubes (at $8
each) to heal him completely. This took about a month. He was
cranky, but was pretty good for having such a sore bottom.
(Louise, 19 - Mark, 5½ months, and Meghan, 23 months)*

It's easier to prevent diaper rash than it is to get rid of it. For your
baby's comfort—and your own—change her often. And clean her
thoroughly each time you change her.

WHEN SHOULD YOU CALL YOUR DOCTOR?

*You call the doctor when you don't know what to do because
there is something wrong with the baby. He might get upset if
you overdo it—mine did once—but better safe than sorry.
Sometimes, if I'm worried but don't think there's much wrong, I
go to another mother before I call the doctor. But if she has a
fever or seems sick, I call. (Melinda)*

When should you call your baby's doctor? If he has a rectal
temperature higher than 100 degrees, call. If you take his temperature
under his arm (less disturbing to the baby than is sticking a thermometer into his rectum), and it reads more than 99 degrees, call the
doctor.

The best way to take underarm (called *axillary*) temperature is with
disposable Tempa-dots. These are not widely available in drugstores,
however. If you can get them, use them to take baby's temperature.
Otherwise, use a thermometer. Hospitals use Tempa-dots almost entirely except for taking baby's rectal temperature once immediately
after birth.

If your baby gets a sudden unexplained rash, call your doctor.

Many babies spit up occasionally during the first two months. This
is generally a combination of lumps of partially digested milk com-
bined with watery-looking fluid. They do this because their digestive

tract is not completely mature. This happens more often with premature babies. He will spit up less if you give him frequent small feedings and handle him extra gently after feeding.

Generally, this occasional spitting up is nothing to worry about. But if baby, after every feeding, suddenly vomits most of his meal, call your doctor immediately.

Diarrhea, which can be a serious problem for a tiny baby, is not diagnosed by the number of bowel movements the baby has each day. Rather, it is a thin, watery, foul-smelling discharge. If baby has this condition for as long as twelve hours, call the doctor. A baby with diarrhea can quickly lose a dangerous amount of fluid.

If you think your baby might have a hernia, check with your doctor. A hernia is a bulge around the navel or the seamline between the leg and the tummy. You're most apt to notice it after baby has cried a lot or strained to have a bowel movement. Sometimes it will go away by itself, but occasionally it requires simple surgery. If your doctor recommends surgery, it is usually done during the second year of baby's life.

Usually doctors have you bring the baby in when he is about two weeks old. At this visit it's good to talk about any troubles at all with feeding. If you have any concerns with the cord, if you suspect hernia, or if you have other worries, tell him/her.

It's a good idea on your first visit to the doctor to learn the names of the various people working there. If you know the names of the receptionist and the nurse, you can call them by name when you telephone. If you do so, you're apt to get a more friendly response.

Above all, don't be afraid to ask questions. Write down everything you want to discuss with your doctor. Is s/he always in a hurry? Stop her/him and say, "Wait. I have these questions, and I need your help."

If you briefly describe whatever is worrying you, s/he'll take time to advise you. If not, perhaps you need to look for another doctor who will answer your questions.

The first two months with a new baby offer a real challenge to his parents. Your major task is simply to meet his needs as much as possible.

As we've stressed before, feed him when he's hungry. Change him when he's wet. Talk to him and hold him when he's lonely. He'll reward you by responding to you more and more as the days go by.

Chapter Three

Breast or Bottle Feeding?

Most child-care books correctly point out that breast milk is physically better for baby. But, they quickly add, bottle feeding is fine too.

Lots of babies do great on carefully measured, carefully sterilized formula. To learn how to make formula, simply follow the directions found in every package/can of prepared formula. If baby is lovingly held while he drinks his bottle, he probably feels about as good emotionally, too, as he would if he were breastfed.

SOME PREFER BOTTLE FEEDING

I decided on bottle feeding mostly because of the time—and because my mother bottle-fed all of her babies. I tried breastfeeding in the hospital, and I didn't like it. I wish I hadn't bothered. Sterilizing the bottles doesn't take much time. My sister and my brother sometimes feed her. I use pre-mixed formula—no mixing to do. (Vicki, 17 - Deanna, 3 weeks)

Check the size of the nipple holes occasionally. They should be just big enough so that milk drips slowly from the bottle when you hold it upside down.

If the milk comes out too fast, the holes are too big. He won't get enough sucking as he drinks. The only solution is to buy new nipples.

If the holes are too small, you can enlarge them. Dip a needle in boiling water, then stick it through the nipple holes to make them bigger.

I decided to bottle-feed Jonita because I thought it would be easier to leave her if I had to go someplace. But when she was about two weeks old, I was still leaking. My friend talked me into breastfeeding her then. I did for about a week, but that didn't work out. If I had to do it over, I think I would breastfeed because I felt really close to her that week. It was neat. But fixing bottles doesn't take much time. (Ellen, 17 - Jonita, 6½ months)

The high cost of formula is a problem for many young parents. Ellen continues:

When Jonita was on formula, it was really expensive. At first I was buying the pre-mix, but that got ridiculous. Then I started buying the half-and-half to which you add water. I put her on milk a couple of months ago when she weighed about 14 pounds.

It was a lot cheaper except I had to take her to the doctor because she has bad congestion problems. So the doctor took her off milk and put her on Soylac. If after a month she's still congested, the doctor will run tests. So that's expensive again. That's another reason to breastfeed. (Ellen)

As Ellen knows, some babies are allergic to cow's milk. Ask your doctor if your baby seems to have problems. She will probably prescribe a formula made of soybean powder.

Bottle feeding is a lot easier because I'm always going someplace. (Ginny, 17 - Juan, 4½ months)

In a few situations formula is actually better for baby. If a mother must take medicine which would harm her baby, she shouldn't breastfeed. If she is on drugs or if she smokes a lot, feeding her baby formula would be wiser than breastfeeding.

Bottle feeding just seemed normal to me. I was smoking a lot, and they told me I shouldn't breastfeed because I'd give Mona the nicotine. (Ellie, 17 - Mona, 11 months)

MANY CHOOSE BREASTFEEDING

More and more young mothers in the United States are choosing to breastfeed their babies. For many, it may be because they have been told it's best for the baby. They feel they "owe" their baby the best care possible. For them, this means breastfeeding.

I didn't give Karl any formula for at least a month. He was completely breastfed. I stopped because I was going to work. Mostly I liked breastfeeding—I felt I was doing a little more for him, that I was giving him something directly from me. (Kimberly, 17 - Karl, 2 months)

I breastfed Dennis the first two months, and I'm glad I did. I think it was worth it because it was more convenient then. I also felt closer to him. That's probably why he slept so much and was such a good baby. But I changed to formula recently mostly for my own convenience. With summer here, I wanted a little more freedom. And I wanted Ted to be able to feed him. (Andrea, 17 - Dennis, 2½ months)

Knowing how good breastfeeding is for baby, it is also perfectly all right to choose this method *because it's easier than bottle feeding!* Having no bottles to sterilize, no formula to mix, and no heating required can make life much simpler for a tired new mother. And, of course, breastfeeding is cheaper.

It's really handy. When I go places, I pump because I almost always use breast milk. I've tried formula once in awhile, but Patty spits it up. I'm breastfeeding because they say it's good for the baby. But it's also handy and saves money. You don't have to get up and heat the bottle. That's when I especially like it.

Patty wasn't a very good nurser. I wondered if she was getting enough, but she was. My breasts didn't get very sore, just a little. They gave me stuff at the hospital to put on them, and that helped. (Beth, 18 - Patty, 3 weeks)

It's so easy. We didn't have to drag bottles and milk along when we went camping. (Alison, 18 - Stevie, 2½ months)

Erin, whose first son was born seven years ago when she was 16, now has a nine-month-old son. She described her breastfeeding experiences with the two children:

> *I wanted to breastfeed Kelton (7), but I thought I was doing it wrong. But I wasn't. He wanted to eat every two or three hours, but I thought he should be on a four-hour schedule. I figured maybe he wasn't getting enough to eat. (Grandmother: We were afraid we were starving him.) I had enough milk, I'm sure, but I thought he should just eat every four hours, so I switched to bottles.*
>
> *I'm breastfeeding this one completely. I finally found out they want to eat every two or three hours because they digest breast milk faster. Right now I'm trying to wean Wayne to a cup.*
>
> *Breastfeeding is so much cheaper. Do you know how much that formula costs? You're also supposed to lose weight while you're breastfeeding, and it makes you rest. That's good.*
>
> *I wish I had known with Kelton, but he wanted to eat every two or three hours and we were on that strict schedule. Dumb! You're supposed to feed them every two to 2½ hours because each time they nurse, it stimulates the breast to produce more. I really recommend breastfeeding for anybody. (Erin, 23 - Wayne, 9 months, and Kelton, 7 years)*

BREASTFEEDING TAKES EFFORT

Breastfeeding her first baby hasn't been easy for Holly, but she insists it's worth the effort:

> *I had problems at first. Orlando constantly wanted to suck, and my nipples were getting sore. And my mom kept telling me I was running out of milk. She couldn't breastfeed her own kids, so she seems to be totally against it. I thought about trying a bottle, but Orlando is a breast baby. He loves it, and I do too. He's already 4½ months old, and he won't take a bottle at all. He really should so I could get out once in awhile. But within a month he'll be able to drink some milk from a cup.*
>
> *He loved to breastfeed. I tried a pacifier when my nipples were sore at first, but he didn't like that. Then he started sucking his thumb and that helped. (Holly, 17 - Orlando, 5 months)*

> *I'm breastfeeding Jenny. Once in awhile I give her a bottle. I figure God intended me to breastfeed, that it's the right kind of*

milk for my baby. And I haven't had any problems with breastfeeding.

It seems like I'm closer to her when I breastfeed her because she looks at me and sometimes she smiles. And in the night I don't have to warm any bottle, just breastfeed her. (Rosita, 18 - Jenny, 4 weeks)

Stevie slept a lot the first couple of weeks, but the breast-feeding was hard at first. He wanted to eat constantly, all the time. He nursed at least once every hour or two. My nipples didn't get sore, which surprised my mother. I think it was because I massaged them and tried to get ready for nursing while I was still pregnant.

I'd try to feed him, but sometimes those first two weeks I'd get nervous, and the milk wouldn't come. This made him feel worse, of course. So we bought a can of formula, and he drank some of that. I got more milk, perhaps because I relaxed and quit worrying about him starving.

Some people say you shouldn't offer formula until after breastfeeding is going OK, but this worked for us. Soon I could satisfy him with just breastfeeding. He still hasn't finished that first can of formula. I'd nurse him first, then offer him formula if he still seemed hungry. (Alison)

If Alison had offered the formula first, she probably wouldn't still be breastfeeding. The more the baby sucks, the more milk one's body produces. It made sense to feed him formula if he was still hungry *after* nursing. He had already, through his sucking, "told" her body to produce more milk for next time.

However, for a good start with breast-feeding, it is probably best not to give the baby a bottle during the first month. This gives your breasts and your baby a chance to get well started with breastfeeding. Remember, your breasts create more milk only if stimulated by baby's nursing—or if you express milk (squeeze out) by hand or with a breast pump.

After the first few weeks, it's a good idea to give the baby a bottle occasionally so she'll know how to suck from one. There may be an emergency sometime

when you can't be there. This will also give Grandma and Dad a
chance to feed the baby.

People will tell you to give your baby water. Breastfed babies don't
need additional water. Of course, it's OK to give it to her if she appears to want it.

Is there a La Leche League chapter in your community? La Leche
League is an organization of breastfeeding mothers. A local group will
usually have a series of several meetings dealing with the how-to of
breastfeeding. Members are available to help each other find answers
to questions or problems with breastfeeding.

Check your telephone directory. If you find the League listed, you
may want to call to learn of meetings of possible interest to you. If
you have problems with breastfeeding, you can usually get help by
calling their number.

BREASTFEED IN PUBLIC?

Obviously breastfeeding is the natural way to feed a baby. Since
babies have a habit of getting hungry no matter where they are, ideally mother and baby "should" feel comfortable nursing almost
anywhere. Surely most people would agree that when baby is hungry,
she should be fed.

In some areas, however, breastfeeding is not often done in public
places—a custom which can make life hard for a hungry baby and her
mother if they don't happen to be home at mealtime.

Sometimes mothers choose to bottle feed because they think they
would have to stay home to breastfeed the baby. Many mothers,
however, feel comfortable throwing a blanket completely over the
baby while she nurses. Usually, people assume she's asleep.
Occasionally, you might find a person with a problem. Jeanne described her experience nursing two-month-old Eric in public:

> One time we were at Mike's baseball game, and I went to the
> car to feed Eric. When Mike and his friends came back, I had
> him all covered up with a blanket while I nursed him. They said,
> "Sh-h, he's asleep." I smiled and nodded.
>
> I thought that would work in restaurants. The first couple of
> times I threw a blanket over him and fed him. But people seemed
> to look at me, so I decided to start going into the restroom or out
> to the car.
>
> Mike used to get mad because people did that. One lady actually
> said, "How disgusting. How could you do that while we're

eating?" Mike said, "You know what, lady, you think the breast is for sex. God put it there to feed children." I was embarrassed, but I decided it was she who had the problem, not us. (Jeanne, 16 - Eric, 2 months)

GETTING STARTED

The breasts don't contain real milk for two or three days after delivery. Instead, they produce "colostrum." This is a yellowish substance which contains water, some sugar, minerals, and many important antibodies. This gives the baby some protection against illness. Even a few days of breastfeeding will give your newborn a good start.

If a newborn baby is hungry, he will turn his head toward a gentle touch of your finger or nipple on his cheek. This is called the rooting reflex. As he turns his head, his lips will get ready to suck, a reflex action all ready to go at birth.

So when you're ready to nurse baby, hold him and touch the cheek next to your breast. He'll turn to suck. You can help by holding your nipple between your fingers so baby's nose isn't buried in your breast. Be sure he gets as much as possible of the areola (dark area around the nipple) into his mouth as he sucks. Just two or three minutes on each side are enough the first day. Gradually increase the time until, within a week, your baby will probably nurse about 15 minutes on one side, 10 to 15 minutes on the other.

If you offer the left breast first at one feeding, start with the right one the next time so that baby will empty each one completely. This is important so that your breasts will "know" to produce more milk on both sides.

The more often you nurse your baby, the more milk your breasts will produce. But be careful not to let your nipples get too sore those first few days. If your nipples get sore, keep them dry and expose them to air. Putting pure lanolin on them may make them feel better.

If your breasts get hard and uncomfortable, nurse your baby and/or express the milk. You can freeze this milk for later use as needed.

If milk leaks from your breasts between feedings, you can use purchased pads to protect your clothes. Probably more effective are pads you can make yourself. Cut a cloth diaper into small pieces about three inches square. Sew several layers together, then put in your bra as needed. They're easily washed.

Burp your baby after he finishes nursing at each breast. Just hold him up to your shoulder and pat his back gently. He probably won't

burp as much as he would if he took
a bottle. Breastfed babies don't usually swallow as much air as bottle-fed
babies.

Another very important reason to
choose breastfeeding is the fact that
breastfed babies tend to be ill less
often during their first year of life
than are bottle-fed babies. A breastfed baby is less apt to catch a cold,
for example. Have you ever cared for
a tiny baby who couldn't breathe
because he couldn't blow his nose? If
so, you know how hard it is for both
mother and baby.

*I know how much easier breastfeeding is for me compared to
my mom's friend. She had a baby about the same time I had
Stevie, and she's bottle-feeding him. He's had three colds already,
and Stevie's had none. Her baby cries a lot, too. (Alison)*

Of course, breastfeeding your baby doesn't guarantee no colds for a
year. And if you bottle-feed, you aren't guaranteed a certain number
of colds! All we know is that breastfed babies are *less apt* to get sick
than are their bottle-fed friends. They are also less likely to develop
allergies.

With these facts in mind, make your own decision. If you prefer to
bottle-feed your baby, fine. Above all, don't feel guilty. You certainly
can be a "good" mother, no matter which feeding method you choose.

If, while you are pregnant, all of this seems confusing, perhaps you
simply will decide not to decide. If you breastfeed baby for just a few
days, he'll get the colostrum. If you then decide you don't like
breastfeeding, switch to bottles with a clear conscience.

*I breastfed Danette for a couple of months, but I didn't care
for it. I was leaking through everything, and it just wasn't for
me. It was neat being close to her, but I didn't really like it. I
prefer bottles myself. Every time I wanted to go out, I would
miss one of her feedings. My breasts would be so sore, and they
would hurt so bad. (Caroline, 18 - Danette, 10 months)*

Babies under two months of age don't need and shouldn't have anything to eat except milk.

Their digestive systems aren't ready yet for other foods. In fact, it's best to wait until baby is at least four months old before giving him solid food.

Feeding a two-month-old baby cereal at night is not going to make him sleep all night, according to Jean Brunelli, Infant Center nurse. It may make him cross and fussy the next day because of problems with digestion caused by the cereal. If so, he may be so tired by night that he will sleep better! But don't give the cereal credit for the sleep.

IS SHE GETTING "ENOUGH"?

How do you know if your baby is getting enough milk? If you bottle feed, your doctor will tell you about how much formula your baby needs.

At times, baby won't finish her bottle. You don't need to worry—she probably wasn't as hungry as usual. Her appetite will vary from feeding to feeding. "Enough" at one meal may not be enough next time. But you will find she eats about the same total amount of formula each day.

If you're breastfeeding, your baby will "tell" you. If she has at least six to eight wet diapers each day, if she seems satisfied for at least one or two hours after each feeding, and if she seems to be gaining weight and is active when she's awake, she's undoubtedly getting plenty of milk.

Babies go through times when they suddenly are growing faster and need more food. This often happens at about the following times: one-two weeks, five-seven weeks, and three to four months. If your baby has been nursing every three or four hours, she may suddenly start demanding food more often. She's not telling you you've lost your milk. She's simply saying she wants more.

Nurse her more often—"on demand"—and soon your breasts will be producing more milk to keep up with her increased needs. Then you'll be back to your three- or four-hour schedule. . .and baby will again be getting enough milk.

I pretty much fed him on demand every 3½ to four hours. He was really a good baby. He'd get up to eat at night, then go right back to sleep.

My cousin doesn't believe in feeding on demand. She says Orlando will get fat, that he'll be obsessed with food when he gets older. But Orlando knows when to eat. (Holly)

NO PROPPED BOTTLES—EVER

Whenever you give your baby a bottle, *always* be sure you hold
him. Don't ever lay him down and prop his bottle in his mouth, then
leave him to drink alone.

First of all, he needs the love and emotional support he'll feel from
being in your arms. He also needs eye contact with you while he's
eating. These happenings are all extremely important to baby.

In addition to the loving he gets from being held while he eats, he's
also less likely to have an ear infection if you don't ever prop
his bottle. Most ear infections are caused by baby drinking from a
propped bottle. The passageway from the ear to the throat is still open
in infancy. Milk, if not "served" properly, can go back to his ears
and cause an infection.

Have you ever taken care of a baby who had an ear infection? He'll
cry and cry because he hurts. Even when you've taken him to the doctor and gotten a prescription, it takes a while for it to take effect.
How much easier to hold him while you feed him and not run the risk
of that painful ear infection!

If you need another reason for holding baby while you feed him,
remember that a baby can choke on a propped bottle.

*I blew it with my mother-in-law yesterday. She's been wanting
to keep little Eric for a few hours, and I finally took him over
there. I thought he would be all right while I did some shopping.*

*I came back about two hours later, and I couldn't believe my
eyes. My mother-in-law was working in the kitchen, and there
Eric was on the couch—with a bottle propped in his mouth! You
should have seen him. His little hands were all clenched, and his
whole body looked tense and uptight. Usually when he's eating,
he waves his arms and has such a good time.*

*I was furious. I took a deep breath and said, "If you don't
have time to hold him while he eats, I do," and I picked him up
and went home!*

*Babies need to be held while they're eating. They need that love
and attention. Besides, bottle-propping is dangerous—he could
choke, and it could cause an ear infection. If she ever keeps him
again, she'd better not prop his bottle! (Jeanne)*

LET BABY SET MEAL TIME

How often should you feed baby? A generation ago some "experts" recommended feeding baby by the clock. She should eat every four hours, according to this theory. Or occasionally an extra small baby might need to be fed every three hours.

In that era, you were supposed to wake a sleeping baby if the clock said it was time to feed her. Far worse, you were not to feed her if it wasn't "time." If a baby woke up 30 minutes before her scheduled feeding, you were to let her cry until the "right time." If you couldn't stand that, you could give her a little water—but no milk!

Mother was 16 when she had her first child. She lived with her brother and his wife, and they told her she had to feed her baby every four hours. The baby would lie there and cry and cry while they waited for the four hours. She knows that's not the way to treat a baby. (Erin)

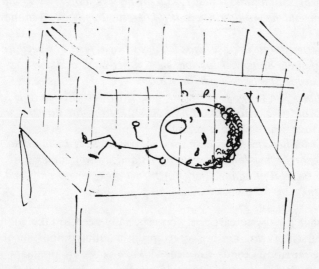

We now think this was a terrible theory. Tiny babies need to be fed when they're hungry. They can't tell time very well for a few years yet, so their hunger pains are not clock-directed. They're simply hungry when they're hungry.

Paula only cries when she's hungry or when she's cold. I don't think she bothers me. Last night she was waking up every 15 minutes. She wanted me to hold her until she went to sleep.

Breastfeeding is working fine. I didn't have much soreness, on- ly the second day when my milk came in. I gave her a little water once, but she doesn't seem to need that.

I feed her about every time she cries—about every two or three hours. The nurses wanted me to feed her every four hours in the hospital. If she was sleeping, I was to wake her up and feed her. I did it there but not here. Sometimes she wants to eat every 1½ hours. They gave me some cream to put on my nipples, but they didn't get sore enough to use it. (Deanna, 15 - Paula, 3 weeks)

During the first couple of months, most of your baby's crying may be due to hunger. Offer her your breast or a bottle first. If she doesn't want food, naturally you don't try to force her to eat. You look for other reasons for her crying. But first you offer milk.

When Nick was little, if he wasn't hungry, he would push my breast away. Sometimes when I thought he was hungry, I would push it in, but he wouldn't take it. (Theresa, 16 - Nick, 6 months)

Patty cries about the average. I don't always feed her because I can tell if she's hungry. I just pat her on her back and she goes back to sleep. She likes a pacifier, too.

Sometimes she sleeps four or five hours. I'll feed her at 10 P.M., and she won't wake up until 3 or 4 A.M. During the day she goes three to four hours without eating.

I don't let her cry for a long time. My mom says I should so she can exercise her lungs, but I can't stand it. Sometimes she cries a little while I change her, but then I pick her up and feed her. (Beth)

If you have a baby to care for, you especially need to take good care of yourself. If you are breastfeeding, it's doubly important that you eat the nutritious foods you needed while you were pregnant.

Drink enough liquids, too—12 to 16 glasses each day of water, milk, fruit juices, etc. "Liquids" is the key word. You probably will drink a lot of milk while you're breastfeeding, but if for some reason you can't, you can still breastfeed. You need to get enough calcium some other way, but it doesn't necessarily take milk to make milk.

It's best for baby if you can limit your drinking of coffee, tea, and soft drinks to two cups each day.

It's absolutely necessary that you get enough rest if you're taking care of a little baby. If you get too tired, you may not be able to produce as much milk. Even if you're bottle-feeding, your baby doesn't need an exhausted mother. *Take care of yourself!*

Chapter Four

How Do Parents Feel?

For two or three weeks after delivery, mother may feel tired. Her stitches will hurt for a few days. If she has no help with baby care, she may wonder how she can do it.

I didn't really want to go home from the hospital. I guess I felt more secure there—I was scared. When I did go home, I wasn't sure what I'd do with him. I was all by myself that first day. Orlando just ate and slept, so we stayed in bed all day. (Holly, 17 - Orlando, 5 months)

It was hard when I first came home. You're in pain at first. Sitting was hard. Nick wasn't that much trouble, except the whole first month he had his days and nights all mixed up. He was up all night and slept all day. (Theresa, 16 - Nick, 6 months)

I'm happy that I had a baby. I wanted one, but after that first week I said, "Oh God, I shouldn't have had this baby." But after the first week, Joe started helping. And I suppose it was after-baby blues, too. (Rosita, 18 - Jenny, 4 weeks)

Don't get upset when he cries. Andrea used to hate it. If Dennis cried for a whole minute, she'd be crying, too.
That first day she was trying to change him, get him dressed, feed him—and he wouldn't shut up for anything. (Ted, 18 - Dennis, 2 months)

AFTER-BABY BLUES

A lot of mothers are unhappy at least part of the time during these
first few weeks. To make things worse, a young mother may think she
should be delighted—this baby for whom she waited so long is finally
here. So why isn't she thrilled?

I had 19 hours of labor, so I was exhausted. I was so happy it
was over that I didn't care about much of anything. I held Karl
while they sewed me up, and while they rolled us back to the
nursery. Then I didn't see him again until the next morning.
I think the hospital was too strict. Next time I want rooming-in
so I can hold the baby whenever I want to. They would bring him
in every three or four hours. All I could do the rest of the time
was look at him through the nursery window—that wasn't very
satisfying.
Because I didn't see much of Karl in the hospital, I wasn't
prepared for the crying when we got home. He cried all night at
first, and I didn't have enough sense to sleep when he did during
the day. I had all these things to do, so when he slept, I'd work
furiously. But then he would keep me up all night. I was
miserable. (Kimberly, 17 - Karl, 2 months)

Because so many mothers get these unhappy feelings after
childbirth, doctors give the condition a name—post-partum depression
or after-baby blues. Realizing how much work a baby takes and how
tied down she is with this tiny helpless creature are two of the reasons
she feels sad. But she also has a physical reason—her body is adjusting to being non-pregnant. Her hormones are working hard trying
to "get over" the nine months of pregnancy. This may make her feel
pretty mixed up sometimes.

Each time Elaine cried, I cried. Not being able to get back in
my clothes bothered me, too. I was pretty depressed from the day
I came home with Elaine until she was about three months old.
Then I started being a little happier, calmer about things. I was
only 16 then. With Susan, I haven't had much depression. (Maya,
21 - Susan, 7 weeks, and Elaine, 5 years)

I would think about everything—the father, how is it going to be
for Patty as she grows older, if she doesn't have a father? Some-
times I would cry and didn't know why. (Beth, 18 - Patty, 3 weeks)

The best cure for after-baby blues is to get some help with baby care and to take some time to do things you want to do for yourself. It also helps a lot to talk to someone. Don't keep those unhappy feelings all bottled up!

If you have just had a baby, and you feel sad even as you look at your beautiful infant, remember that you're not weird. You're perfectly normal, and you'll probably feel better soon.

Have patience with her. The first couple of weeks I was really impatient because I wanted to sleep, and Jenny wouldn't sleep. You should sleep while your baby is sleeping. I had to wash clothes, hang them up, fold them, wash the dishes. You don't have time to sleep, but you have to make time. Sleep was really important to me. (Rosita)

LIFE-STYLE CHANGES

Often a teenaged mother—any mother and most fathers, for that matter—finds caring for a tiny baby changes her style of living a great deal.

I can't do the things I used to do like go to the beach. I have to stay home with the baby. I'm not as free as I used to be. I have to wash clothes and make formula. I don't get as many calls from my friends as I used to. That bothers me. I like to shop and I can't go shopping as much. I'm not dating because I have to be with Chandra all the time.

Sometimes I want to go someplace. I get ready to go, and then . . . suddenly I see the baby there beside me. I've just forgotten her! (Maria, 18 - Chandra, 6 weeks)

I think Deanna knows what I'm thinking. When I get ready to go someplace, she'll be asleep. But when I'm ready to walk out the door, she wakes up and starts crying. Yesterday I went swimming, and she woke up at the last minute just as I was ready to go. Then she woke up again five minutes after I was in the pool. I sit down to eat and she wakes up. (Vicki, 17 - Deanna, 4 weeks)

But as the baby matures, young parents will be able to include her in some activities. Life may never again be quite as simple and carefree for them—no more deciding on the spur of the moment to take off for the beach or the river. Even shopping with a small child is complicated. But with extra planning, it can be done.

My life style is entirely different. Before, I could just get up and leave and do things on instinct. But now we have to plan ahead and take about an hour getting ready to go. You plan your life, too—she's with you so your life has to be different. Especially money—you can't just be spending your money on anything you want now. (Cheryl, 16 - Racquelle, 8 weeks)

My girl friends used to ask me to go with them. They used to call me when he was about two weeks old, and they would say, "Let's go out and have a good time."
I would say, "I can't because I have to take care of Eric." So they would call again and again for about a month, but then they stopped. They knew I couldn't go out with them.
They come over to see me, and they talk about parties and stuff. Then they look at me and say, "I'm sorry," because they're talking about it in front of me. But I don't mind. When Eric's older, he can go with me some places if there isn't drinking and pot. (Jeanne, 16 - Eric, 2 months)

HANDLING STRESS

Bonding with your baby means falling in love. It has all the same ups and downs about it. Anybody who has ever fallen in love with anyone knows there are times when the person you love the most can make you terribly angry as well as lift your spirits remarkably. This can be true of your baby.

Sometime during the first two months you should feel this surge of love, that this baby is truly yours.

But it's all right if sometimes that baby makes you feel angry and frustrated. It's all right that some mothers sometimes want to run away from home.

But all mothers (and fathers) need to learn ways of dealing with this stress. Sometimes it means someone else giving you a break. Sometimes it means leaving the housework and going to visit a friend for a change of pace. Sometimes it may mean calling a hot line. Every mother is going to have some of these feelings at some time.

I remember some nights I just wanted to go crazy because I didn't know what to do.
Being alone is hard. I used to wish that Norm just had half the

responsibility—just to let him have a baby for a week, for a night. But of course I would never do that. But it was hard. It's hard to remember now the times I stayed up at night and just pulled my hair and wanted to run away. I'm at home with the baby most of the time now. (Julie, 16 - Sonja, 7 months)

Girls are often reluctant to ask their fathers to baby-sit, but sometimes a grandfather is a fine person to watch the baby. It gives him a feeling of participating and helping his daughter through a difficult time. It gives him a way to involve himself.

If you start feeling tense and uptight, and you have no one else to take care of the baby, what can you do? Sometimes it's better to put her in her crib where you know she's safe, then walk away from her for a short time. This may be better for baby than if you try to cope with more than you can handle right now.

You may need to get out of the house. Go out in the back yard and walk around. Or run around in circles until you feel the stress go.

There are times when you just want to spank her butt so hard. What I've done a few times is lay Sonja down and take a walk. There have been a couple of times at 2 A.M. when I couldn't do anything with her, so I'd lay her down and walk around the block—even though it's not the safest neighborhood in the world. (Julie)

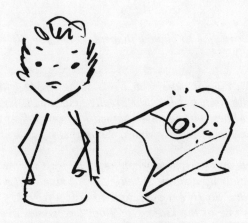

Don't feel guilty about it. Sometimes mothers do that. They know they have to get away, but they still feel guilty. It is OK. It may be very necessary occasionally, especially for a single parent who can't poke a father in the back and say, "It's your turn."

Of course, if you can possibly avoid it, you should never leave your baby alone in an empty house. Julie, who mentioned walking around the block in the middle of the night, lived with her parents. Because they were home, she could leave occasionally when she was upset.

A mother living alone might ask her next-door neighbor to stay with her baby for a short time when she needs to get away. The point is, if you need to get out for awhile, find a way to do so.

WHAT ABOUT FATHER?

How does baby's father feel? About one-third of all teenage mothers are not married when they give birth. Some of these young mothers are quite alone. The baby's father may have left when he learned of the pregnancy. In some cases, he may not even know about the baby.

Often, however, the baby's parents have a close relationship whether or not they are married. Perhaps they took prepared childbirth classes together. He may have been deeply involved coaching the mother throughout labor and delivery.

Once baby and mother come home from the hospital, father may feel he isn't really needed. If he has been brought up to feel that baby care is woman's work, he may not make much effort to help even if he'd like to.

Dennis doesn't like to change diapers. ("Do you?") Well, no . . . (Vicki)

He was always telling me what I was doing wrong with Myles. He's good with him, but he didn't really help much. He was there to play with Myles, but he never bathed him or took any real responsibility. (Janette, 18 - Myles, 7 months)

Bob isn't always here, and when he is, he isn't that much help. Last night I blew up at him. When he gets home, I like to sit down and relax. So I went next door to visit a friend.

As soon as one of the kids says "Boo," he comes over and gets me. I just told him, "Can't I ever leave this house to take a break without having you coming after me, or Meghan tagging along?"

But if he goes out that door to visit some of the guys in the complex here, I'm not to bother him. It seems like Mother is supposed to do everything with the kids. (Louise, 19 - Mark, 5½ months, and Meghan, 23 months)

If you are a young mother, and your baby's father is with you, you may be able to help him take some of the responsibility of caring for his baby. Encourage him to help change, bathe, feed, and rock baby.

Be careful that you don't suggest through words or actions that only you know what to do when baby cries. If you criticize your husband/boy friend, he may soon decide that caring for baby is, indeed, your job, not his to share.

You'll end up getting very tired and perhaps feeling upset. He may decide he's not needed, and that he's being left out of this whole parenting business.

Perhaps he hasn't had much experience with tiny infants. If he seems afraid of doing the wrong thing, show him how to diaper, feed, and rock baby. Before long, he may feel better about the whole situation. Baby will, of course, be better off if both Daddy and Mommy are caring for and loving him. And you will certainly feel better if you can share some of the tasks of baby care.

Theresa, an exhausted young mother, explained:

When you first get home, you have so many things to do. If you're married, you have to fix your husband's clothes, wash and iron them and your own clothes. You have to fix meals. You have to dress your baby, feed him. It takes all your time. I didn't have any help from my mom except she would keep my little brothers away from the baby. (Theresa)

If parenting is a good thing, it must be good for both parents. Often child-care books report that new fathers sometimes feel left out after the baby is born. Mother spends her whole time taking care of baby and doesn't seem to have time for father.

Rather than worrying about "making time for father," she's surely better off including him in the whole scene. New babies need so much loving care that, if both parents are there, both parents can feel—and certainly are—needed.

The first week when I got home from the hospital, I took care of Jenny in the night. But then when I didn't get any sleep and I

was all tired, my husband helped a lot.
He got up in the night and took care
of her. He still gets up with her at
night sometimes, changes her, and
feeds her. They're real close.

A lot of times he tells me, "I know
you have to get out of the house. Go
with your friends, go shopping."
(Rosita)

Babies just want all your attention.
Jay's father lives with us and does his
fair share. He changes his diapers,
gives him a bath, feeds him. He's a
real good father—he loves him very
much.

We're still young, and we have a lot
to learn. That's why I'm still going to
school. When Jay is older and he has
a problem, I want him to come to me.
It's nice having him, but there are a lot
of hard times.

It's hard for Vince, too. By the time I get home from school,
he has to go to work. He comes home about 2 A.M. Then at
5 A.M. he has to get up to look after Jay. Right now (1 P.M.)
he's taking care of little Jay, probably with his eyes half shut.
Usually when I get home at 3 P.M., he goes to sleep. Then he has
to be at work by 6 P.M., and three hours is not enough sleep if
you're 18 years old. (Bev, 17 - Jay, 8 months)

I rock him to sleep. Now that he takes bottles, I can feed him.
I take him when Andrea gets frustrated. I'll probably get more in-
volved when he gets older. Right now he's Mommy's baby. (Ted)

If baby's parents are not married, how much "should" father be included? If the young family lives together, they probably feel much
the same about joint parenting as do married couples. If they don't
live together, there is no pattern cut and ready for them to follow.

Mother and baby may live with mother's parents. They may have
firm opinions about how much—if at all—the young father should be
involved. This can be a difficult situation for everyone.

What about the father who is no longer involved with the mother?

Should he be a part of his baby's life?

> *I'd feel even more alone perhaps if the father had been with me throughout pregnancy, then left. But he left three months after I got pregnant. I'm not in touch with him at all. He's entirely out of the picture.*
>
> *Sometimes I see a friend with her boy friend and baby, and wish Orlando had a father. But other times I wonder if I'd want to share! (Holly)*

> *At first Al saw the baby about every other day, or called up to see how she was. But then I decided I didn't want him to see Patty any more. I told him, and we argued about it. He has the right, I know, and he really does care about her. I had thought he was the type of guy who would say, "So I have a baby, so what?" but he's not.*
>
> *Al had planned to coach me during labor, then we started arguing. The subject wasn't brought up again. I found another coach, a friend of mine, and she did it.*
>
> *I haven't seen him much for quite awhile. When I was first pregnant, we were going to get married. But I didn't want to get married just because of the pregnancy—I think that's a big mistake. Maybe when he works out what he wants to do with his life, maybe . . .*
>
> *Perhaps the real reason I don't want him to see Patty is because I still like him. When he's around here I get really upset. So maybe if/when I don't have these feelings, it will be the right time for him to come around. But now I still care for him a lot, and when I see him with his daughter, I feel sad. I wish things could have worked out. I know he has the right to see her, but I'm not ready for it, that's all. (Beth)*

If the baby's father is providing some financial support—and sometimes even if he's not—he has a right to see his baby. Legally, he may be able to have his child with him part of the time. If the young parents disagree on this matter, they should talk to a lawyer or legal aid group.

About half the children in the United States today will spend at least part of their lives in a one-parent household. Most people still think it's better for a child to have two parents who care about each other. But a single parent can certainly be a loving, "good" parent. It just takes a little more effort.

THREE-GENERATION LIVING

Teenage parents, married as well as single, are more apt to live with their parents than is an older family. How does this change their approach to baby care and child rearing?

The following dialog is typical of the young families interviewed:

Andrea (17): I'm taking most of the responsibility—it's the way it works. They all (sisters, mother) drop little helpful hints, but that's about it. I can ignore those.

Grandmother: At first it was hard because I wanted to hold him. But I tried not to be too overbearing because I didn't want to upset Andrea.

Ted (baby's father): Look at the pictures—you're in every one of them!

Grandmother: I couldn't wait to get him home.

Andrea: Everything upset me that first week. It upset me that Mom took Dennis and was running around the house showing him off.

Grandmother: He was the most beautiful baby in the entire hospital.

Andrea: Mom with the baby and Ted with the camera—that was the first day. I was upset. But I was kind of glad she took him for awhile so I could sleep.

On the positive side, it is often reassuring as well as less tiring to have some help with baby care. So often new parents discover they don't feel they know how to take care of this small creature.

When I came home from the hospital, sometimes I'd feel really scared. I didn't know what to do. I was even scared to carry Racquelle. When she cried and cried, I cried myself because I didn't know what was wrong. (Cheryl)

I could baby-sit easily, but when it came to my baby, I needed my mom. She was too bossy, but I did need her. I wish she could have sometimes asked me instead of telling me what to do.

I'm a new mother and I need help. But I have my own instincts, and I think I know what is best. She thinks her way is much better because she's older and a nurse. But I'm a mother too, and I think I should try my way to see if it works.

If I were living on my own, I think I'd be a nervous wreck. I

wouldn't have anyone to ask for advice. But there are times when I want to try something myself because I want to be the responsible person. (Holly)

Having your mother in the same house can be reassuring. During the early weeks of night feeding, she may even be willing to take an occasional turn at getting up with the baby while you sleep.

She loves me and she loves the baby, but the baby is my responsibility. But a couple of times Sonja would wake up at night and cry and cry. I would cry, too, and Mom would come in and help. But I want Sonja to know me as her mother. (Julie)

"WHO'S MY MOTHER?"

If grandmother takes over in the beginning, it may be hard for baby's own mother to take charge later. The result in many families is a baby who thinks Grandma is her mother. Baby's mother then feels left out and resentful. Most hurt may be baby who isn't sure who mother really is.

I've caught my mother a few times playing the mother role. I can understand that because she has the experience. Besides, I really need that when I'm tired or don't feel good. But other times I don't like it. I'll be playing with Karl, and she'll come in and pick him up and take him off with her. I don't like that at all.

I take Karl with me everywhere I can, and my mother is constantly telling me I shouldn't do that, that I'm not being fair to Karl. But if I had to stay home all the time with him, I'd be miserable. And if I'm miserable, so is Karl. I think it's all right—he's seeing new things, being with people. He's learning more from going places with me.

Sometimes I have to explain to my Mom that I have taken on

*this responsibility of being a mother, and I want to do it the
whole way. I know when Karl is hungry, when he needs a bath,
etc.—but my mom still tries to tell me to do all these things. I try
not to let it bother me—but it does.*

*Because I'm underage, it would be hard to live alone. I
wouldn't have anybody around when I'm sick, I wouldn't have
anybody to talk to—and I couldn't afford a place of my own.
(Kimberly)*

*Sometimes my sisters want to give me advice. I let them say
what they want. I can ignore them.*

*For example, just lately Stevie gets crabby when he's having a
bowel movement. When they see him fussing, they tell me to feed
him. Or they think we should "do" something. They'll shake toys
in front of his face. But he's too little to care much about toys.*

*When he was just two weeks old, they wanted to shake rattles
in his face. He didn't want that. He's just a little baby. I'd tell
them that, and they'd go running to tell my mom, "Alison just
doesn't want us to do anything with her baby." My mom would
laugh and tell them I know what I'm doing.*

*I think my sisters do get annoyed at my being here all the time
with the baby. But when I ask them to baby-sit so I can go out
for a little while, they usually refuse. (Alison, 18 - Stevie, 2½
months)*

Beth realizes how important it is to take care of her baby herself:

*I really can't go anywhere now, especially since I'm breast-
feeding. I'm limited in the things I do, even though I have my
mother around. She loves taking care of Patty, but I don't want
to become dependent on her. I want to take the responsibility.
That's where my older sister kind of messed up. She depended on
my mom to take care of the baby whenever she wanted to go
someplace, and I don't want that to happen. It's nice to have
Mom around though. (Beth)*

Cheryl has also seen the problems in letting Mother take over:

*I thought it would be my mom taking care of Racquelle all the
time. With my two sisters who got pregnant at 16, she took over.
They didn't know anything about taking care of their babies.*

But when I brought her home, I took care of her by myself all

*the time. I showed my mom I could do it. So now that she knows
she doesn't have to take care of her, she will baby-sit sometimes
when I want to go out. (Cheryl)*

If a young mother doesn't want Grandma to take charge, the
secret seems to be in showing that she is indeed capable of caring
for her own child. Alison's mother explained:

*Alison does everything. If I weren't working it would be harder
not to take over. I'm surprised at myself that I haven't done that.
That was a concern I had when she was pregnant. I knew this had
to be her baby, her responsibility. I love babies, and I like to take
care of them, but I've not gotten up even once with Stevie. In
fact, I don't hear him cry at night!*

Her daughter added:

*Stevie's such a good baby—but I do think I have to keep him
quiet. Dad can take quite a bit, but I know he doesn't like to
hear babies cry. It would be a lot harder if he were a fussy baby.
Then I think my family might get irritated. But since he sleeps in
my room, I just pick him up and nurse him when he wakes up at
night. He goes right back to sleep. (Alison)*

If you are a young parent living with your parents, you may feel
you have no choice. You probably also appreciate their help very
much. An extended family of baby, mother and/or father, and grandparents at its best means more love and TLC (Tender Loving Care)
for baby—and that's great!

*It should be easier because I live with my parents. I guess it's
because I don't have to clean the house, wait on a husband, or
cook food. That would be even harder because a baby takes all
your time. Eric likes to be held, walked around the house.*
*I figure if I were married and lived on my own, there is no way
I could make it. Oh, we could, but the house would be a mess
and we'd starve! It takes two hours to clean a house. You can't
just set the baby down for an hour and let him scream.*
*You can't be cooking something and running off to check on
the baby. If you like burned food, you might make it—but I
don't like burned food!*
I don't let my mom watch him because the baby is my respon-

sibility—she has already raised her kids. I'm home most of the time.

My parents don't tell me what to do. I can come and go as I want. I could stay out until 3 A.M.—but how could I? Who would take a two-month-old baby out in the cold until 3 A.M.? When I want to go someplace, I have to pack a diaper bag, and take a bunch of diapers, two sets of extra clothes, and a heated bottle in a thermos. (Jeanne)

WILL EVERYONE AGREE?

With more people in the house, there will be more interacting —more people who may wake up when baby cries, and more people who resent the mess of wet diapers and other baby things around.

With more people, there will be more disagreement, too, as to whether baby needs to be picked up when she cries, or whether she is simply trying to get to sleep. "Don't pick her up, you'll spoil her" can be fighting words if it's Grandma talking to a young mother convinced that a newborn's crying means something is wrong.

My mom is really good, and she helps me a lot. But there are some things I disagree with her about. I don't think you can spoil a newborn baby, and that is one thing I feel strongly about. I just don't feel you can spoil a newborn. She needs all the loving she can get.

My mom tells me I shouldn't pick Patty up when she cries, but I won't let her cry very long. I tell her times change, she raised five, but I've learned some things, too. (Beth)

Three generations—baby, parents, and grandparents—living in the same house or apartment means everyone must give a little, sometimes a lot. When you get uptight, try to remember that all that extra love can be a real advantage for your baby.

Chapter Five

Two-Five Months:
Your Infant-Person

I got a lot done those first few weeks because Dennis slept so much. It was almost boring at first because all he did was lie there—compared to now, anyhow. People told me it wouldn't last, and now I know. He's 2½ months old, and suddenly he's awake a lot.

He has a real personality, and he's almost always happy. He only cries when he's hungry. All along, I've fed him about every time he cried, and that's worked well.

We take him with us almost everywhere. Last week we took him camping for three days. Another friend with a baby went with us, and we took turns taking care of the babies. We had a good time. (Andrea, 17 - Dennis, 2½ months)

Now at five months, Orlando is more alert, more a person. When he was little, he just lay there and really couldn't see me clearly. Now he rolls over, coos, growls (really!), plays with his feet and his hands, and laughs. When he was a newborn I held him a lot, and he loved that. Now, I hold him and play with him. I spend about as much time playing with him now as I did holding him, perhaps a little more. He's teething now, and is a little fussy. (Holly, 17 - Orlando, 5 months)

Your newborn's main interest is his own comfort. When he's hungry, he wants and needs to be fed—now. He may hate wet or messy diapers, or he may not seem to notice. If he doesn't like them, he lets you know by crying.

Even if he has been fed and changed, and you know he is neither too warm nor too cold, he may still cry. Often it's because he's lonely. Or he may be a colicky baby who just cries more than some babies do.

When Lance was a baby, he always had to be held. He was colicky, and we walked with him a lot. Then overnight at about four months, he changed and was the best little baby. Then he was happy, didn't cry much any more. What a change. I could leave him alone, or set him in his chair, and he would watch me fold clothes. I could never do that before. (Celia, 21 - Lance, 18 months, and Laurel, 4 years)

Your main job as a parent of a newborn infant is to help him be as comfortable as possible. You feed him when he's hungry, change his diaper when necessary, hold him when he wants you to. But most of his days and nights—16 to 18 hours daily—the newborn spends sleeping.

When he is awake and needs you, you are the one who talks, smiles, interacts with him. He responds, but far less at birth than he will a month or two later.

HIS WORLD CHANGES

By the time he is two months old, baby's world—and yours—is changing rapidly. During the next three months, that usually sleepy infant turns into a little person who can "do something."

Juan tries to talk back to you, and he makes noises. He's usually happy and has a big smile. He laughs out loud now and it's cute.

He sleeps through the night. When he woke up in the morning, he used to cry right away. Now he plays awhile until I wake up. He sleeps with a bear, and when he wakes up, he talks to it. He goes all over the place on his bed turning back and forth.

Picking him up before, he was just there, but now he has a lot more personality. Now he's a real person. He's so strong you wouldn't believe it. He got hold of my ear this morning until it really hurt!

He loves his bath—even likes his hair washed. It makes him tired, too, makes him go to sleep. (Ginny, 17 - Juan, 4 months)

Perhaps the most exciting thing a two-month-old does is to smile. If she feels good, she'll smile at almost anyone.

Four months is a popular age for taking pictures for baby food advertisements—and for sending to grandparents. You can almost depend on baby to smile and look great while doing so. By this time, too, she will probably be giggling and laughing out loud.

Kerry just started laughing out loud. I was washing her under her neck and she started laughing. I really got excited. I think that's something special. (Leslie, 20 - Kerry, 4 months, and Amy, 27 months)

Between two and five months, your baby is mainly exploring things in relationship to her own body. She discovers her hands, her feet, the joy of rolling around, the thrill of finding herself in a new place.

About a week ago Gary discovered his feet. He pulls on them, tries to stick them in his mouth. He coos, yells, screams all the time.

He's starting to laugh out loud now. He's happy all the time except when he's wet or hungry. (Lecia, 18 - Gary, 3½ months)

HANDS ARE BIG DISCOVERY

A big and important change occurs when he starts looking at his hands. Sometimes this is called "hand regard." At first, his hands are fisted, and he doesn't seem to be aware of them. He puts his fist in his mouth and sucks on it soon after birth, but this is more a reflex action, not a learned activity.

But soon, usually during his third month, he will truly notice his hands. He will hold one hand in front of his face and stare at it, sometimes for several minutes.

Stevie is beginning to look at his hands. Yesterday he looked down and got almost bug-eyed staring at his hand. (Alison, 18 - Stevie, 2½ months)

Carol sticks her hands in her mouth, looks at them, clasps them on her stomach. She started staring at her hands last Thursday. (Kristyn, 17 - Carol, 3 months)

She looks at her hands now partly because she can see them more clearly. During her first month or two of life, she couldn't see small nearby objects very well. The world was a little hazy for her. But by the time she is three or four months old, she probably can see about as well as any adult.

As her hands become less and less fisted, she will be able to move her fingers. This gives her something more to study. You may see her staring at her hands, moving her fingers back and forth, for five to ten minutes at a time.

You can make looking at her hands even more interesting for baby by making little wristbands for her. With brightly colored yarn, knit little wristlets. Or use red and yellow pieces of fabric. Make the wristbands either by using elastic (not too tight) or sewing on snaps to fasten the band. Put one on baby's right hand for a few minutes. Next time, put it on her left hand. But leave it on her wrist for a very short time. Her attention span is extremely short.

Sometime during this three month period, baby will bring her hands together. Up until now, remember, she hasn't had much, if any, experience with those two hands feeling each other. Soon she will be able to pass objects from one hand to the other—a complicated behavior indeed.

A week or two after baby starts staring at her hands, she may begin to bat at objects. If you hold a rattle five or six inches from her eyes, she will not only look at it, but she may also raise her fist and try to hit it.

When she is three or four months old, she will be able to hold her legs up. When she's on her back, she'll soon start kicking. If she feels pressure against the soles of her feet, she may push against this pressure over and over.

You can provide pressure to her feet in two ways. First, if the end of the crib is solid, place her so she can push against it with her feet. Second, you can briefly stand her on a hard surface. She may enjoy pushing down with her feet for a minute or two.

CURIOSITY DEVELOPS

His curiosity is growing fast, and he wants to touch and handle everything possible.

Juan likes to feel and chew on things. He knows different textures, and if it's coarse, he doesn't like to hang on to it. He likes his little bunny and dog because they're soft—he puts them all over his face. Buffy (poodle) is really good around him. He licks Juan's foot. (Ginny)

No longer can you give him a flimsy paper plate face to look at. Now his mobile must be strong enough to be hit, pulled, and abused—if he can reach it at all. And it's less frustrating to baby to have the mobile placed close enough to be touched and handled.

Delphina has a mobile of bears with music, and she grabs them. She loves sitting in a swing and watching the mobile go around. (Tiffany, 18 - Delphina, 4 months)

Your baby will enjoy a well-designed mobile, preferably one he can reach and touch. This, of course, means a very sturdy mobile. When you make or buy a mobile for baby, look at it from his angle. Most mobiles look pretty to an adult entering the room. However, baby probably can't see much of anything except the feet of the animals on the mobile.

At this age, he needs a crib toy. It must be "battable" and safe. It also should make a noise—such as several rattles hanging within batting range. Don't use something hanging from a string. Baby will get too frustrated trying to grab it and finding it's apt to fly out of his reach. Think of yourself in the dark trying to turn on an old-fashioned electric light bulb—the kind with the string you pull to turn it on—and the string always seems to jump out of reach. Baby will have the same problem with a toy that is not attached fairly solidly.

An inexpensive cradle gym is a good purchase. It should have a few simple objects that a baby can hit, pull on, and handle.

Sometime during this stage, or soon after, baby will be able to reach for things he sees. This is quite different from his earlier batting at objects. Now he sees the object, reaches for it smoothly, and either opens or closes his fingers before he touches it.

> *Juan pulls on the handle of the cradle gym in the playpen. He pulls it down, then lets it go. He got frustrated this morning because he tried to crawl to get what he wanted, and he just couldn't do it. (Ginny)*

SHE LISTENS AND "TALKS"

By two or three months, baby will hear a sound, then look to see where it's coming from. Sometime during this stage, the sound of your footsteps coming toward her room may quiet her while she watches for you. She may enjoy soothing music, although she undoubtedly prefers the sound of your voice singing to her.

> *I put my radio on to put Juan to sleep, and he moves his foot up and down in rhythm to the music. (Ginny)*

A four-month-old hears as well as most adults, and she will have a good time making sounds with her own saliva. Sometimes she will entertain herself for fairly long periods of time by making these delightful noises.

> *Carol plays with her saliva, makes sounds by spitting it out. I heard her say Dada once, I really did. I screamed and ran to get Mario, but she hasn't done it since. (Kristyn)*

Baby is becoming much more active now. It's even more important that you talk to her, but talk to her, don't lecture. Hold a dialog even though she doesn't "answer" in words. Ask questions, then pause for her answer. That's how she learns about speech patterns. Before long she will be responding to you with her brand of talking.

Don't use "baby talk" with her. She will learn faster if she hears words pronounced correctly. Learning baby talk is not what she needs. She wants to talk like you do.

> *I talk to Gary and he goos back at me. He looks at my mouth and tries to copy my expressions and what I do with my mouth. (Leica)*

Kerry is talked to all the time. We have two other people living here, and I take her over to my mom's about three times a week. Everybody talks to her. I like talking to her because she smiles. (Leslie)

BUILD TRUST BY RESPONDING

It's still important to respond to your baby's cries as promptly as possible. Letting him learn that he can trust you to take care of his needs is not going to spoil him. Unhappy, dissatisfied, "spoiled" babies are far more apt to be babies who are already learning that mother can't be depended on to come when needed.

Jay is a good baby. Some babies cry for no reason, but he just cries when he wants something, has messy pants, or wants to eat. But he has his fussy days when he just wants to cry. Yesterday was one of those. I barely got home from school when he started crying, and he didn't stop until 10 P.M. when he went to bed. I think he's cutting teeth. Sometimes it's hard having a baby. (Bev, 17 - Jay, 8 months)

Continue to hold your baby and to rock him. But now you will be able to do a lot more with him. This stage is usually delightful for parents. Babies are generally happy, as happy as they will ever be. They generously reward you with big smiles when you give them the attention they want and need.

Pedro laughs a lot more than he did, and he's awake more now. He looks at animals and smiles. I took him to the San Diego zoo, and he liked it. He'd wave his hands.

Yesterday I took him to the store because I was buying him some toys. He liked it because all the toys are bright. He stared at them and started laughing. (Maria, 17 - Pedro, 2 months)

Mark giggles and that thrills me to death. I try to get Bob to hurry and listen. I tickle his belly and he giggles. (Louise, 19 - Mark, 5½ months, and Meghan, 23 months)

This stage is the last time your baby will spend most of his time on his back or on his stomach. He will soon learn to turn over from back to stomach and from stomach to back. He's probably awake about half the time now, and he may seem happy much of the time. Illness, indigestion, and cutting teeth, of course, can cause unhappiness. Generally, however, things look good to a two- to five-month-old individual.

For a couple of weeks recently we had problems. Dennis caught a cold, then he got his shots. I decided to put him on formula (I'd been breastfeeding), and he was allergic to it. But that's all worked out now. He's over his cold, and the second formula we tried works fine. (Andrea)

Everybody says it's like a piece of cake taking care of a baby this age. I don't quite agree—but the only time I've gotten really upset was once when Juan was sick and I was staying up all night rocking him. I had bronchitis, and then he got a cold. Then he got a lot of congestion. I put his bed up with a humidifier in there. He slept about 15 minutes that night. I rocked him all night. It was a long night! He finally went down about 5 A.M.—giving me two hours of sleep before I had to go to school. (Ginny)

Don't ever leave your baby or toddler alone in your house or apartment—even if he's sleeping. Don't ever leave him alone in your parked car either, even if you're just running into the store for one quick item.

SELF-ESTEEM IS CRUCIAL

Self-esteem is extremely important for all of us. Parents must think well of themselves before they can truly think well of their baby. To feel good about someone else, you start out by feeling good about yourself.

But you can help baby gain a good sense of self-esteem. Whenever she does something different, learns a new skill, cheer her on. If she bats at an object and manages to hit it, praise her. When she can finally grab that object, get excited with her.

Juan will be playing on the floor while I'm doing the dishes. I'll turn to him every couple of minutes and say his name, and I

*think he's beginning to know it. I don't ever call him names like
Fathead, because when he gets bigger, he'd believe it. When he
burps, I always say, "Good boy." (Ginny)*

Babies come equipped with a delightful urge to learn. Watch the
baby who has just learned to turn from her back to her stomach. She
will practice her new skill over and over and over again. She'll be
thrilled each time she does so. Being able to do something today that
she couldn't do yesterday excites her—especially if you're excited, too,
and show her you are.

*Delphina started turning over about two weeks ago. I leave her
on the floor, and she turns over. She loves it. (Tiffany)*

*Mark just started turning from his back over to his belly last
Friday, and he does it constantly. He's really thrilled at learning
something. He thinks that's super. (Louise)*

An infant seat is a good purchase for this age. You can overuse it,
however. Baby prefers to be carried in your arms or in a back or chest
carrier rather than in a cold plastic seat. But when you're working,
you can place her infant seat near you. She'll love watching you and
the other activities around her.

By three or four months, baby can sit up with support. Sitting
upright gives her a much better view of her world. Think about
it—how much could you see if you were usually lying down? What a
difference it makes to be able to sit up!

*Now Delphina likes to be propped up on the couch. I think it
makes her feel big. (Tiffany)*

*Carol scoots. Sometimes I put her down on one side of the
blanket. Then if I go put clothes in the dryer, she is off the
blanket when I come back.*

*She rolls over both from back to stomach and the other way.
We help her with pillows. She can sit up for a second, then she
falls back down. (Kristyn)*

If the weather is pleasant, baby will love going outdoors. Lay her
on a blanket under a tree where she can watch the sunlight coming
through and hear the rustling of the leaves. Don't leave her outside
alone, however, unless you're working by a window very close to her.

PLAY WITH BABY

Now is the time to start playing regularly with your baby. If he is awake about half his day, he has time for a lot of interaction with you. Playing with him, however, doesn't mean you get nothing else done all day. To baby, talking and singing to him while you work and he watches you is play.

Specific games with baby are fun, but at this stage, they need take only a few minutes. Patty-cake and peek-a-boo are the old standbys.

He'll also love having his skin gently massaged. Several books are available which describe simple exercises you can do with baby. The most important thing is your interaction with him. It doesn't mean complicated, time-consuming games—baby wouldn't like that yet. It does mean giving him your full attention part of the time.

Perhaps you'll gently tickle him, move his legs slowly up and down, or give him a variety of objects to hit and grab. He'll appreciate the attention.

Babies like excitement—their version of excitement. Instead of going to sleep right after eating, he now wants to play. "Play" means rocking, talking, laughing, listening. Start playing games with your baby for brief periods of time.

I play with Orlando—clap my hands, play patty-cake, sing to him, talk to him. He holds his head up now. He doesn't like to play by himself yet, so I lie on the floor with him. When he gets bored, I squeak the toys for him. He plays with his feet when he's in the infant seat. He loves to chew because he's teething. He's hanging on to things pretty well, and he chews on everything. (Holly)

I lay Gary in bed with me sometimes, and he pulls on my nose or pulls my hair, just to get me up. He kicks and he loves to stand up. Everything goes in his mouth. I set him in his little stroller in the room where I'm working, and he watches me. (Leica)

Mark stares and touches and tries to grab things. Last night Meghan had a bowl of dry cereal about six inches out of his reach. He managed to reach it and spill it all over! (Louise)

Give your child a chance to do a lot of looking, feeling, and handling of objects. Perhaps more important, give him plenty of opportunities to socialize with you and other people. He will learn more easily later than will the child who spends these early months of life lying in a crib or sitting in an infant seat, not doing much of anything.

If you have been around babies, you know how different each one is from the others. They develop at different rates in different ways. Some are very active, some are quiet.

Too often parents, and especially other people, think the quiet baby is the "good" baby. In fact, the quiet baby may need more from you than does the very active baby. She needs more stimulation to help her learn about her world because she's not apt to do as much active exploring on her own.

HE LIKES MIRRORS

Babies love mirrors. Hold your baby in front of a full-length mirror and watch his reaction. He may be puzzled at seeing you there, apparently a second you. His own reflection will intrigue him because he will soon learn he can make that "person" move when he moves.

I've held Kerry up to the mirror, and she just looks and wonders what is going on. She's able to distinguish me from her. She knows who she is, but she isn't sure what to think of two mommies. (Leslie)

One of the best "toys" for this age is an unbreakable mirror placed six or seven inches from baby's eyes. Glass mirrors are dangerous. Look for a good quality stainless steel mirror four or five inches in diameter. If it isn't fairly good quality, his image will be distorted.

Placing a mirror over the crib or beside the changing table gives him something very interesting to watch. Don't put it too far away, however, because his image will be reflected at twice the distance of the mirror.

If the mirror is seven inches away from his eyes, for example, his image will be 14 inches away. If it's further away, it won't hold his interest as well.

*Upstairs in Gary's room on his changing table there is a big
mirror. He smiles and looks in the mirror, and he'll turn his
head, then look. (Leica)*

A mirror by the changing table might help Tiffany:

*Delphina loves to look in mirrors. I hold her up in the
bathroom and she smiles. I can hardly change her any more
because she kicks so much. She grabs her rattle, combs, anything
you give her. (Tiffany)*

KEEPING BEDTIME PLEASANT

Have you visited friends at their child's bedtime? Were you ever
horrified at the problems they had getting their child to go to bed and
to sleep? You probably would like to make bedtime a different kind
of experience for your child.

If you satisfy baby's needs most of the time—feed her when she's
hungry, pick her up when she cries, often visit with her when she's
lonely—she'll probably adapt to going to bed with no great fuss most
of the time.

Don't use bedtime as your most lively play period with baby. That
won't help her accept being put to bed by herself. This is a good time
to start reading to her.

At four or five months, she isn't going to listen to a long story, or
even to a few Mother Goose rhymes. But she probably will enjoy
looking at some big clear pictures with you. Our favorite for this stage
is a book with sturdy cardboard pages with a picture of a baby farm
animal on each one. Our son, when he was a little older, "had" to
say "night-night" to the baby pig every night for many months.

Sitting on your lap and looking at a few pictures now may help her
feel ready for bed. It is also the first step in encouraging her to enjoy
books, to know that a book can be a joy to her.

*I think Juan will learn a lot faster if I read to him. Right after
I feed him before he goes to bed at night, I read to him. He likes
the sound of my voice. I was reading "The Three Little Pigs,"
and I was using a gruff voice. He started to cry. Of course I
changed to a softer voice. (Ginny)*

By two or three months of age, your baby will probably be sleeping
through the night, a real blessing for exhausted parents. She probably

will still need a late night
feeding. But if you give it to
her right before you go to
bed, it may last her through
the night.

Most babies suck their
thumbs, some much more
than others. When she does,

it's satisfying her need for more sucking. Early thumb sucking will not
harm her teeth. If she's not nagged about it, she will probably quit
when she no longer needs the sucking.

> *Juan sucks his thumb and was trying to suck his hand. He
> couldn't get it in, so I gave him a pacifier. My mom didn't want
> me to, but it was the only way I could get him to sleep. I didn't
> want him to cry. (Ginny)*

Can you imagine telling a baby not to crawl because if she does, she
may never want to walk? That's pretty silly. But it's about as silly to
tell a baby not to suck her thumb because if she does, she may never
want to stop. She'll stop when she's ready.

OTHER CAREGIVERS

Some parents stay home most of the time with their newborn baby.
Especially if she's breastfeeding, mother may find it easier as well as
pleasanter for both herself and the baby if she doesn't try to take him
out much or attempt to leave without him during those first weeks.

By two months, however, you will want to go out, do things on
your own occasionally. Unless you have a live-in baby sitter, you'll
need to let your sitter know where baby's things are kept and the style
of care baby needs. Does he expect rocking after feeding? Is it hard
for him to burp enough? Does he whimper a few minutes before falling asleep?

In addition, be sure to leave phone numbers for your doctor, a
caring neighbor, the fire department, and the police department. Put
the numbers where the sitter can find them easily. *Always* let him/her
know exactly how to reach you while you're gone. Some parents leave
Medicaid stickers with a sitter if they're going to be gone long.

Whenever you leave your child with someone else, it's wise to give
that person a signed medical emergency card. You could state,
"_____ has my permission to obtain emergency

medical care as needed for my child, (child's name).'' Generally, medical care may not be given to a child without his/her parent's permission.

Some parents take their baby with them wherever they go. Many parents will have baby along at least part of the time. This can be a problem for couples whose friends don't have children. A young single mother may find it especially hard, although many find that friends will cooperate:

I have two really close friends. I can call them any time. When they say, "Let's go to the movies," I say, "Well, I have to take Juan." They tell me that's all right. A boy I was dating asked me out, and I said I would have to take Juan. He said, "Some other time." So that's it with him. I don't need a friend like that. (Ginny)

Taking baby with you can be tiring, too. Babies usually are creatures of habit. If their routine is changed, they usually let you know how they feel about it:

I was very tired at first. Stevie is 2½ months old now, and sometimes I still get tired. We went camping this weekend, and because of the change, he didn't sleep as much at night as usual. I had a great time camping all day, but then I was up at night with him. I'm tired! (Alison)

If Daddy is around, how involved should he be during this stage? A tired mother needs his help—and doesn't always get it:

Vince hasn't been as involved as I would like him to be. He says he'll enjoy Jay more when he's potty trained, and he can ask him what he wants. When he needs changing, he hands him to me. But he has been getting up lately with him when he's crying a lot because of teething. (Bev)

Fathers, however, can get deeply involved in child care. A four-month-old baby is a charming little person much of the time. Caring for him can be very rewarding for his father and for him. In fact, this can be a very special relationship for father and baby.

Mario feeds Carol, changes her, and plays with her. He even got up to feed her last night. He put her in her crib, and she

started crying. So he picked her up and put her next to him, and she fell asleep. I'm glad she's like that. I'm glad she's attached to her dad.

Mario wanted to go fishing the other night. I said if it was cold, the baby and I would stay home. He went outside and decided it was warm enough, so we all went to the lake. He caught a fish and showed it to little Carol.

Let the baby get close to her father. It's really neat. (Kristyn)

EXTENDED FAMILY LIVING

Your extended family—brothers, sisters, parents—may get even more involved with your child at this stage than immediately after birth. Sometimes it may be hard, especially if you're tired, to understand their viewpoints:

Mother tried to put Gary on a schedule, but I wouldn't let her. It's hard—they make you feel like you're incapable of being a *mother. They think they can do it better. After they keep harping on you for awhile, you get to wondering if they might be right, that maybe you aren't a good mother. I keep trying to remember the real mother is probably the best mother.*

Even when they're home and I go out, I have baby sitters here—unless Mother volunteers. I don't ever want that thrown up in my face—"Well, I had to watch your baby." It's my responsibility, not hers. But on the other hand, when they're in those funny moods—sometimes I'll get a baby sitter and she will say, "You mean I'm not good enough to baby-sit?" Then I ask her to watch Gary, and she'll say, "I have plans tonight." You've got to keep your sense of humor! (Leica)

My mom is too cautious—she always takes off Juan's clothes when she comes home from work. I ask her why, and she says, "It's so hot. He doesn't like it with his clothes on." Juan has two plaques above his changing table, and he reaches for them. Mom tells me to move them.

She doesn't like him to go out at night. If I'm going someplace, I try to take him with me, and she doesn't like that. I try to tell her how I feel, but I don't want to hurt her feelings because I still live with her. (Ginny)

Sisters, too, have opinions on baby care:

Now that Stevie's older, sometimes I do have to let him cry. Just this morning I was folding the wash. If I didn't fold it right away, it would get wrinkled. He started fussing. After I checked to make sure he was all right, I went back and finished folding clothes. Then I picked him up. But my sisters kept telling me I should take care of him immediately. (Alison)

COPING WITH CRYING

This may be the happiest time in your baby's life. But that doesn't mean she is always happy and easy to care for from the minute she's two months old until she's crawling. There will be difficult times with any baby.

When the kid is crying and crying and you don't know what he's crying about, you do start climbing the walls. I just remember that Nick is my baby, and I want him. He didn't ask to be born. He is here because I wanted him. So I take care of him. I do get upset sometimes when he cries and cries, but I don't show it to Nick. Sometimes my sister will hold him for five to ten minutes, and by that time I'll be all right.

Everybody gets those times. If you don't know what to do, and you can't handle it, you should give him to somebody else for at least five or ten minutes. (Theresa, 16 - Nick, 6 months)

As Theresa said, everybody has those times. You, or someone close to you, may think you shouldn't feel like that. But these feelings are normal, are OK. The trick is to keep the feelings from spilling over into unwanted action. Having someone else there to take the baby for awhile may help.

If he cries a lot, it bothers me. I can't handle crying very well. If I can't handle it, I just go into the other room. Before we split, my husband would say this isn't right, to have those feelings. My mom helps me. (Janette, 18 - Myles, 7 months)

When I get really upset, I hold it in. I can't yell at Jay. He doesn't understand. He doesn't know right from wrong. I can't yell at him; it just makes him more upset. A lady down the street used to yell at her baby, and now that she's 5, you say something to her and she'll start crying. Sometimes I'll give Jay to Vince. He'll hold him for ten minutes while I go outside. (Bev)

If a four-month-old baby isn't happy much of the time, perhaps her mother and others around her aren't very happy. Babies are great mimics. They are also extremely sensitive little creatures and may mirror the attitudes of those around them.

If mother is unhappy, is she perhaps too tired? Does she have any help with baby? Can Father or Grandma give her some assistance?

Is she perhaps feeling she is only giving, and not receiving much in return for her role as mother and, possibly, wife? Perhaps she is trying to keep up in school or perform a full-time job in addition to taking care of baby and home. No wonder she doesn't feel ecstatic very often!

Louise tried hard to give her two children and her husband everything they needed. But she was trying to finish school, Meghan was only 17 months old when Mark was born, and Bob didn't help her very much.

I was quite upset with myself when Mark was first born because I didn't spend much time with him because of Meghan, and because I was trying to clean. And then I went back to school. Mark was a very demanding child—he wanted me 24 hours a day.

When he was young, he wasn't very happy. I hardly ever saw a smile on his face until about three weeks ago. It worried me that no matter what I did with him, he was a crier.

I would change Mark, feed him, try to play with him, but he didn't want to play.

He didn't like to be cuddled a lot. I would take him to a different spot in the house thinking he was tired of one place, but it didn't work. So I would just have to let him fuss to sleep after I had tried rocking.

I got upset, and so did Meghan. She would come and tell me the baby was crying. I would tell her I knew. She couldn't understand why I would let him go, but I had tried everything. He was just a crier.

At first I thought he was a person who needed lots of attention, but he didn't like that either. He didn't like to be rocked, he didn't like to be cuddled. He liked to be held out away from me. So the only thing I could do was let him fuss and go to sleep, and he did sleep a lot. He apparently just didn't feel very well during that time. (Louise)

Then several things changed. Louise graduated from high school and was able to stay home with the two children. Mark started eating better. And then he giggled at his mother:

I think that's what brought me around. I was getting so upset because Mark didn't want to be close to me. It had gotten to where Bob was doing a lot for him because I couldn't do it. But when he finally giggled, that was the breaking point. Ever since then, Mark will smile at me no matter whether he's in a good mood or not.

It's very important to baby that mother be satisfied with her life. As a matter of fact, his mother's satisfaction is a big part of his own happiness. A young mother was talking to a class of non-parents:

I don't think you guys know how hard it is—you think it's like playing dolls, but it's not like that. When you have a doll, you feed it when you want to, but with a baby, you can't put him up in a closet and say, "I'll see you later." Sometimes you feel like you're going to climb a wall.

For me, sometimes Mike takes care of him and I go out and take a walk or do something for an hour. I'll go to my girl friend's house for awhile, and I'll feel better. But there are a lot of hard times in having a baby. I have to be at school at 8 A.M., and I have to get him cleaned up. I have to feed him. I put him in his crib while I get ready, and I have to keep checking to be sure he's all right. It's back and forth all the time. (Jeanne, 16 - Eric, 2 months)

If you feel frustrated, perhaps you need to get away by yourself occasionally. Share your feelings with a friend or relative. Someone will be willing to baby-sit for a couple of hours.

It is absolutely normal to want to get away from the kids sometimes. Don't feel guilty about it. We all need to be alone sometimes. I love my kids dearly, but sometimes I need space. (Thelma, 20 - Janeen, 18 months, and Melissa, 4 years)

Sometimes a young mother isn't happy with her appearance. Perhaps she still has weight to lose from her pregnancy. Maybe she doesn't feel she has time to take care of herself.

Yes, this summer is different. Last year I went to the beach every day. I see pictures of me all tan and slim. It's kind of disappointing to me. I wish I could do that again, but I can't this year. (Alison)

Exercising regularly and following a sensible weight reducing diet may improve her self-image. Perhaps a minor shopping spree—minor because most young parents tend to be short of money—will help her feel better about her world and her baby. Spending time with friends can help. Many young mothers report a feeling of isolation and being "fenced in" with their baby care duties.

BABY EXPENSES VARY

Expenses during this stage vary a lot. If you already have the equipment you need—crib, highchair, car seat, and stroller are most important—and you use cloth diapers and are breastfeeding, the cost may be fairly low. If you had a baby shower, your baby is probably just now growing into the clothes you received. (Just a few months later, you'll find her clothes get expensive.)

But a three-month-old baby can be quite expensive, especially if she's allergic to cow's milk. Any formula is expensive, but the cost of special soy-base non-allergenic formula is very high. If you use paper diapers, they'll cost about $85 to $100 during this three-month period.

A mother who starts feeding solid food to a very young baby will find it expensive if she buys jars of baby food regularly. See Chapter Six for suggestions for making your own. But most babies should not be eating solid food until they're at least four months old anyhow. Buying jars of strained food for a two-month-old baby is expensive. Feeding them to her could cause food allergies and stomach upsets.

ANOTHER BABY? WHEN?

Couples need to think and talk about future family plans. How soon do they want another child? Many young mothers, married as well as single, don't want another baby right away. From a physical standpoint, their bodies need time to recuperate from the last pregnancy.

I'm going to have two children at the most. I think two is enough. I think ideally I would have another one when he is about three—when he more or less does things on his own. (Arlene, 17 - Dale, 11½ months)

It's really hard—a second kid seems like five more. I guess I shouldn't have had her. I tell Charles, "You were right—I should have had an abortion." I wanted to get everything over with—

graduate, get my license, have the two kids. But now I don't really have anything. I'm tired and nervous all the time. (Colleen, 18 - Ruby, 7 months, and Hilda, 21 months)

From baby's standpoint, waiting three or even four years before the next child is wise. In many ways, the two-year-old child needs about as much care—in different ways, of course—as does an infant.

When we brought Leon home from the hospital, DeeDee was almost three. She wanted to hold him, so we set her down on the couch and propped a pillow on her so she could. Ever since, he has been her baby. We've had very little jealousy.

If we had had him sooner, DeeDee would not have been able to enjoy being a baby long enough. I wanted her to be just a little more independent so she would be used to my not spending so much time with her. A lot of mothers I've seen have their kids real close together. It kind of makes the oldest child feel a little bit neglected. It just seems the little baby has to grow up so fast instead of enjoying being a baby. (Tamera, 21 - Leon, 20 months, and DeeDee, 4½ years)

The money cost of having a second baby soon after the first can be overwhelming:

You don't think the expense of a second baby is that much, but it is. It costs a lot more with Ruby. Charles used to work over-time last year just for extras like Christmas. Now he has to work overtime so we can make it through the month. Maybe it wouldn't be so bad if we were living in a house and had a lot of things, then said, "We're broke." But it shouldn't happen when we're in a one-bedroom apartment. It takes a gallon of milk every day, diapers, soap to wash clothes. (Colleen)

Babies do come by accident. If you don't want another child right away, birth control is essential. This could be simply not having sex, but most mothers will want some other kind of contraceptive. And if you are breastfeeding, *don't* count on that to keep you from getting pregnant. *You can get pregnant even though you are breastfeeding your baby.*

If you are breastfeeding, you shouldn't take the birth control pill because it would cut down on your milk supply. This might be a good time to ask your doctor about inserting an I.U.D. (intra-uterine device).

Many young women are using the diaphragm. For whatever reason, they prefer it to having an I.U.D. inserted in their uterus or taking the birth control pill. The diaphragm takes some planning since it must be inserted not long before you have sex. It must be left in place at least six hours after intercourse.

If the man uses a condom (rubber) and the woman uses foam, the two methods together are as successful at preventing conception as is the pill or the I.U.D. Both the condom and foam can be bought at a drugstore with no prescription from the doctor.

If you aren't pregnant now, and you don't want to have a child soon, you have two choices. One, of course, is not to have sex. If you're having sex, use birth control—*always.*

About half of all couples who have unprotected intercourse a dozen times will become pregnant. If you don't want to have a baby, and you are having intercourse, using a contraceptive consistently is essential.

IMMUNIZATIONS—ABSOLUTELY NECESSARY

Babies have to put up with adjusting to all kinds of germs and bacteria. Sometimes babies will be sick, have colds, fevers, and other illnesses.

But there are other serious childhood diseases that your grandparents will remember well. When they were children, many people had such diseases as polio, whooping cough, mumps, and measles.

In the early part of this century two of the leading causes of death for children under two were diphtheria and whooping cough (pertussin). This doesn't happen anymore because of the DPT shots your child should start getting at age two months. The name "DPT" refers to the series of immunizations against three diseases: diphtheria, pertussin, and tetanus. He will have a series of three of these shots, usually two months apart. Tetanus is a disease related to accidental injury. He'll get occasional booster shots against tetanus throughout his life.

Polio vaccine has been available in this country for about 25 years.

Before that time, thousands of children and adults became ill with polio every summer. Many of these victims died, others became paralyzed, handicapped for life.

The polio vaccine available to your child during the first six months of life can prevent this horrible disease. Polio is still prevalent in many parts of the world including Mexico, so it's very important to have your baby immunized against it.

Your baby will need another DPT and polio immunization when he is twelve months old, fifteen months, eighteen months, and before he starts to kindergarten.

In addition, he will need to be immunized against "red" measles, rubella (German measles), and mumps at fifteen months of age.

People often wonder why we bother immunizing children against measles and mumps. Perhaps they had these diseases themselves without serious effects when they were young. However, many babies have suffered very serious illness and even death from measles and related disorders. Some have become permanently deaf from mumps. Your baby need never run these risks.

Red measles cause lots of complications to young babies. They can get pneumonia. Meningitis is another common complication of measles. Babies sometimes die from meningitis.

Rubella (German measles) generally doesn't make babies too sick. But a pregnant woman exposed to rubella during the first three months of her pregnancy may have a baby who is deaf, has heart disease, or some other birth defect because of the rubella. If the woman has had rubella herself or was vaccinated before she was pregnant, her baby is not in danger.

Your children need never have any of these diseases because they can be completely prevented by immunizations.

Immunizations are free at any health department. They are also often given by the Health Department at local parks. If you don't know where to take your baby for his shots, ask your school nurse for a recommendation.

Most babies have some reaction to immunizations. Usually the reaction lasts only a day or two and is generally mild. Giving your child a baby aspirin will help relieve these symptoms.

When Nick got his shots, he got a lot of fever—that really bothers him. He woke up at midnight with a fever, and I gave him aspirin. That helped. (Theresa)

See page 178 for suggestions about caring for a feverish child.

Of course, if your baby has a severe reaction to his immunizations (high fever for more than twelve hours or other severe symptoms), you should call your doctor.

BE SURE to keep a record of your baby's immunizations. When you enroll him in school later on, you'll need that record. In fact, you'll need it each year for school enrollment.

Chapter Six

Good Food For Baby

Your baby doesn't need—and generally shouldn't have—solid food until she is *at least* four or five months old. Almost all babies get along best on breast milk or formula during this time.

VITAMIN/MINERAL SUPPLEMENTS

If you are breastfeeding your baby, you should continue taking your prenatal vitamins for two or three months after delivery. If you do, your baby won't need an extra vitamin supplement. She gets her vitamins through your milk, and an extra dose would not be good for her.

By the time baby is three months old, you shouldn't need to take prenatal vitamins any longer. At that time, ask your baby's doctor about a vitamin supplement for her. S/he will probably prescribe a vitamin D and fluoride supplement. Each day you will give baby a certain number of drops of this mixture. Give exactly as prescribed. Don't overdose!

If you are eating enough nutritious, iron-rich foods, your breast milk will provide enough iron for your baby for about four months. At that time, your doctor may suggest an iron supplement. Or s/he may tell you it's all right to start feeding baby an iron-fortified cereal.

Commercially prepared formula contains enough vitamin D for baby. You'll need to give vitamin C separately, usually through vitamin drops. These drops should also include fluoride—or fluoride may be prescribed separately. The amount of fluoride needed, however, will vary depending on the fluoride already present in the water used with the formula.

We know that enough fluoride in our diet will help prevent cavities in our teeth. This is the reason for adding the fluoride supplement to baby's diet soon after her birth. But too much fluoride can also be a problem. It can lead to discolored teeth. The amount of fluoride in your water supply may be high or low. Therefore, it is important that you ask your doctor how much, if any, fluoride supplement your baby needs.

Some commercial formulas contain iron. Others do not. Your doctor will help you decide which is better for your baby.

DON'T RUSH SOLID FOOD

Sometime between four and six months of age, baby needs to start learning to eat solid foods. Trying to feed him solids earlier offers no benefit to him, according to the latest report (1979) from the Maternal and Child Health Branch, California Department of Public Services.

Too-early feeding of solids sometimes causes problems for baby. He is more apt to develop food allergies if he is given solid foods too early. He will probably have more digestive problems than will his completely breast- or bottle-fed friends.

Feeding solids to a very tiny baby is usually time-consuming and often frustrating to mother and to baby. Mother spoons it in, baby rolls it right back out! Before he is four months old, baby has a well-developed sucking reflex. He sucks before he swallows his milk. But food put in his mouth from a spoon is usually spit right back out. This is called the *protrusion reflex*. By about four months of age, this protrusion reflex is gone. Then he is much more able to accept food on his tongue. He can swallow it instead of letting it roll back out.

In addition, if you buy strained baby food, the cost can be rather high—high, at least, when you realize this is money spent which gives no benefit to baby during these early months.

So why do so many parents start feeding cereal and other solids to their very young baby? They may have several reasons.

A widely accepted idea is that feeding him cereal in the evening will make baby sleep through the night sooner than he would otherwise. But research shows this is simply not true.

Often mother, tired of getting up in the middle of the night for two months or so (a very natural feeling!), decides to try cereal. Maybe that will help baby sleep. So she feeds baby cereal at 9:30 P.M. Lo and behold—he sleeps until 6 A.M.

But at two months, that baby was probably ready to sleep all night without requiring a middle-of-the-night feeding. Feeding him cereal may have happened right at the time he was ready to give up his night feeding anyhow.

In Chapter Two, Jean Brunelli, Infant Center nurse, states flatly that cereal does not help baby sleep at night. Instead, it may cause indigestion. The indigestion makes baby fuss more the next day. If he fusses more, he gets more tired. If he's tired enough, perhaps he will sleep all night. But daytime indigestion seems a rather high cost for nighttime sleep.

"But the baby next door started eating solids when she wasn't even a month old," you may say. Sometimes, putting baby on solid food very early is considered a great achievement. "If my baby eats cereal before yours does, then I must be a better mother." Don't you believe it!

There are exceptions, however. All babies are different. Occasionally an extra big baby needs more food earlier. It's possible that a three-month-old baby will adjust well to eating solids. But start with the idea that he probably doesn't need them, and will be better off with only breast milk or formula. Then, if you and your doctor decide he is the exception that proves the rule, that he really does need solids added to his diet, go ahead and feed him.

Another reason for early feeding of solids is the urging of grandparents and other relatives. The research which shows that babies are better off without early solid food is quite new. When you were born, there was a trend toward very early feeding of solids. At that time, neither doctors nor the rest of us realized that early feeding can, and often does, cause allergies and stomach upsets.

Even your doctor may tell you that it's all right to start feeding solids to baby when he is very young. If this happens, talk to him/her. Some doctors seem to think all mothers want to rush solid feeding. After discussing it, you and your doctor may agree baby doesn't need cereal yet, and that it certainly is all right to wait until he's at least four months old.

Sometimes people you love—perhaps your own mother—urge you to start early feeding. Most of the young mothers interviewed for this book are taking full responsibility for caring for their babies even though many are still living with their own mothers. However, if Grandma is convinced that baby is starving if he drinks only milk, you (and your doctor) may decide it's important to go along with her wishes in order to avoid a family argument. Many babies can tolerate solid food.

*I breastfed Orlando completely. I knew he didn't need anything
else. But when he was a month old, my mother started telling me
I should give him some solid food. Mom is a nurse and worked
with the newborns at the hospital several years ago. She thinks
she knows exactly what to do with every baby, especially
Orlando.*

*She kept telling me he wasn't gaining enough weight. She was
surprised when the doctor weighed him and said he was just fine.
But Mom still thought I was starving him.*

*To make matters worse, I made the mistake of quoting the
nurse at school. That really upset her. I guess she thought I was
going over her head or something. When Orlando was about 2½
months old, I decided it wasn't worth the hassle. And the nurse
at school agreed with me. A little cereal and strained fruit each
day would hurt Orlando less than the fussing between Mom and
me. (Holly, 17 - Orlando, 5 months)*

SOLIDS BY SIX MONTHS

Ideally, then, you don't feed baby solid food for at least four
months. It's just as important, however, that you DO start spoon-
feeding her and giving her finger foods by the time she is six months
old.

By this time, she needs nutrients she isn't getting from breast milk
or formula. Even breast milk won't supply enough iron much after
four months.

She also needs to learn to eat solids. This is quite different from
getting her food through sucking. Four to six months seems to be the
ideal age to help her learn this new method of eating. It's also important by this time that she learn to eat a variety of foods.

*I waited about five months to give Nick solid foods. He likes to
be nursed after he eats, and then he falls asleep. I used to leak,
and I wanted to nurse him, but I think it's best to feed him solids
first. I give him cereal in the morning, and then I bring him here
to the Center and I nurse him. (Theresa, 16 - Nick, 6 months)*

Infant rice cereal is probably the best food to offer first. Use the
dry, iron-enriched kind that you buy in a box. Rice is less apt to cause
allergies than other kinds of cereal such as wheat. Above all, don't
start with the mixed cereal. If she's allergic to one of the ingredients,
you won't know which one it is.

Mix the dry rice cereal with a little formula. If you are breastfeeding, you can pump enough milk for her cereal at first. She will be more willing to accept the cereal if it smells and tastes somewhat like her formula or breast milk. Mix enough milk with the cereal to make it quite thin at first.

Carefully choose the "right" time for teaching baby to eat solid food. Don't attempt spoon-feeding at first when she is terribly hungry. She would be furious at the delay in getting the bottle or breast that she wants. But she needs to be reasonably hungry or she won't bother trying this new food. About half-through her breast or bottle feeding is the best time.

Try to get a small, narrow, shallow-bowled spoon with a fairly long handle for these early feedings. To baby, eating from a regular tea-spoon feels like eating from a huge tablespoon would feel to us. (Try it sometime. You'll understand why she needs a little spoon to match her mouth size.)

If baby doesn't sit up by herself yet, put her in your lap for her first solid food experience. She has learned to accept food when she's in your arms. Hold her a little more upright than you would for breast or bottle feeding.

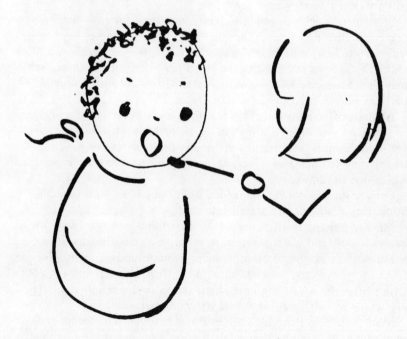

Next step is for you to relax! If she doesn't like cereal the first time, that's OK. Try again tomorrow—and the next day. If she still resists, wait a few days before trying again.

If she does swallow a bit of cereal, congratulate her. Be thrilled—show her you're pleased. But if she doesn't eat it, don't make a big deal of it.

Sometimes mothers mix cereal and formula together, then feed it to baby from a bottle. *Don't!* Your baby needs to learn to eat from a spoon. An infant feeder which practically "injects" the food into her mouth is bad too. Don't buy it.

If baby "drinks" her food, she can't experience the texture and flavor of individual foods. This is an important part of learning to eat different foods.

Still another reason not to feed solids from a bottle deals, believe it or not, with speech development. Certain facial muscles needed for good speech later on don't develop if baby continues to drink all of her food.

Let her drink milk, water, and juices from a bottle. Help her learn that solid foods are eaten from a spoon. Fairly soon, of course, she will also learn about finger foods.

Start feeding baby vegetables, fruits, and their juices sometime between her fifth and seventh months. Traditionally, babies have eaten white fruits first, usually applesauce or pears, perhaps because almost all babies like the taste. After the sweet taste of fruit, however, baby may balk at vegetables. So you may decide to start with a vegetable—perhaps squash, sweet potatoes, or carrots.

At first, offer baby only one new food each week. If she's allergic to that food—if she gets a rash or seems to have a digestion problem—you'll know that particular food is probably causing the problem. If you fed her a new food each day, you wouldn't have any idea which one to remove.

Orange juice is not recommended until baby is about a year old. Some very young babies are allergic to it.

Mashed banana is often one of the first foods given to baby. Most babies like it, and it's super-easy to mash to a smooth consistency.

Between six and eight months, offer protein foods to baby. Choose from cheese, yogurt, cooked beans, meat, fish, chicken and egg yolk. Don't offer the whole egg until she is ten to twelve months old. The egg white doesn't agree with a lot of young babies.

Many babies like cottage cheese. Put it through the blender at first or through the baby food grinder. Before long, just mash it with a fork.

Plain unflavored yogurt is also good for baby. Don't choose the heavily sugared items. Many children prefer the tart flavor of plain yogurt.

The above foods, along with formula or breast milk, can supply most of baby's vitamin and mineral needs. Iron-fortified cereal can satisfy her need for iron. Fruits and vegetables, of course, are good sources of vitamins A and C. Your doctor may want baby to continue taking her vitamin drops, however.

MAKING BABY FOOD

Many people buy ready-prepared strained baby food. Either they don't know how to fix it at home, or they feel they don't have time to prepare it.

Juan has cereal and fruit for breakfast, fruit and vegetables at noon, fruit and vegetables at night. The doctor is starting him on beef and lamb mixed with vegetables. He doesn't like the dry cereal so he eats the kind in the jar mixed with fruit. I don't know how to fix baby food myself. (Ginny, 17 - Juan, 5 months)

There are two big advantages to preparing baby food at home. First, it has to be cheaper to buy a carrot and cook and mash it than to pay 21¢ for a jar of strained carrots. When you're tempted to start buying prepared baby food, check the prices in your store.

I recently bought a piece of squash for 29¢. I steamed it and put it through the blender. The result was 1½ cups strained squash, the amount in six baby food jars. Price that week was 21¢ for a jar of strained squash. Six jars would cost $1.26, a saving of $1.05—not bad for about three minutes work.

Do a little arithmetic. How much would it cost each week or each month to buy several jars of baby food every day? Wouldn't you rather have some new clothes for yourself or for baby? Or money for furniture or a night out on the town?

The second, even more important reason to fix your own baby food is nutritive value. You won't be using fillers to stretch the amount of food. You won't be adding salt and suger that baby doesn't need.

Several years ago the commercial baby food companies got a reputation for adding a lot of salt and sugar to their baby foods. They now are much more cautious about using these additives.

If you decide to buy strained baby food, read the labels carefully before you buy. Choose basic fruits, vegetables, and strained meats. Don't buy combination meals because you get less protein per serving than if you mixed together a jar of meat and a jar of vegetables yourself. If the label tells you the food contains a lot of suger and modified starches, don't buy it. Skip the baby desserts because baby doesn't need them any more than the rest of us do.

When you fix baby food yourself, of course, you know exactly what is in it—quite an advantage for baby.

Fixing food for baby is easy. You don't even need a blender. You can buy a baby food grinder for just a few dollars. With it, you prepare small amounts of food for baby. The blender is easier for fixing big amounts.

You need nothing but a fork and a saucer to mash a banana. Choose a ripe banana, one with yellow and brown peel. If, after you mash it, it seems a bit thick for baby, mix it with a little milk.

It might take 40 seconds longer to mash a banana than it would to open a jar of strained banana. Prices at my store were 8¢ for one banana, 21¢ for the same thing in a jar. You can fix half a banana, cover the other half and refrigerate it. It will keep for two days.

Other fruits should be cooked until they're soft, at least until baby is six or seven months old. Just wash, peel, and cut apples, peaches, pears, plums, or apricots into small pieces. Add one-fourth cup boiling water to one cup of fruit. Simmer until tender, ten to twenty minutes. Don't add sugar. Blend until smooth using your baby food grinder or the blender.

Or you can cook the fruit in a steamer for fifteen to twenty minutes. Wash and peel the fruit before steaming it. Steam, cook, and remove pits. Blend to a smooth consistency.

Cook vegetables for baby either by simmering in one to 1½ inches of water or steaming over boiling water until tender. To get the right consistency, add some of the cooking water as you mash or blend the vegetables.

Important vitamins are lost when you cook foods in boiling water. The steam method of cooking will save more of those vitamins. The food is held above the boiling water so it will cook only in the steam.

A steam basket, available in most department stores for less than $5, fits into most pans. You need to use a pan with a tight-fitting lid. Many adults prefer steamed vegetables because foods cooked this way retain more natural flavor.

If baby is at least six months old, try fixing uncooked fruit for her. Wash and peel an apple, pear, peach, or apricot. Add a little water, then blend.

Meat you have cooked for your family can be blended to a smooth consistency. You may need to add a little water or juice.

If you're cooking for the whole family, be sure to take baby's portion out before you add salt, sugar, and other seasonings. She won't mind. A craving for extra salt is probably learned by eating foods with added salt. Don't season her food to meet your taste.

Too much salt in one's diet can cause numerous health problems including hypertension. Eating sugar may cause a craving for sweets. Help your baby avoid these problems by having as little salt and sugar as possible in her diet.

FINDING TIME TO FIX IT

Many mothers say they don't fix baby food at home because they don't have time. If you're working full-time or going to school, or if you have other children, of course you're very busy. Most of us will even agree that one baby keeps a mother overly busy. So how can you find time for all this blending and grinding of baby food?

If possible, use your family's meals as a start. If you're having a vegetable, put a small amount (without seasonings) through a baby food grinder. Perhaps you're having a meat that is also suitable for blending. Do you like applesauce? If so, share it with baby.

I broil hamburger and put it in the blender with a little bit of milk. We'll have chicken for dinner and sometimes I'll put it in the blender, or I'll just give her the drumstick to chew on. (Julie, 16 - Sonja, 7 months)

Perhaps you're not fixing meals for adults that include food suitable for baby. You can still prepare her food without spending several hours each day. Best approach is to cook and freeze ahead. If you spend a Saturday morning preparing baby food, you can be set for a month. Or invite another mother over and have a cooking-for-baby party one evening.

Unless you know exactly what and how you want to cook, investing

in a baby food cookbook would help. My favorite is Vicki Lansky's
Feed Me—I'm Yours. It's published by Meadowbrook Press and also
by Bantam Books. It's available for $3 or $4 at most book stores.

But first, the bad news about *Feed Me—I'm Yours.* It makes one
very wrong recommendation. Honey is suggested as a substitute for
sugar, and is recommended in several recipes for babies. *Don't* feed
baby honey. It is not sterilized and can cause botulism (food poisoning). It doesn't bother children who are older—perhaps three or four
years old.

If you cut out the suggestions for using honey, the rest of *Feed
Me—I'm Yours* is excellent.

Ms. Lansky describes two methods of freezing baby food. For the
food cube method, you simply pour prepared food into ice cube trays.
Freeze it quickly. Then store the cubes in plastic freezer bags. Be sure
to label and date the food. Use it within two months.

To freeze baby food by Ms. Lansky's "plop" method, "plop" it by
spoonfuls onto a cookie sheet. "Plop" the amount you think baby
will eat at one meal. Freeze quickly, remove from cookie sheet, and
put in plastic freezer bags.

She suggests you keep protein food, cereals, vegetables, and fruits
in separate containers in the freezer.

When you are ready to serve the cubes or "plops" of food, thaw in
a warming dish or in an egg-poaching cup over boiling water. The little individual egg-poaching pan is a convenient size and is relatively
inexpensive.

You don't need to warm the food beyond room temperature.
Baby's taste buds are not fully developed, and what seems warm to
you may seem hot to baby.

Small amounts of frozen baby food are handy for short trips. By
the time you arrive at your friend's house, baby's food will probably
be thawed and ready to serve.

With a little planning, you can have a nice variety of food stored in
your freezer. If you fix a different vegetable for your family each

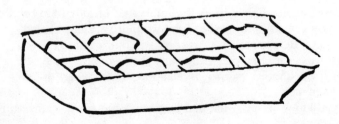

night one week, simply cook at least twice the amount you need. Prepare the extra amount for baby, then freeze. Do the same with fruits. You may find it easier than running to the store to buy jars of baby food.

If you wait until he's six months old to start baby on solid food, you'll need to use strained food for only a couple of months. He can be eating table food, much of it mashed, by the time he's eight months old.

He may be able to hold and gum a teething biscuit by the time he's five months old. A six-month-old baby can handle little pieces of hard-boiled egg yolk. (No egg white yet.) When he's seven months old, he can have dry unsugared cereal, soft toast, French toast, cooked carrot and potato pieces, peas with the skins broken, even diced liverwurst sandwiches! He can handle all these things himself by eating with his fingers.

By the time he is eight months old, you'll be able to mash his food into small pieces. If you're serving chicken, get rid of the bone and cartilage. Then cut the meat into very small pieces for him. Fish is excellent because it just falls apart. Of course, you have to be very careful to get all the bones out first.

Even if you don't want to prepare strained baby food yourself, you surely won't buy jars of junior food. Feeding him from the family meals is so little bother to you, and it's better for baby.

Raw, crisp fruits and vegetables aren't good for baby until past the first year because he might choke on them. Until he is two, in fact, if you want him to have raw carrots, you should grate them.

Corn is not for infants or toddlers. It goes right through in the BM without changing color or shape.

FAT-PROOF YOUR BABY

Have you ever been too fat? Or is your mother or father constantly trying to keep her/his weight down?

You know the reasons most people would like to be slim. They feel better and they look better if they're not fat.

Yet many people still think a fat baby is "so-o-o cute." "He's the picture of health," according to Grandma. But the truth is that fat babies are no healthier than fat adults. Obese (fat) babies have more respiratory infections and other illnesses than do slim babies.

It is just as important for baby to "keep her figure" as it is for mother. In fact, it's even more important because now we know that a fat baby is more apt to become a fat adult, an adult who has trouble losing unwanted weight. Many experts believe a fat baby develops more fat cells than does a slim baby, fat cells that stay with her the rest of her life. If, as an adult, you have more fat cells than your friend does, you will undoubtedly have much more trouble keeping your weight down where you want it than s/he will.

You can save baby from a lot of unhappiness throughout her life if you help her avoid forming a lot of those extra fat cells.

The first and most obvious rule is, "Never force-feed her." Don't encourage her to eat more than she wants. She's born wanting about the amount of food she needs. If she's breastfeeding, she isn't apt to get too fat because you won't coax her to drink that last ounce. She won't nurse unless she's hungry.

If she's on formula, you and your doctor will decide about how much she needs each day. As long as she gets about twenty ounces daily, the final decision as to how much she drinks should be hers. It's a temptation to urge her to finish each bottle. Don't do it! Feed her until she seems satisfied—and not a bit longer. Insisting she finish the last drop in each bottle probably means you're over-feeding her.

Too-early feeding of solid food can make your baby fatter than she should be.

She's eating fruit and juice now. She just started solids last week. She weighs 16 pounds and seems a little too big for her age. Feeding solids sooner wouldn't have been good. (Tiffany, 18 - Delphina, 4 months)

If your bottle-fed baby is gaining weight too rapidly, ask your doctor about diluting her formula with extra water. If she's drinking whole milk, it could be diluted. Most doctors don't want a child under two years of age put on skim or low-fat milk. Diluting the whole milk or formula is better for her. Of course, she should have at least 20 ounces of undiluted milk each day.

Fat-proofing babies also means cutting out empty calories— foods which contain only calories with little or no vitamin, mineral or protein content. She can afford an occasional sweet treat later just as you can. To feed her candy, cake, cokes, or potato chips during her first year, however, is foolish.

Sometimes people try to pacify a child with a sweet treat when a hug would work just as well. In fact, hugs are always better than junk food.

Jello water and other sweetened drinks are in the empty calorie category too. Babies and toddlers need milk, water and unsweetened fruit juices to drink—and seldom anything else.

She has always eaten good things. I let her munch if she wants to—whole wheat and peanut butter crackers, but no junk at all. I used to have problems with my teeth, and I don't want her to. I think junk food is so bad for you. I used to always eat stuff like that. No cokes. My doctor said if you pour coke on a car, it will eat the paint right off! (Caroline, 18 - Danette, 10 months)

Coffee, tea, and cola drinks contain caffeine which is a drug. Your baby doesn't need drugs.

DRINKING FROM A CUP

When she is five or six months old, offer baby a little milk in a cup. You can buy a cup with a lid and a spout as a bridge between bottle and cup. Before long, she will be able to drink a little milk, water, and juice from her cup.

Nick is learning to drink from a cup. Yesterday I gave him a training cup, and he is learning how to use it. He eats flour tortillas. He eats crackers and holds them himself. (Theresa)

I'm trying to give Orlando a bottle occasionally, but he doesn't want one. He does good already with a cup. He holds on to it, and he can take it right to his mouth although his coordination isn't very good yet. (Holly)

If you are still breastfeeding her, you may decide to wean her directly to a cup in the next three or four months. If you haven't used bottles much yet, weaning will probably be easier for you if you let her go from your breast to the cup.

If she is bottle-fed, she still needs to learn to drink from a cup. She'll spill it, even try pouring it out if you give her too much. But with patience, she'll learn. Remember, she needs about 20 ounces of milk daily, whether by cup or bottle.

Did you know that putting a baby to bed with a bottle is very hard on her teeth? If the milk film stays on her teeth at night, it breeds decay. Many toddlers have rotten front teeth as a result of sucking on their bottles as they go to sleep.

If, at the end of the first year, she still needs a bottle when she goes to bed, fill it with water. Give her a cup of milk—or a bottle on your lap—at bedtime. Brush her teeth. Then, if she wants it, give her the bottle of water to take to bed with her. She'll still be able to suck to her heart's content, but her teeth will survive.

WHEN HE FEEDS HIMSELF

If baby wants to help feed himself, let him. He won't be able to get much food to his mouth at first. He can put his hand on yours as you hold the spoon. Or he can have his own spoon while you get most of the food to his mouth with yours.

He's trying hard to use the spoon—doesn't quite have it yet. He puts his food on his spoon, but has trouble getting it to his mouth. (Arlene, 17 - Dale, 11½ months)

When she's eating, she likes to get the spoon and bang it for awhile, then eat for awhile, then bang it again. She doesn't like me to feed her unless she's in a good mood. She likes to feed herself. She drinks by herself from a training cup although she still takes a bottle. (Joleen, 17 - Maelynn, 9½ months)

Give him finger foods as early as he can handle them. By the time he is six or seven months old, he can pick up small slices of banana or Cheerios. Before long he will be ready for graham crackers, pieces of toast, teething biscuits, even little bits of meat and cheese.

Alice won't eat out of a spoon. She refuses. She'll pick it up and eat it with her fingers. She doesn't eat a lot because I guess she's attached to the milk.

First I fed her fruits, bananas and applesauce. Then at eight months she went to regular food. String beans are her favorite. She eats any kind of meat herself—turkey, chicken, anything. She has ten teeth. She can chew the bone from the chicken wing without my cutting off the meat. (Melanie, 15 - Alice 13 months)

Cheerios are a marvelous early food-toy. He'll pick one up in each hand, look at it, stick it in his mouth. They contain some nutrition and, most important, are very low in sugar.

Don't give him sugar cereals. Such "cereals" should be labeled breakfast candy. Some are actually more than half sugar!

According to *Today's Child*, December, 1977, the ten cereals with the greatest amounts of sucrose, the form of sugar that is the chief cause of tooth decay, are: Super Orange Crisp (68 percent sucrose), Sugar Smacks (61.3 percent), King Vitamin (58.5 percent), Fruity Pebbles (55 percent), Cocoa Pebbles (53.5 percent), Apple Jacks (51.5 percent), Lucky Charms (50.4 percent), Cinnamon Crunch (50.3 percent), Pink Panther (49.2 percent), and Honeycombs (48.8 percent).

In contrast, Cheerios are only 2.2 percent sugar.

Are you a fairly neat person? If so, don't expect baby to follow your example! A baby learning to feed himself is at his messiest. Don't be shocked. Expect it and be prepared to cope with it.

Sonja bangs her cracker on the table and it smears all over and flies everywhere! (Julie)

Gilbert likes to feed himself, and he makes the biggest mess. He eats mashed potatoes, string beans. He has six teeth and he can even chew on meat already. (Gaye, 14 - Gilbert, 7 months)

The easiest way to feed him is to put him in a sturdy highchair. When he starts feeding himself, lay newspapers under the chair. A piece of heavy plastic protecting your floor might look better than newspaper. But you don't want something you have to clean. After each meal, just bundle up the newspapers and throw them out.

She skins her own hot dogs with her teeth, and spits the skin out. We don't know how she does it, but when we go to clean her up, the skin is on the tray and the hot dog is gone. (Melinda, 16 - Robin, 9 months)

Dale is on table food. He doesn't much like eating meat, but he likes vegetables. I don't have to mash them—if I do, he gets mad because he can't pick them up. He gets mad if I try to feed him, too, so I just put food on his tray. (Arlene)

Remember how much baby likes to explore, to touch, to feel? That's exactly what he will do with his food. Some of it will go in his mouth, but at first more seems to end up on his face, in his hair, any place but where you'd like it to go. He will be delighted with the whole mess.

When he wants to help, give him bits of toast or banana to hold while you feed him. He may get some food to his mouth by smearing it there with his palm. Looking at, handling, tasting and smelling food is part of the same exploring that begins earlier with inedibles. If he is allowed to work out his own eating habits, he learns the world is not a restrictive forbidding place where showing his own feelings and wants only brings trouble.

Keep cool and go along with his sheer enjoyment of the whole eating process. This is the best route to making his mealtimes the pleasant events you want them to be.

Chapter Seven

Five-Nine Months: Ready To Go

Five-month-old Sara stays pretty much where you put her. Lay her on a blanket with a few toys. Go back ten minutes later and she's in the same general area. She may be able to dig her toes in and scoot a little. She can turn from her back to her stomach and back again. But she's not moving all over the apartment yet.

Nine-month-old Sam is an entirely different being. Lay him on a blanket on the floor, turn your back for a second, and he's across the room! He has learned to crawl.

The physical changes happening between five and nine months in a baby's life are startling. Until he's four or five months old, baby is limited to lying on his back or his stomach or being propped up by someone else. He depends completely on others to move him from place to place.

SITTING—STANDING—CRAWLING

By about 6½ months, many babies sit up by themselves. Many start creeping or crawling about a month later. But, as in every kind of development, each child is different. Don't worry if your baby isn't sitting up or crawling this soon.

Nick sits up by himself for a long time, then he collapses. Then I set him up again. When he gets tired, he lies down. He entertains himself for a longer time now. (Theresa, 16 - Nick, 6 months)

Sonja was sitting up at four months, but she would fall over. By 5½ months she was sitting up really good. (Julie, 16 - Sonja, 7 months)

Wayne's been crawling since seven months, but he didn't sit up until about that time. I liked the crawling because then he could do something. (Erin, 23 - Wayne, 9 months, and Kelton, 7 years)

The age at which she sits up, crawls, and walks seems to have nothing to do with her I.Q. when she is older. The baby who doesn't move off the blanket during much of her first year may be one of the brightest kids around.

To some parents, baby's intellectual development is very important. But intellectual development really can't be measured until about age three. Besides, there are many different kinds of intelligence. The child who doesn't read well in kindergarten may be repairing the family car a few years later, a task her reading brother may find impossible.

As Sally McCullough, Infant Center teacher, puts it, "Your child is important, your child is a fun person to be with. So enjoy him. Whether or not he is an Einstein is not terribly important."

Sometime toward the end of this five-to-nine-month period, baby may pull herself to a standing position. She'll hang on for dear life to her crib railing or to the arm of the couch. At first she's pleased with herself, but in a minute she may start crying—she doesn't know how to sit down again!

You can help her learn to sit down. Show her how. Gently bend her knees as you talk to her. She'll sit down—and two minutes later she's up again. It may take several days for her to learn to get down by herself.

CURIOSITY LEADS TO CRAWLING

As baby lies on the floor or sits in his infant seat, his curiosity is building rapidly.

Put yourself in his place. Imagine what it must be like not to be able to move. You see all those exciting things around you, and all you can do is look at them. Imagine the frustration!

Dr. Burton White, author of *The First Three Years of Life*, says wanting to satisfy his curiosity is baby's biggest reason for learning to crawl. Sure, he likes the exercise, and he likes being able to move his body, but satisfying his curiosity is the big incentive.

This past couple of weeks Jonita has started pulling herself up on the chair. She likes to stand, does not like to sit very often. This morning my sister got her up and set her in the living room. She went in the bedroom, and when she came out, Jonita was clear across the room! (Ellen, 17 - Jonita, 6½ months)

Before they walk, babies get around in a variety of ways. Classic crawling is getting up on his hands and knees and moving around. But some babies pull themselves along on their tummies. Others stand up on their feet and hands, then "walk" like a little puppy. Whichever method your baby chooses, he is delighted that he can finally get around.

Throughout most of this period, baby may be happy most of the time, just as he was in the less active two-to-five-month stage. He giggles and laughs, mimics what you're doing, and generally has a wonderful time throughout much of his day. But he wants you to be nearby.

Maelynn doesn't really like to be left alone even if I put a lot of toys around her. She'd rather I would be there to watch her and comment on what she's doing. (Joleen, 17 - Maelynn, 9½ months)

I leave the room and Robin follows me because she's so nosy. She wants to know where I'm going. She'll follow me into the bathroom and stand and beat on the tub. You say "No" to her, and she'll give you a real dirty look, then cry.

If somebody does something she doesn't like, she will crawl over to me and want me to pick her up. She doesn't just cry, she screams. (Melinda, 16 - Robin, 9 months)

DON'T TRUST STRANGERS!

He still loves people—for awhile. But by about eight months of age, your friendly baby may suddenly refuse to look at strangers. Perhaps he won't even go to Grandma. Has he turned into a frightened, timid child?

Not really. But he has matured enough to know exactly whom he trusts. He generally trusts the people he lives with and who take care of him most of the time. But now he doubts the others.

> *Maelynn likes to play with people she knows, but she's afraid of other people. She'll smile at them, but when they come up to get her, she'll hug me and not let them pick her up.*
>
> *She's been afraid like this for about three weeks. It doesn't bother me. You can see she's afraid, but she won't cry if she knows I'm there. I explain to her, and she seems to understand. (Joleen)*

Give baby time. If he hides his head in your shoulder as Grandma holds out her arms to him, tell her he needs a few minutes to adjust. He'll go to her under his own terms.

> *Men scare Danette more than women. She takes to some women pretty good. Sometimes she gets afraid of everybody. It all depends on the mood she's in. If I'm there, it's all right, but if I just hand her over to somebody, she gets scared. (Caroline, 18 - Danette, 10 months)*

"Stranger anxiety" happens to most babies although a few don't seem to experience it during the first year. When/If your baby does, be patient. He's just showing you he needs a little time to get used to people.

It may be hard to leave baby with someone else during this stage. He may protest loudly if Mother goes away:

> *Robin doesn't want me to leave. She cries when I do even though she isn't afraid of people. (Melinda)*

If Mother leaves for more than a few hours, the separation may be hard on both her and her child:

> *I went to the mountains for three days without Lynn, and it*

was hard. I couldn't really have fun because I was always think-
ing about her and wondering if she was all right. I knew she was
being taken care of OK, but it still bothered me. When I got
back, she wouldn't let me out of her sight. (Sheryl Ann, 17 -
Lynn, 7 months)

This doesn't mean it's wrong to take some time for yourself. It does
mean you will choose carefully the person who will care for your child
while you're gone. You also need to be prepared for a short period of
increased dependence on you when you return.

Some babies develop other rather strong fears. Sometimes it is the
vacuum cleaner. Or it might be the lawn mower or some other loud
noise. He may decide he wants nothing to do with new places or different situations. A trip to the store may upset him.

If it's the vacuum cleaner, you could try using it while he sleeps.
But a better way is to let him look and explore the vacuum cleaner
before you turn it on. Then hold him with one arm (lovingly, *not*
scoldingly) while you clean for a few minutes. Don't overdo it, of
course, but he may accept the noise under these conditions.

Always, whatever his age, treat your child's fears as the realities
they are. It absolutely does not matter that you know "there is
nothing to be afraid of." The fact is that he is afraid. You need to
help him deal with his fear, not scold him.

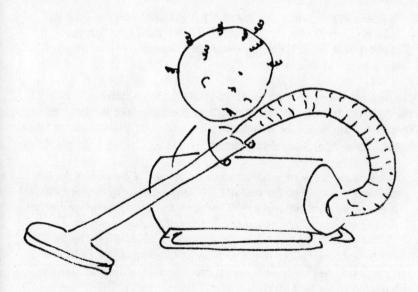

BABY LEARNING

Along about this time, while she's sitting in her highchair, baby will have her first physics lesson. She'll drop a spoon or a toy to the floor, then lean over to see what happened to it. This is serious learning on her part, and she'll try it again and again.

Of course Mother is supposed to hand the item back to her. Mothers vary as to how long they're willing to continue this game. Most, however, will go along with it for awhile, especially when they realize it's a learning time for baby.

During the last two weeks Sonja has been dropping things from the highchair. Then she looks over and sees where it goes. I pick them up for awhile, then I just say "No." (Julie)

We set Carlos in highchairs at restaurants and he'll throw things down, then look where they go. He can turn himself around, and if something is out of reach, he tries to figure out how to get it. (Renette, 16 - Carlos, 6 months)

Later, you can tie some toys to the highchair with a heavy string. Baby will learn to pull it back up herself. But at first she won't be able to do that. She needs you to do it for her.

Robin drops something from her highchair, watches it drop, then screams for me to pick it up. Then I tie it on a string so she doesn't hear it hit the floor. Now she's learning to pick it up with the string. (Melinda)

She's beginning to see that she can make things happen. Let her flip the light on and off. When she realizes she can make the light go on, then off again, she'll be delighted. She may want to continue practicing this magic for several minutes.

He knows how to work a light switch now. I'll put him by one, and he'll make it go on and off. At first he didn't know he was turning the light on and off. Then I said, "Look," and he started paying attention. He was thrilled. (Bev, 17 - Jay, 8 months)

Jay is learning he can make something happen. After awhile he'll realize that if he does one thing, something else will occur. He has discovered cause and effect.

My mom has sheets over the sofa. When Maelynn wants something up there that she can't reach, she will pull on the sheet until she can get it. (Joleen)

Did you know that baby needs your help to learn to crawl? No, you don't need to show her how to move her legs and arms. But it is important that you give her lots of opportunity to move around. That means not caging her in a playpen or setting her in her highchair for long periods of time.

Instead, put her on the floor on a blanket. Dress her so she won't hurt her knees and let her go. And before you know it, she will go—all over your house! Of course, you need to baby-proof your home by this time. See the next chapter for suggestions on this important topic.

When Lynn started crawling, I couldn't sit around any longer and not watch her when she was on the floor. She's going all the time—and so am I! (Sheryl Ann)

Clark didn't crawl two weeks ago, but now he speeds all over the place. (Kathleen, 18 - Clark, 7 months, and Aaron, 2½ years)

You'll probably see your baby staring intently at tiny tiny particles. As she crawls across the floor, she will pick up that speck of dust or the crumb she dropped from her highchair earlier. During this period, you may find yourself keeping your floors cleaner than you ever dreamed possible.

The other day I put Maelynn outside, and there were ants crawling up this pole. She dropped something and looked at the ants. She forgot the other thing and started watching them.

Sometimes when I clean her walker after she's eaten, I'll miss a spot. When I put her back in there, she'll try to get that last spot.

She likes to watch flies and bugs, little things. (Joleen)

Jay picks up fuzz balls off the floor, string, that one little thing is what catches his eye. He loves newspapers, loves tearing them up. (Bev)

CONTINUE TALKING TO BABY

Baby will begin to understand a few words during these months. He may even say "Ma-ma," "Da-da," and "Bye," but don't count on it. What you can count on is his ability to make delightful sounds. You'll hear him in his crib "talking."

This is a beautiful time to put a tape recorder by his crib. Try to turn it on just before you think he'll wake up. If you walk in to see him, however, his jabbering will stop because your face and voice are even more interesting to him than the sounds he's making himself.

Your child needs you to help him develop language. You need to talk to him and read to him long before he learns to talk himself. It is especially important now to talk about the things he knows. As you change his diaper, talk about it. As you dress him, say "Now I'm putting your shoe on your foot. Your hand goes through your sleeve." Name the parts of his body as you bathe him. Talk about the toys you're handing him.

I talk to Nick all the time. My mom talks to him and so does my dad. He's very talkative—maybe he takes after me. We've all talked to him since he was tiny. Maybe that's why he's usually happy. (Theresa)

As you carry baby around the house, show him different objects. Name and describe such things as chair, door, table, dish, picture, TV, couch. Take him outdoors and name the sidewalk, tree, fence, grass. As you do this again and again, he'll learn a lot about his world. He'll enjoy your attention, too.

Different sounds—music, an airplane, a dog barking—interest him.

Maelynn likes music—sometimes it puts her to sleep. She tries to sing along with it.

When she hears an unusual sound like an airplane, she'll stop whatever she's doing and look around to see where it's coming from. She turns around when you call her. (Joleen)

Sometimes when you're talking to baby, whisper in his ear. He'll enjoy the change, and he'll learn to listen to different levels of speech.

Some people don't talk to babies because they don't like talking and getting no spoken response. But if you wait to talk to baby until he can talk to you, you'll wait 1½ to two years. If this happened, baby would miss out on a lot of learning.

I talk to Robin all the time because she likes it and it keeps her quiet. She understands what "Come here" and "Bye" mean. I think she also knows what "eat" means. (Melinda)

READING IS IMPORTANT

If you aren't already reading to your baby, start now. Choose very simple stories, preferably with pictures of things he knows. At this age, you may have trouble getting his attention. Reading at bedtime is ideal. If baby is sleepy, he'll be more willing to sit still for a story. And if he sits or lies still long enough for a story, he'll be more apt to go to bed without causing a lot of commotion.

Carlos loves his books—he'll sit there and look at the books and talk to them. I told him the story of the Three Bears and he liked it. (Renette)

I read to Jay at night after I give him his bath. It calms him down a little. (Bev)

I read to Sonja. We have cardboard books with big pictures of dogs, cats, and other animals. I sit down and we look at it together. (Julie)

You don't need to buy all of baby's books. You can make them yourself. Cut big colorful pictures out of magazines. Choose pictures of things familiar to baby—a dog, airplane, car. Pictures of babies will intrigue him. Paste the pictures on cardboard. Punch holes in the "pages" and tie together with brightly colored yarn.

Or you may want to invest in an inexpensive photograph album, the kind with the plastic over the pages. The plastic has adhesive already on it to hold the pictures in place. After you put the pictures in place and relay the plastic, tape down all loose edges carefully with cellophane tape.

Again, choose pictures of subjects that are of particular interest to your child.

SIMPLE TOYS ARE BEST

Your little pre-walker may often play alone for as long as an hour—*if* Mother is nearby. Talk to her as you work. Give her a different object to play with every so often.

Collect small objects for your child to play with and to explore. Let her spend a lot of time on the floor on a blanket. In front of her, put several small items and a container for them. Choose things that are two to five inches in size and with a variety of shapes and textures. She'll spend a lot of time exploring these objects and practicing simple skills with them.

These small objects don't need to be expensive toys. She'll undoubtedly prefer items from your kitchen drawers. For example, plastic measuring spoons and cups, a shiny can of sardines, a plastic freezer container, and a big pan will delight her. She'll look at each thing as she takes it out of the pan. She'll feel it, chew it. Then she may bang several things together.

When she's tired of these items, you'll find more in your kitchen. Just be sure each thing you give her is smooth and safe for her. Nothing should be smaller than 1½ inches. Remember, anything you give her will be mouthed if at all possible.

Jay likes pans and lids. He'll sit there for hours and bang them together. (Bev)

Nick likes the Playtex bottle and other containers. I cleaned out one container and put pennies in it, and he loves that. Of course I taped the lid on really tight. (Theresa)

Sometime during this stage, baby will be ready for simple stacking toys. You can give her plastic cups that will nest. Be sure they don't stick together.

TIME FOR GAMES

Even though baby can now play alone, give him attention when he's happily occupied as well as when he's fussing. As he plays, talk to him, throw him a kiss, hug him as you walk by. Smiling often at him will be easy.

He'll love to play games with you. Give him a few minutes of your time several times a day for games. Hide-and-seek can change. He may hide behind a chair and ask you to find him. He'll go into gales of giggling as you look behind each chair until you "find" the right one.

Maelynn likes to play choo-choo. She does it herself sometimes. When she's in the walker, she'll go behind something, then look out at me to surprise me, and I'll laugh.

She was trying to make me laugh the other day—she bumped her head lightly on the padded headboard. She didn't get hurt, and I laughed. So she did it again to make me laugh again. (Joleen)

Get on his level. Play on the floor with him when he learns to crawl. He'll love having you chase him across the living room floor. Soon he may decide to chase you instead.

Sonja loves to play peek-a-boo. My mom says to play it with her a lot because it's like me disappearing and then coming back. She'll hold covers over her face, then drop them. I'll say "Boo!" and she'll laugh. Or we'll play peek-a-boo around the corner. (Julie)

I play peek-a-boo with Myles on the bed, and he laughs out loud. He cracks up giggling. (Janette, 18 - Myles, 7 months)

Make him some small rice bags and show him how to throw them. Use a different textured fabric for each little bag—fur, satin, corduroy and vinyl, for example. Simply cut two circles of fabric for each rice bag. With right sides together, sew tightly (preferably on a sewing machine) around the edge leaving a one-inch space for turning and stuffing. Turn right side out. Fill with rice. Sew up the hole with tiny stitches.

Using rice to stuff these little bags is far safer than using beans. He could choke on a bean. He could have a real problem if he stuffed a

bean in his ear or nose. Don't
risk it.

He would also like a feel-box.
Use a box for the container. Put
in a linoleum square, a playing
card, big rubber sink stopper,
and squares of different kinds
of textured fabric.

Baby will still enjoy a mirror
above his changing table.

Would you like to sleep a
little later in the morning? A
mirror beside his crib may
keep him intrigued for a
short time after he wakes in
the morning. Be sure it's
firmly attached to the wall.

Balls are the best toy of all
for baby. He can roll them and
throw them. Once he can crawl,
he can go after the ball. Soon he'll enjoy a big beach ball as well as
smaller ones.

> *Maelynn likes to play with her beach ball and a little tennis
> ball. She throws it, then wants someone to bring it back again.
> (Joleen)*

> *Clark loves my brother's basketball. He tries to put his mouth
> on it. He likes to put everything in his mouth. (Kathleen)*

> *We sit on the floor and I roll the ball to Sonja. She can't roll it
> back yet, but she laughs. (Julie)*

A small metal pan with a lid is a great toy. It takes patience and
skill for baby to fit the lid on the pan. If you put a small object inside
for a surprise, he'll be even more interested. After he has carefully ex-
amined the pan, you may need to show him how to take the lid off
and put it back on.

You can also show him how a block sounds when you hit the pan
with it. Show him the different sounds it makes when you tap his shoe
with the block, then the floor. Noise is an important part of baby's
life.

Sonja bangs everything. She loves to make noise. She wakes up at 5 or 6 A.M. and screams—not crying, just noisy. (Julie)

Jonita bangs toys. I have a huge keychain that she likes to play with. Once I gave it to her in a restaurant when she was in a highchair with a metal tray. That wasn't a good idea—it was so loud I had to take it away from her! (Ellen)

Robin takes cans and rolls them down the floor. She bangs toys all the time. The other morning she got up and crawled into the kitchen, opened the door—and I heard all the pans fall out. Then she screamed because it scared her. (Melinda)

You can make a fine toy using a one-pound coffee can and the old-fashioned non-spring clothespins. Make sure edge of the coffee can is smooth. Simply set the clothespins on the edge of the can. You might want to use a non-toxic paint to paint them red, yellow, and blue. You don't expect him to learn his colors yet, but you begin to introduce the idea of color when you say, "Let's put the red one on the can."

A coffee can with a plastic lid can also be used for a "drop the spool in the hole" game. Cut a hole in the plastic coffee can lid a little bigger than the spools. Then show baby how to drop the spools into the can.

Baby will enjoy going outdoors with you. If he isn't crawling yet, lay him on a blanket near you while you work in your yard. When he starts crawling, let him play in the grass. A little dirt won't hurt him. You do need to watch him rather closely, of course.

Sunshine is lovely and provides some vitamin D for your child if his skin is exposed to it. But too much sunshine is harmful. Babies should have very limited doses. Start out with two minutes of sun a day, front and back. Don't expose baby to midday sun in the hot summer. Sunning sessions should be before 10 A.M. and after 3 P.M.

If you take your baby or toddler to the beach, you'll need an umbrella unless you're staying for only a few minutes.

NOT MUCH MEMORY YET

Does baby have a memory yet? Not very much. You can "test" her memory yourself.

Sit with her on the floor. Let her play with a toy for a few minutes. Then pick it up and put it under a scarf. Does she reach for it or look for it? If she doesn't, you can figure she simply doesn't remember the toy. It's gone as far as she is concerned.

Make a game of it. Put the toy partly under a blanket. Say "Find your toy." Does baby reach for it? She may not at first. Later, as her memory develops, you'll be able to cover it entirely and she'll remember to look for it.

I'll put my hand over the plastic keys Sonja's been playing with. She pulls my fingers off and looks beneath. Or I'll put the keys behind an album cover. First she'll hit the cover, then she'll go around it. (Julie)

Jay has this thing for pens and pencils. He grabbed one the other day. I took it and put my hand over it. He remembered and tried to get my hand off it. Or I'll hide it behind me and he'll try to see it. He has some memory now. (Bev)

WATER PLAY

Babies love water play. It can be relaxing for them, too. If you can't put baby outside with some water, perhaps you can arrange it in your kitchen without too much trouble.

First, put down a good padding of newspapers, then spread an old sheet over them. Put some water in a plastic dish. One or two inches

of water is enough—you want him to splash, not flood the place.

You'll find he first splashes the water, tastes it, and has a good time finding out all he can about it. You can add to his fun by giving him a couple of ice cubes. Take them out when they get so small he could choke if he put them in his mouth. You can even put a little food coloring in the water.

> *Once in awhile I put Maelynn down, and I get her a dish with some water in it. She will start playing with that. When I give her a bath in her little tub, she'll hold on by herself and turn around and around. It worries me because she might fall. One day she put her whole head in the water and it scared me. (Joleen)*

When baby can sit up by himself, you'll probably bathe him in the big bathtub. He'll love having a few floating toys in with him. Tell him to wash the fish's hair while you wash his.

A plastic sieve for water play can be made from the lower half of a plastic milk jug. Just poke holes in it with an ice pick.

Make him a bath mitt with a washcloth. Cut two pieces of cloth the shape and size of baby's hand. Sew them together and, if you like, decorate them. Let him help wash himself with his mitten. Of course you'll never turn your back on him for a second while he's in the water.

TIME FOR TEETH

The "average" baby (yours may be quite different) cuts her first teeth when she is six or seven months old. She will probably get her lower incisors first. By eight or nine months, she may have all four of her upper teeth.

Some babies fuss when their teeth are cutting through their gums. Others seem to notice very little, if any, discomfort. One mother reported she knew her child had cut his teeth when she heard the spoon clanking against the tooth.

> *When Dale was teething, I didn't even know he was. He would be cranky once in awhile, but I just thought he was tired or something. (Arlene, 17 - Dale, 11½ months)*

But for some babies, teething is a painful experience. She may want to bite everything in sight. Give her a teething ring. Store several in the freezer. If the ring is cold, she'll like it better.

A teacher in one infant center recommended freezing thin slices of cantaloupe for teething babies. Of course you carefully remove all seeds and rind from the melon. Baby can suck on the frozen piece and, when it thaws, gum it and swallow it if she likes.

You can buy teething lotion which may help soothe painful gums. Put it on baby's gums a few minutes before feeding time. It may take away some of the pain so that she can eat more comfortably.

Jay has a tooth that's not all the way in. He's keeping me up for hours. Nothing seems to work. I put teething lotion on it, whiskey, ice cubes, but nothing helps. (Bev)

Baby may drool while she's teething. If so, put a terrycloth bib on her.

These first teeth are not chewing teeth. They won't help much when she's trying to chew food. She'll still have to gum solid food with lumps in it. But she may try to chew the nipple on her bottle.

If you are breastfeeding, she may try biting your nipple. But if the nipple is well back in her mouth as it should be for sucking, she can't bite. The only problem is when she stops sucking and decides to play. If she bites, remove your nipple from her mouth with a firm "No." Pause for a few seconds even if she's whimpering because you have taken her food away. Then if she wants to eat, let her. But don't let her bite you. Many breastfed babies learn not to bite after only a few days of this approach.

By the way, if your baby gets a fever, don't blame it on teething. She may fuss, she may even have a tiny bit of fever if her teeth are bothering her. But if she has a "real" fever, she's sick. A fever indicates an infection. Call your doctor.

Guard against cavities in those little teeth from the beginning. Encourage her to drink water. It's certainly better for her teeth than are sweet drinks, and water helps rinse milk and other foods out of her mouth.

Avoid sweet foods. During this period you should be able to keep candy and other sweets almost entirely away from baby. If she doesn't know about them, she won't cry for junk foods. The same suggestion applies to cokes and other soft drinks. Don't even give her a taste. Her teeth will thank you.

Even a bottle of milk can be a problem for baby's teeth. True, her teeth need a lot of calcium in order to develop properly and to stay healthy. The best source of calcium is milk. She needs about 20 ounces of milk each day at this stage.

A bottle of milk is a problem if she keeps the bottle nipple in her mouth as she falls asleep, and it stays there. Milk dribbling into her mouth during the night keeps her teeth covered with a film of milk. Milk, nutritious as it is, has enough natural sugar in it to damage teeth if it stays there hour after hour.

Dentists see so many toddlers with rotten little teeth in front that they have given this condition a name: Nursing Bottle Syndrome.

The solution, if baby wants a bottle in bed with her, is to fill the bottle with water. Fruit juice is even worse than milk because it has more sugar in it. If she needs the sucking when she goes to sleep, she can get it with a bottle filled with water.

Most experts recommend the bottle of water instead of milk from ten months on. They feel the milk won't cause a lot of damage before that time. But taking a bottle of milk to bed can become a very strong habit, a habit that is hard to change.

Because she can hold her own bottle doesn't mean you can no longer hold her when you feed her. She still needs a lot of love. Holding her while she drinks her bottle is a great way to give her some of that love.

BEDTIME ROUTINE

The habit of holding him while you give him his bottle is especially helpful as he begins to resist going to bed. At six months, baby will usually go to sleep if he needs to. By about nine months, however, this is not always so. By this age, baby is interested in so many things that he may not want to take time for sleep.

You can help matters by setting up a nightly routine for him. Does he have a favorite blanket or stuffed animal? If not, encourage him to take one special thing to bed with him. Help him find that object every night at bedtime.

Most babies have a security blanket or other object that is very important to them. Perhaps it's a loved teddy bear. I remember our son, four years old, losing his teddy bear in an airport on our way to a new home in another state. Disaster seemed inevitable—until his brother found it in the men's room minutes before departure time.

One little girl had a certain corner of her blanket which she rubbed on her cheek while she sucked her thumb. To her parents' amazement, she could find that one corner even in the dark.

Attachment to the security object may begin in this five-to-nine-month stage, although it will become much stronger later. Many mothers report that it's almost impossible to get that special blanket

away from the child long enough to put it through the washing
machine.

As mentioned earlier, reading to your baby at bedtime can calm him
down so that he will be able to fall asleep a little easier. Rocking him
to sleep is a method used by many parents.

> *If we don't rock Sonja before we put her to bed, she'll scream
> for an hour—but we can rock her to sleep in about 15 minutes. I
> don't mind, except I don't want her to be two years old and I still
> have to rock her to sleep. I want to be able to lay her down and
> she'll go to sleep. (Julie)*

Probably the majority of toddlers aren't willing to have mother
simply "lay her down and she'll go to sleep," however. Much older
children like to follow a routine and to be tucked in at night. Your
baby still needs some special attention at this time.

Sometimes a change in beds or rooms will disrupt even a small
baby's sleep schedule:

> *Jonita was sleeping really good through the night. Then I
> changed bedrooms with my sister and put her in a new crib. The
> past two weeks she has been getting up at night. I usually give her
> a bottle. Sometimes she'll go to bed at 9 P.M., then get up at 11
> P.M. If I'm still up, I let her play herself to sleep. (Ellen)*

Jonita may not really be hungry when she wakes up. It would probably be better for Ellen to try other methods of soothing her before
resorting to an extra bottle. She might go in to Jonita, reassure her
that she is there, perhaps pat her back for a few minutes. Jonita might
go back to sleep at that point. If not, the next step might be to offer
her a drink of water. Check her diaper. If she's wet, change her.

Letting her stay up to play when she wakes up is probably a habit
Ellen would rather Jonita didn't acquire. Letting her stay up "if I'm
still up" will cause real problems next week if Ellen is tired and wants
to go to bed at an earlier time.

WALKERS? PLAYPENS?

During the early part of this stage, your child may still use her infant seat. Place her in the seat near you so she can watch you work.
Be sure you set her in a safe place on the floor. As soon as she can sit
up by herself, however, she won't want to sit in it. By that time, she

probably would not be safe in it, either. She might be able to tip it over.

Nick will sit up in the infant seat, but he won't stay long in it anymore. (Theresa)

Unless he's sitting straight up, Carlos bounces right out of his infant seat. If he's not doing it by himself, you might as well forget it. (Renette)

Many families purchase a walker for their baby. This is fine if you are going to supervise her closely. A walker is a crutch which lets a child get around before she can do so by herself. She may go into dangerous areas, or pull things down onto herself. So watch her!

We don't have a playpen. I'd rather put Maelynn in a walker and let her do whatever she wants. She moves around, but only when she's really interested in something. She isn't getting into things yet from crawling, but she does when she's in a walker.
I put her in the walker and open the cupboards and let her get stuff out to play. (Joleen)

Robin jumps up and down in her walker and runs around. It's good except it gives her too much support front and back. She won't want to learn to walk if she's in it too long. (Melinda)

Playpens are also used by many families. If you take a poll on your street, you'll probably find several babies caged in playpens. In fact, some babies put up with spending several hours a day in a playpen.

A playpen is a handy item to take to the beach. A seven-month-old baby is not ready to be turned loose in the sand. At home, the playpen can be a safe and fun place for a baby for perhaps ten minutes—long enough for you to take a shower.

Playpens are all right, but not for a long period of time. I would feel caged in if I had that little area. But when I'm cleaning the house, sometimes I put Sonja in there for a little while. It gets hard trying to do something now that she goes everywhere.
When she's playing in her playpen and she gets restless, I put that picture of me right outside her playpen. Sonja looks at it and gets quiet. My sister started that, and it was a great idea. Or I put a big mirror outside the playpen. (Julie)

But babies generally are bored in playpens. Some scream until you let them out. Others may not fuss so much, especially if they have been stuck in their pen since they were tiny.

But how much do you learn when you're bored? Not much! Your bored baby doesn't learn much either. If you use a playpen, do so as little as possible. Your baby needs to be able to satisfy her curiosity.

See Chapter Eight for suggestions on baby-proofing your house so you and baby can survive her creeping/toddling months with as little use of the playpen as possible.

> *I'm not going to make Mark stay in a playpen where he can't touch things. I don't think they can learn much in a playpen with nothing but toys. He's very curious. (Louise)*

> *Now that Jay's crawling, he wants to pull himself up and get into things. I have a playpen but he doesn't like it. I don't really want to put Jay in a playpen anyway. I would rather he would crawl around and get into things and I'll watch him.*
> *Vince's mom thinks I should put him in the playpen. (Bev)*

Your pre-toddler has changed tremendously in these nine months. As she scoots across the floor, you may think she's into everything already. But amazingly soon she will be walking, then running. Keeping up with her will be—already is—an exciting challenge.

Chapter Eight

Child-Proofing Helps
Baby and Parents

"Nothing is more fundamental to solid educational development than pure uncontaminated curiosity," writes Dr. Burton White in *The First Three Years of Life* (page 112).

Put another way, if your child's curiosity is spoiled (contaminated) by too many "No's" and other kinds of restrictions, she won't learn as well as she could. She may not learn to read well when she goes to school. Bluntly, she won't be as smart as she could be.

On the other hand, if she can satisfy her curiosity most of the time, and if she has a lot of different kinds of experiences and things to explore, she's getting a good foundation for future learning. If her early eagerness to learn is encouraged, she'll probably still want to learn when she goes to school. And isn't that the way you want it?

As you think about providing a good learning environment for your child, "child-proofing" your house or apartment is a key issue. You need to make your home safe *for* her. You also need to protect some things *from* your child. A child-proofed home encourages her to explore and to learn more than does an environment of constant "No's."

CURIOSITY IS HARD TO SATISFY

Is "satisfying his curiosity" easy to do? Let's look at a typical living room complete with a couch, coffee table, lamps, chairs, television, and bookcase.

The floor lamp has an unsteady base and could be tipped over quite easily. One of the chairs is a fragile rocker Mother doesn't want damaged because it was her grandmother's chair. On the coffee table is a glass ash tray, a bouquet of artificial flowers, and several china figurines. Several family pictures framed and covered with glass are on the television. Against the wall is a little table. A pitcher and six glasses are setting on top of it. Books in the bookcase are not meant for children.

Now picture a ten-month-old baby in that room.

He has been crawling for several weeks. He is now learning how to pull himself to a standing position.

Next time someone tells you, "Oh, they have to learn. If he's old enough to touch it, he's old enough to be told to let it alone," think of this room. The flowers, the ash tray, the pictures, the figurines, the glasses, all are inviting. He is eager to explore, and here are all these items seemingly waiting to be explored.

But what happens? "No, you can't touch that." "I told you, let those pictures alone." "Get away from those glasses." "Put that ash tray down this minute." "Don't you dare touch those flowers."

Put yourself in his place. Do you still want to learn as badly as you did? Or does the situation remind you just a little of the strange state our schools would be in if teacher said, "Now don't you dare open that book." "Stay away from those microscopes." "Don't touch your clarinet. It might break."

> *Maybe you want to leave the stuff out so you can teach the kids, but after it's too late, it doesn't do any good. Of course we teach them not to get into light plugs, some of the cupboards, etc.*
>
> *But just to put knick-knacks where he can get them, then tell him he can't have them, is cruel. It's like putting a hungry person in front of a table of delicious food, and then telling him he can't eat. Naturally a kid is curious—they want to see and touch the pretty things. (Erin, 23 - Wayne, 9 months, and Kelton, 7 years)*
>
> *Shelly goes all through the house finding everything. But it's always somebody telling her, "No, you can't touch that." (Dixie, 18 - Shelly, 17 months)*

Ira J. Gordon, author of *Baby to Parent, Parent to Baby*, writes (page 69), "Some people believe that the best way for a baby to learn the value of property is to leave things out for her or him to get. Then punish the baby for handling them. While it is true that the child will eventually learn to leave those objects alone, she or he will also learn that exploration is dangerous, good books are to be avoided, parents can hurt you, force is an effective way to control people.''

Gradually, of course, your child must learn that some things are his and some are not. Some things can be played with and others can't. Before he's a year old, however, he really can't cope with deciding just what he can explore and what he can't. First, his memory only recently started to develop. How could he possibly remember today that you told him yesterday to leave the ash tray alone?

During his second year, too, he needs to be able to continue to explore as much as possible. But he'll be a little more capable then of following your directions.

"But how will she learn what 'No' means if I never tell her 'No'?" you ask. I can't imagine a home where a crawler or a toddler doesn't have to hear "No."

You'll stop her from burning herself on the stove. You won't let her stand up in her highchair because you don't want her to fall and break her neck. You can think of dozens of other things she'll have to learn even if you child-proof your home as completely as possible.

It's important to realize that she'll learn the meaning of "No" much better if she hears the word only occasionally. If she's told "No" all day long, no wonder she doesn't pay much attention. But if, when mother says "No," she removes baby from the forbidden activity immediately, she will understand so much better.

PLAYPEN PREVENTS EXPLORING

Playpens were discussed briefly in Chapter Seven. Penning your child up for more than a brief period is guaranteed either to bore him or infuriate him. Boredom is also a killer of curiosity, of learning. He doesn't learn much when he's infuriated, either.

I don't think you should leave babies in playpens. They won't develop if you just put them there with toys and you do your work. My aunt does that, and I think it's wrong. (Theresa, 16 - Nick, 6 months)

I don't like playpens. I'd feel like I was caging Shelly in, just as if I were putting a leash on her. My mother always told me to get a playpen, that I would regret it, and that she would be into everything. But she knows more. I know she would have learned

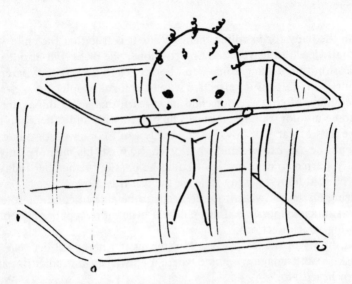

things later if she had been in a playpen.
  When she was getting into things, my mother would throw it in
my face, but I think it worked. I don't think she needed it. (Dixie)

"A child who has been in a situation where he has had to be in a
playpen a lot does show delayed motor functioning compared to other
children," commented Sally McCullough, Infant Center teacher. "It's
not a serious thing. He can catch up if he has a chance soon enough,
but it does happen. If he is penned up too long, intellectual development can also be delayed because of the lack of opportunities for
exploration."

  No playpen. I don't like them. I don't like seeing a baby penned in.
If you have them penned up in a playpen all the time, they don't learn
what they can and can't get into. I just don't like them. My mom said
I didn't like it at all, either. (Sheryl Ann, 17 - Lynn, 7 months)

  I had a playpen but I never used it. I guess if you are going to use
it, you have to put them in when they are small so they can get used
to it.
  At first I was totally against it unless you just had to have them in
it. So I never put Todd in until he was six months old. I almost never
put him in then either, mostly because I knew he couldn't explore. I
read a book that said it was like caging them.
  I still feel that way, but I think you should probably put them in a
playpen a little more than I did so you could get some things done,

*too. I couldn't even take a shower. I would wash my hair when he
was asleep. I couldn't even put him in the playpen with a new toy
because he'd scream. (Jill, 18 - Todd, 16 months)*

If you already have a playpen, use it for a toybox. Put one side
down so your baby can crawl in and out of it.

CHILD-PROOFING YOUR HOME

So if you choose not to use a playpen, or to reserve it for short
periods of time, how can you cope with your terrifically curious, still
clumsy, whirlwind of a child? After all, your sanity and the sanity of
other family members is also important!

*We child-proofed our apartment, and this has almost totally
eliminated problems because almost anything Troy can get into is OK.
If you eliminate the cause, you don't have the problem.*

*When we go to someone else's house, he is pretty good. I usually
bring along a couple of toys, or point out things he can play with
rather than saying "No."*

*We had a playpen, but I didn't keep him in it much. The doctor
said, "You're dumb. It won't hurt him to be in there two or three
hours a day, and it will give you a chance to get things done." But
Troy learned to entertain himself, and I could get things done without
him being penned up. (Rebecca, 20 - Troy, 2½ years)*

Child-proof your home! Take a weekend if necessary. Start out by
crawling through the house at your child's eye level. What does she
see? What will look inviting to her?

You're looking for two kinds of things. First, you want to remove
things that would hurt her. Second, you want to remove as much as
possible the things you don't want your child to damage.

If you like breakable decorative objects, find a high shelf,
preferably one close to the ceiling, for them. If you must leave ash
trays out, choose unbreakable ones. Then take the responsibility of
never leaving ash-filled trays where your child can reach them because
the cigarette butts are poisonous. Expect the smokers at your house,
not the baby, to figure out a way to cope with this rule.

Check your electric cords to make sure they are in good condition.
Frayed cords are not good any time, but are especially dangerous
when handled by a curious baby who puts everything she touches into
her mouth.

Get all cords out of the way as much as possible. Be sure to cover all unused electrical outlets with masking tape or special plastic covers. The plastic covers are probably better because your child might be able to pull the tape off.

I'm putting things up. She knocked over a plant the other day and broke it. She was trying to stand up by hanging on to the table, and it pulled over. (Sheryl Ann)

When you are child-proofing your living room and other areas, perhaps you can figure a way to hang cherished plants from hooks in the ceiling, well out of your child's reach. Many house plants are poisonous. Even if the plant is not poisonous, pulling a heavy plant off a table onto herself could hurt your child. The plants, too, would appreciate being out of her reach!

Some young couples box up most of their wedding gifts and store them for months, maybe years. They don't have space for their china and extra appliances in their tiny apartments. This procedure, as far as I know, has not caused a great deal of pain and grieving among these young couples.

Perhaps you can do the same thing as you are baby-proofing your house or apartment. Box up the bric-a-brac, the breakable dishes that aren't stored securely in cabinets, the artificial flower arrangements, the irreplaceable books.

We just put everything up. There is nothing on the coffee table, for example. (Jill)

LEAVE SAFE ITEMS OUT

As you're putting away the things you don't want your baby to handle, be alert for things she really couldn't hurt. If she can touch, handle, and explore the item without upsetting you or the rest of your family, and without danger to herself, leave it out. Don't forget how much she needs to explore. If you child-proofed to the point of having your living room and kitchen empty, she couldn't do much exploring.

Do you have a lot of bookshelves? You may decide to empty them up to a three-foot height. Or you may realize that books won't hurt your child. If so, make sure the books on those lower shelves aren't especially valuable or hard to replace. Baby may tear a few as she explores, but if you can handle that, leave them in place.

Leave at least one bookshelf for baby's own books. Perhaps

another can house magazines she may look at without being scolded. If she has her shelf, she'll learn much faster not to bother yours.

> *There is nothing on the bottom shelves of our bookcases. All the cupboards are child-proofed with baby locks on them. There is one bookcase in the den where we left all the books on the bottom.*
>
> *I have a couple of drawers in my bedroom that Todd can get into. He can't get into the ones in the kitchen and that aggravated him. But he gets a lot of freedom. (Jill)*

This principle of giving her a drawer or shelf of her own applies to other areas in the house. If you have at least one kitchen cupboard she may explore to her heart's content, don't feel guilty about putting child-proof fasteners on the other cupboard doors. But let her play in the cupboards containing pans and sturdy plastic ware. Cans of food also make delightful toys. In fact, she'll probably prefer your "toys" to her own.

I let Alice run through the house. I put a rubber band on the one cupboard I don't want her in. The rest of the lower cupboards she can explore all she wants. I shut each door in the long hallway. (Melanie, 15 - Alice, 13 months)

IF GRANDPARENTS DON'T APPROVE

But what do you do if you aren't in your own home? If you're living with your parents, they may not especially want to baby-proof their house or apartment. After all, they did all that when you were little, and that was enough!

You can probably understand their feelings. If you're finally able to decorate your home as you want it because your kids are grown, it can be hard going back to the toddler stage, especially if you're "only" the grandparents.

Sometimes people forget how curious and carefree crawlers and toddlers are. Or perhaps you were a quiet baby who didn't get into things very much. But your child may be extremely active, and may be constantly investigating everything possible. You may feel that child-proofing as much as you can is the only way to go, but your parents think he should "learn" by being told "No."

If it's their house, this can be a real problem for everyone.

My mom's house was not made for babies. When I lived there—I moved out when Heidi was ten months old—she was crawling and starting to hang on to the furniture to walk. When my mom wasn't around, sometimes I would put things up. When she was there, she didn't want to because she thought Heidi could learn not to touch. (Jenny, 18 - Heidi, 13½ months)

Ideally, you'll start talking about this situation long before your child is old enough to need a child-proofed house. If your seven-month-old crawler has just broken your mother's favorite antique vase, it isn't the best time to deal with the child-proofing problem!

If your family is firm about not wanting to disrupt their living area with child-proofing, perhaps you can arrange your bedroom to be as attractive and challenging as possible for your child.

Fix things so he won't have to hear "No" constantly when he's in that room. You'll need to spend a lot of time there with him, of course, but this can work pretty well for the first year.

In the meantime, do all you can to be responsible about rearing your child. Don't leave diapers in the toilet or baby things setting all

over the house. Wash out baby bottles and clean up after feeding
baby.

If you're careful about keeping this kind of mess cleaned up, your
family may decide it's OK to rearrange the house for baby after all.

> *That's what my dad said at first, "Todd is going to have to
> learn." But Dad is the one who ended up putting more things
> away. I started putting things up, but he left some books out. He
> kept saying, "No, no," but finally he put his books away like the
> rest of us. (Jill)*

If your family doesn't see it this way, continue to allow your toddler as much freedom to explore as you can. Plan to spend a terrific
amount of time supervising, far more than you would have to spend
in a child-proofed apartment.

If you distract him—give him a substitute toy for the forbidden object—he'll gradually mature. Constant supervision for a few months
should result in more freedom for you as well as for your child by the
time he is two.

If you make time to teach him—slowly and over several months'
time—that he can play with this but he can't touch those things, he'll
finally learn to follow your direction. See Chapter Ten for more ideas
on discipline.

ACCIDENT-PROOFING IS ESSENTIAL!

Your family will undoubtedly realize that all of you must work
together to guard baby against accidents. This is the part of baby-
proofing that permits little compromise.

Accidents injure and kill many young children every year. In fact,
accidents are by far the greatest cause of injury and death for this age
group. Thousands are permanently crippled or killed annually because
of accidents.

The chief causes of fatal accidents for children under one year of
age are suffocation and choking. For toddlers and preschoolers, cars,
fires, drowning, and poisoning cause the most fatal accidents. About
40 percent of all injuries are caused by falls.

Accident-proofing your home as much as possible is well worth
your time. It is absolutely essential if you have a baby, toddler, or
preschooler living there.

Infants as well as toddlers can be the victims of damaging accidents.
Never leave a baby alone on a changing table, bed, or other off-the-

floor surface even for a second. The baby who couldn't turn over yesterday may be able to do so today.

When you visit friends, put your tiny baby's blanket on the floor. She can nap there as well as she could on the bed, and she will be much safer.

No baby needs or should have a pillow in her bed. A pillow could cause a breathing problem if she got her face buried in it. If Grandma made a beautifully embroidered pillow for her, appreciate it, but keep it out of her crib.

The propped bottle is another common danger for infants. Baby could choke from her milk coming too fast from that propped bottle. Propped bottles, of course, are also a no-no for two other reasons. They cause most of the ear infections that babies have, and the propped bottle doesn't provide the loving human contact baby needs at mealtime.

START WITH YOUR KITCHEN

Dangers multiply rapidly when your child is crawling, then walking. Accident-proofing involves far more now that he can plunge almost deliberately (it seems) into risky situations.

The kitchen is a marvelous learning laboratory for babies and toddlers. Designing it so it's safe for your baby is an important challenge.

Probably 90 percent of us keep cleaning supplies in the cupboard under the sink. Yet most, perhaps all, of these materials are dangerous

to a baby or toddler. For example, if he gets dishwashing detergent on his fingers, he'll then put his fingers in his mouth as usual. Because dishwashing detergent is so powerful, it can burn his mouth badly. Don't let it happen!

I keep a lock on the door under the sink so Gary can't get into it. (Jan, 15 - Gary, 12 months)

My mother always said not to put my soaps and things in a low cupboard, so I have always kept them up high above the stove. (Olivia, 20 - Henry, 23 months)

During the years you have a baby or young child, it is terribly important that you put such dangerous items in a high cupboard. Even there, if he is a climber, you should use a secure lock.

Leon pushes a chair up to the counter and gets up in the top cupboard looking for little goodies. I have glasses up there, so I suppose I will have to fasten the doors shut. I keep him locked out of the bathroom. (Tamera, 21 - Leon, 20 months, and DeeDee, 4½ years)

Knives need to be stored where a small child can't reach them. Check kitchen drawers and cupboards for other dangerous items. Your child could get a nasty cut from a vegetable grater. An ice pick is literally a deadly weapon.

Keep all pot handles turned toward the back of the stove. If you have your baby in someone else's house while cooking is being done, check that those pot handles are safely out of baby's way. Keep all coffee pot, toaster, and other appliance cords completely out of his reach, too, whether you are at home or someplace else.

Do you iron? (Some of us get through life with no-iron clothes.) If you do, notice how unsteady your ironing board probably is. Even if you remember to keep the iron cord up, baby can knock the whole thing over. Of course, a dangling iron cord is inviting a serious accident. Iron when baby is asleep, then put the board and the iron away.

I always keep the iron and the cord up, and I push the ash trays back so Gary can't reach them. (Jan)

When your child has a minor accident such as touching the stove and burning his fingers slightly, help him understand what happened.

Don't say anything about "the bad stove" burning him, and don't fix
it up with cookies. Sympathize, of course, but also explain that if he
touches the stove when it's hot, he'll be burned.

If you're buying a range, you may be able to get one with controls
on top at the back. If the controls are in baby's reach, you'll have to
watch constantly that he doesn't turn the heat on. A gas stove without
a pilot light is extremely dangerous in a home with little children. If
it's turned on, but not lit, escaping gas can be deadly.

If you have a gas heater, have someone help you check to see if it
has a valve which cuts off the gas if the pilot light goes out. If it
doesn't, escaping gas could cause lack of oxygen and explosions.
Don't heat with a gas oven by leaving the door open because of the
same dangers.

If you ever smell gas in your home, check with the gas company immediately. In most areas, they will send someone out to check it at no
charge to you.

To a creeping baby, tablecloths are to be pulled. If hot foods, even
empty dishes, come down with the cloth, results can be disastrous.
Even placemats can cause big problems. Our second son, when he was
eleven months old, pulled on a placemat early one winter morning.
Over came the cup of freshly poured coffee. His burn required
emergency hospital treatment.

*Sonja pulls on the tablecloth. If it were my own home, I don't
think I would leave it on the table. People tell me kids have to
learn not to touch it. I think when they're babies you can't do
that. (Julie, 16 - Sonja, 7 months)*

You know how baby loves to play peek-a-boo by pulling a blanket
over his face. He might do the same thing if he finds a thin plastic
bag, the kind put on garments by dry cleaners. If he did, he could suf-
focate within minutes because the thin plastic would cling to his face
and shut off his breathing. Cut up and discard such bags immediately
after you get them.

DANGER OF POISONS

About 80 percent of all reported accidental poisonings involving
children take place among toddlers ten to thirty months of age.

You would be smart to lock up furniture polish, kerosene, gasoline,
and all cleaning agents. Keep your cosmetics out of your child's reach,
too, because some of these are poisonous.

It's ironic that something that is supposed to be life-saving can also be life-destroying. Yet accidental poisoning caused by swallowing medicine happens to many babies and toddlers. Some children in their eagerness to explore will eat anything even if it tastes bitter or, in our judgment, plain awful.

Don't ever refer to medicine as candy. If you do, baby may decide to take a whole bottle of "candy" at once. She knows baby aspirin taste good, but she can't understand that a handful of them could kill her.

Even prenatal vitamins with iron, so necessary for the sake of an unborn child, are deadly for toddlers. Too much iron is toxic (poisonous) to children. Taking six to twelve of these capsules can kill a toddler unless she gets medical attention, according to Corrine Ray, administrator, Los Angeles Poison Control Center. In fact, any medication with iron, including children's vitamins, can be dangerous if taken in bigger doses than prescribed. Medical treatment is needed if this happens.

You can get a small strong box with a lock for under $10. Protect your child by getting one and putting all medicines, including baby aspirin, in it. Then keep it locked. Your child's life is worth the effort.

> *Our medicine is all put up. We put them up as high as we could. I have to stand on a chair to get it, but it's better to do that than have to rush them to the hospital. I also have a "What to do in case . . ." taped to the medicine cabinet. (Celia, 21 - Lance, 18 months, and Laurel, 4 years)*

Watch out for guests' purses. The "normal" thing to do with your purse when you're in someone else's home is to set it beside you. If your friend does this, guess what? As you talk together, your toddler, feeling ignored anyhow, starts going through her purse. You're busy talking, so you don't notice. Next thing you know, baby has opened your friend's bottle of aspirin and swallowed them all. Avoid this problem. Insist the purse be put up out of reach when your friend arrives.

If, in spite of all your precautions, your child swallows something poisonous, try to find out immediately what it was. Save the container to take with you to the hospital. Then call your doctor, the nearest hospital emergency room, or your local Poison Control Center for advice on first-aid treatment.

Even if you lock up all medicines, you may decide the bathroom is one room your baby can't enter. If she can't open doors herself, just keep the door shut at all times. Make it as safe as possible inside, however, because you know she will get in there occasionally. But it's probably impossible totally to toddler-proof a bathroom.

Sonja threw a roll of toilet paper into the toilet about two weeks ago. She bangs the toilet seat up and down, too. (Julie)

Heidi likes to play in the toilet an awful lot. I hate that—that's irritating. So I have to keep the bathroom doors shut. And she loves to play with the toilet paper. She'll unroll the whole thing if you let her! (Jenny)

You should never leave a baby or toddler alone in the bathroom. But the day will come when she goes in herself, then locks the door behind her. An outside lock-release on the bathroom door would solve that problem.

CHECK ALL AREAS FOR DANGER

Stairs are an obvious danger to a creeping/crawling/toddling child. Putting a gate at the top and one at the bottom is a solution. But put the lower gate at the third or fourth step up, not at the bottom. Baby will then have a chance to practice climbing a few steps, then coming

back down. But he won't have far enough to fall to hurt himself.

Lance climbs stairs. My in-laws have a two-story house, and that's bad news. He doesn't get down very well, but he can go up them. We have two steps on our porch, and he can slide down on his tummy on those. If we had a two-story house, I would make sure we had a gate. (Celia)

Another room you may decide to shut off, perhaps with a gate, is a place where an older brother or sister plays. Satisfying baby's curiosity there might cause more trouble with big brother than it's worth.

My brother gave Laurel some model cars, and she can't play with them except when Lance is in bed. Sometimes he can be sort of pesty, but Laurel knows not to play with them when he's around. She also has a game with marbles, and of course she has to be super-careful to keep those away from Lance. But most of the toys she has are OK.

When she builds houses with blocks, Lance kicks them down. So I try to play with him with his blocks while Laurel builds with hers. (Celia)

It takes pretty constant watching where I'm living. Quentin (Heidi's uncle) leaves little screws and things on the floor in his bedroom. I've asked him a few times to pick them up, but he doesn't. I get furious and start yelling at him. (Jenny)

If you have a fireplace, open heater, heating register, or floor furnace, put guards in front of and over it. Use furniture to block off radiators.

If your toddler has learned to open doors, you can attach fasteners, the hook-and-eye kind, up too high for him to reach. You'll need some method of keeping doors closed if they lead to stairways, driveways, and some storage areas. Your window and door screens need to be locked or nailed securely in place.

Sometimes Heidi will go out the front door. She takes her ten-month-old cousin with her into the front yard. Luckily we're on a dead-end street where no cars come. (Jenny)

Do you have a pet door, a little door your dog or cat can open? If it's big enough for your baby to get through, expect him to use it!

*Sometimes I will be doing something, curling my hair or
polishing my nails. The next thing I know, Heidi has gone out the
doggy door and is playing with the dogs in the back yard. I'll
bring her back, and she'll do it maybe three times more. (Jenny)*

ACCIDENT-PROOF OUTSIDE AREA

A fenced-in yard is a marvelous luxury for a toddler and her
parents. If you are lucky enough to have one, enjoy it, but keep an
eye on your child as she plays there.

Yards, fenced or not, and garages need to be child-proofed, too.
Check for rubbish, insecticides, paint removers, and other poisons.
Get rid of them or lock them up. Also get rid of rusty furniture and
nails. Keep gardening equipment and other tools locked in the garage.
Check hammocks, swings, and other play equipment for safety.

Some plants are poisonous. You need to find out if in your yard
you have shrubbery or other plants dangerous to your child. Also
check any house plants in your home.

Even a lovely rose garden can harm a toddler when she runs into all
those thorns. Putting a temporary, but sturdy fence around your roses
will protect baby. It will also protect the roses.

IS PAINT LEAD-FREE?

Do you have furniture, walls, or woodwork in your home which
were painted some time ago? If the paint contains lead, it can damage
your child if he chews on the painted surface, or if the paint is peeling
and he puts bits of it in his mouth. Lead poisoning could be the
result, a serious problem for babies and children.

When you buy paint, make sure the label on the can states that the
paint is lead-free and safe for children. It should read "Conforms to
USA Standard Z66.1-1964 for use on surfaces which might be chewed
by children."

Lead poisoning is most apt to occur in older neighborhoods. Before
World War II, almost all house paints were made with lead as the
base. Even though more recent coats of paint in old houses are probably lead-free, chipping paint will include the bottom layers of lead-
base paint. Many children eat these chips of peeling paint and plaster.
Apparently they taste sweet, and children like them.

But if children get too much lead, they will show signs of lead
poisoning. "Too much" for a baby may be a very little bit of the
paint. The child may become anemic and lose his appetite. He may be

either listless or hyperactive and irritable. He may find it harder to learn, and may even suffer convulsions and permanent brain damage from the poisoning.

If you suspect lead poisoning, check with your doctor. Through a simple blood test, s/he can detect the condition. If lead poisoning has occurred, the doctor can recommend treatment to get rid of much of the extra lead in your child's body so he won't have the problems described above.

CONSTANTLY SUPERVISE WATER PLAY

Never leave your child alone in water. She can drown in a bathtub or a wading pool as well as in a swimming pool, lake, river, or ocean. Even shallow water is dangerous. A child can drown in an inch or two of water.

Mothers of toddlers need to be constantly alert if there is a nearby swimming pool.

> *I'm so afraid about that pool. I watch Henry constantly. We go in the pool and he paddles his feet. That's about it. (Olivia - lives in apartment complex.)*

> *Right now Shelly can't open the doors, but later on she'll be able to. Then she can get to the pool, and she'll just jump in it. She loves it, and she doesn't know she could drown. I always take her in when I go.*

She has fallen in, but not in the deep part, just the three-feet-deep section. I was in the pool and my cousin had her. Then suddenly she dived in. I brought her up pretty quickly. She came up laughing, with water in her mouth, and I tried not to scare her. (Dixie)

You can't assume that anything designed to keep children from drowning is foolproof. If baby gets upside down in the water, wearing a life jacket may keep her floating—but floating *upside down.*

Life jackets can be dangerous. Mothers buy these and think, "My child is safe." Don't believe it. Meghan had one on, and another child pushed her in. We almost lost her. She had swallowed quite a bit of water by the time I realized it. That life jacket didn't do any good. I swam over there as fast as I could and pulled her out, and she was OK. (Louise, 19 - Mark, 5½ months, and Meghan, 23 months)

Some parents feel it is important for their baby to learn to swim as early as possible. A horrifying number of small children die in family pools each year. Many apartment buildings now have pools, too. They're usually well fenced, but the risk is always there of someone leaving the gate open.

If you have this problem, check with your town's recreation department. Do they offer swimming lessons for toddlers? These can be lifesavers.

I'm teaching Lynn how to swim. I don't like having little kids around a pool if they can't swim. I've been taking her to the big swimming pool, and I'll just hold her hands. She will hold her head up and kick her feet. (Sheryl Ann)

I taught Myles to swim. He goes underwater, and he can dog paddle. (Janette, 18 - Myles, 7 months)

Heidi likes to swim, and she can stay up. We taught her how when she was ten weeks old. She won't sink if you put her in. (Jenny)

Don't ever think your toddler is safe because she can swim, however. She still needs constant supervision. Sally McCullough, Infant Center teacher, tells a harrowing story:

"Our neighbor came over one day with her four-year-old. 'He's learned to swim and he wants to show you,' she said proudly.

"So my husband and I watched. Sure enough, Seth dived into our pool. He appeared to be swimming underwater as most children do. His mother was beaming.

"But suddenly Stewart jumped in the pool and pulled Seth out. He had all at once realized that kid was drowning right before our eyes!"

All children must be watched at all times when they are in a pool. Even good swimmers get in trouble. Children often play games that are really very dangerous. Toddlers, of course, must be removed from the pool if older kids are playing roughly.

Unused pools should be drained and covered when not in use. A swimming pool, of course, should be securely fenced. Back yard holes, old wells, and cisterns should be filled.

CAR SAFETY

Of course you'll do everything you can to keep your toddler from running out into the street. But did you know that more children are hurt inside cars as passengers than are injured on the outside as pedestrians?

Traffic accidents are the leading cause of death in childhood once the critical early months have passed. They claim more lives than any disease.

During the last decade, about 10,000 children under five died as passengers in automobiles. Of the hundreds of thousands injured, many remain permanently disabled, physically or mentally.

Seat belts are real lifesavers for adults and older children (*if* they use them!), but they don't protect infants or children weighing less than 40 pounds. Riding in a car bed or in your arms is not safe for baby, either. Even many car seats designed for young children will not protect them adequately in accidents.

Car seats are available, however, to protect your child from injury while riding in your car. Several different brands are

good, but check to be sure the one you buy meets government standards for safety.

For infants, you need a seat in which the baby rides facing
backward in a reclining position. It should be held firmly in place by
the car's seat belt.

When you choose a car seat for toddlers and slightly older children,
be sure the seat can be fastened securely by the car's seat belt. If it is
a tall seat, the top must also be anchored to keep it from toppling forward.

Each of the major car manufacturers has a good car seat which
should be available through their dealers. If your dealer doesn't know
about it, you may have to insist she find out. You can also buy a well-
designed car seat in some department stores.

Spending money for a good car seat is much more important than
spending it for a bath table, playpen, or fancy carriage. Your child's
life may depend on it.

A car seat, of course, is safe only if the child is buckled in it. When
your toddler decides to be negative about his car seat, it's time for
you to be positive. Fasten him in it very matter-of-factly, even if he's
screaming. Be sure he knows you, too, use a seat belt.

Making sure your child is safe in your home, in your car,
everywhere he goes, is a big responsibility. Creating a safe environment that also allows him to explore and to learn about his world is a
double challenge with double rewards.

You will find more peace of mind knowing your child is not in
danger, and you will be delighted with the bright, happy individual
that he is.

Chapter Nine

Nine-Fifteen Months: She's a Toddler

Dale gets into everything. He's starting to talk, to say words. The other night I said "Good night," and he said "Night!" That's exciting. (Arlene, 17 - Dale, 11½ months)

Gary has been walking since he was ten months old. He says "Ma-ma," "Pa-pa." We talk to him a lot in both English and Spanish. He's curious. If he sees you doing something, he copies you. He'll come over and look. He's very close to me.

He climbs up on a board and then jumps off, but he's not on the couches yet.

He loves playing outside, mostly with other kids. He takes pans out of the cupboard and takes them outside. He picks up a lot of rocks and puts them in the pans and carries them around. (Jan, 15 - Gary, 12 months)

Robin's a monster. She gets into everything. She's crawling around, pulling herself up, standing up, eating table food part of the time. (Melinda, 16 - Robin, 9 months)

Nine to fifteen months—this is the busiest stage yet for both you and your child. She is no longer an infant. She's finally able to move—and move she will. By the time she's fifteen months old, in fact, she may be running.

DIFFICULT STAGE FOR PARENTS

This is a difficult stage for many parents. "She gets into everything," they often say. Because she can get into so many things, people assume she should be able to understand wrong from right. She should be able to follow your orders.

But this isn't true. Her memory is only beginning to develop. If she does happen to remember that you said "No" the last time she touched that ash tray, she still doesn't have the self-control to leave such an inviting item alone. Slapping her hand mostly teaches her that big people hit little people. But she really doesn't know why.

Heidi has been walking since she was 10 months old, and she started taking steps at 8 months. You tell her to come here, and she'll turn around and go the other way. She's very good at ignoring you. If she's entering the negative stage, she's getting good at it! (Jenny, 18 - Heidi, 13½ months)

At this point, removing her from temptation is the smart and loving approach. You can offer her a safe toy or activity instead of the forbidden one. Chances are pretty good that she'll accept the change.

Dr. Burton L. White is director of Harvard University's Preschool Project and author of *The First Three Years of Life.* Dr. White thinks most families do a good job parenting their children during the first six to eight months of life. If they love their babies a lot and satisfy their basic needs to eat, sleep, be comfortable, and avoid loneliness, they're probably doing pretty well.

Dr. White estimates, however, that no more than 10 percent of us do as well as we should with our children during the time they are 8 to 36 months old. He is convinced that a child who doesn't learn as she should before she is three years old will probably never catch up.

His research shows that children

who don't do well in school usually score OK in ability tests until they are a year old. By age two, they are beginning to show problems. By the time they are three years old, they exhibit to quite an extent how well—or how poorly—they will be doing in school a few years later.

Every child, according to Dr. White, is "at risk" during the period from eight months to two years. She is "at risk" as far as learning as much about her world as she should during this period. Being "at risk" means that, unless her parents and other caregivers provide her with enough learning experiences and plenty of freedom to be curious, she won't learn as she should.

Being "at risk" means the desired behavior/learning won't happen automatically. Unless you help her, she may not learn to talk as well as she might. Unless you guide her in learning to get along with people, her social development won't be as good as it should be.

CURIOSITY IS CRUCIAL

Every parent has a huge responsibility to make it possible for her/his child to be as curious as possible. Curiosity doesn't thrive on a steady diet of "No" or constant imprisonment in a playpen.

> *Sylvia likes to get into things, to analyze things. She's very curious. When she sees something on the floor, she stares at it, then puts it in her mouth. Then she takes it out and looks at it again. (Carrie, 18 - Sylvia, 14 months, and Crystal, 31 months)*

> *Dale is curious about everything. He never stops, doesn't want anyone to pick him up. He's independent already.*
> *He has to see what everything feels like, what it looks like. He gets Cheerios, and loves to play with them. As soon as I say "No," his face looks like he is going to break down in tears.*
> *He pulls the drawers open and takes clothes out. He's trying to drink out of a cup, too.*
> *We took him to the beach the other day, and we gave him a shovel. He filled up the pail with water and started drinking it. (Arlene)*

Why is he so curious? Why does he have such a tremendous need to explore? Perhaps because he spent several months lying down, then sitting, but unable to move about. As he watched his world, he became more and more curious. Now that he's crawling, he can do something about his curiosity—he can explore. And explore he will.

Gary seemed to change as soon as he was 11 months old. He's more aware of things. Before, he would just look at something. Now he goes to it, touches it, and examines it with his hands. (Jan)

You'll be amazed at the extent of his curiosity. He may turn the television on and off over and over again until you can stand it no longer. But think of the power he must feel when he pushes that button and the TV comes on!

He may open and shut a kitchen cupboard door dozens of times a day. If he finds paper on the floor, he'll crumple it. He'll investigate anything and everything.

Danette likes the wastebasket. She knocks it over and pounds on it. She opens the cupboard doors over and over and looks in. She'll stare, then sometimes grab something and walk away with it. (Caroline, 18 - Danette, 10 months)

Robin swings doors back and forth. She smacks the bathroom door against the bathtub every morning and wakes my brother up. She'll do that for as long as she gets away with it. (Melinda)

INTO-EVERYTHING STAGE

By the end of the first year, baby may be climbing. At first he will struggle to get on a low footstool. Soon he will master heights of a foot or so. If he can do that, he can climb on a chair. From there, he can climb to the table or to the kitchen counter. If you haven't baby-proofed your house and your habits, you now have a problem.

Dale climbs up on the bed and on the couch, and he's trying to get on the table. I worry about him because he won't stay still at all, and I'm afraid he'll get into something. I watch him constantly.

The last crisis was when I didn't think he was able to open a bottle yet. He was playing with a bottle of alcohol. Suddenly he opened it, and I had to run and get it away from him. (Arlene)

I worry about Robin all the time. She gets into everything, and she's on the go 24 hours a day. She falls and gets hurt because she tries to stand up on everything. She climbs on the couch. She climbs up me when I'm holding her in the rocking chair—she wants to climb up and look over the back.

I use the rocking chair a lot. Every time she has a bottle, or every time she goes to bed, we have to rock her. (Melinda)

Now Alice climbs off beds and is learning how to climb up on the bed. I bought her a little skate toy when she was one year old. Within a month, she learned how to get on and off it. She also tried to stop it from going anywhere by climbing on top of it. She's not really walking, but she'll walk to something she wants badly like her bottle. (Melanie, 15 - Alice, 13 months)

Has he learned to climb stairs? Then it's time to try teaching him to come down safely. Show him how to slide down on his stomach, feet first. Even if you have a gate on the stairs, it may be left open occasionally, and he needs to learn how to cope.

Alice learned how to crawl up and down stairs while we were in Texas, and she did it over and over. At first, it scared me. She went up three stairs, and I panicked and took her down. Then she started up again and fell once. But from then on, she could do it. (Melanie)

A one-year-old child is constantly active and constantly moving. He is always completely absorbed in what he is doing. He can be a fun companion because he is so active. He can also be completely frustrating to you for the same reason—he's so active.

Danette is very squirmy when I diaper her. She loves to play in the toilet. About two months ago she learned how to lift up the lid. She learns fast, but she can't open doors yet, so we keep the bathroom doors shut. (Caroline, 18 - Danette, 10 months)

Changing baby's diaper is quite a challenge during this stage. Putting a toy in his hand may distract him from his violent kicking and wriggling. You may even find you can put a diaper on baby while he's standing up.

It's very hard to change Heidi's diapers. She squirms, yells as if you're killing her. (Jenny)

If all of this sounds as though baby is always in command, don't you believe it! Discipline (not necessarily punishment) is so important from infancy on that Chapter Ten is devoted entirely to this subject.

Of course he will try to do some things that must be stopped with a "No." However, his understanding of "No," if he hears it constantly, may be "Don't try" or "Don't find out."

He won't learn as he should if he decides he isn't supposed to explore, to try new things. But he can certainly cope with the truly necessary "No's."

CRUISING AND WALKING

Soon after baby learns to stand, she may start "cruising." To cruise, she walks around while carefully supporting herself by placing her hands on the couch, a chair, or some other object. A few babies go from crawling directly to walking. But most cruise, sometimes for several weeks, even months. At first she's extremely cautious, but before long she skims along hand-over-hand the entire length of the couch.

Alice isn't walking yet, but she takes a couple of steps. She holds on to the couch and reaches, then goes from the couch to the table. She's been doing this since she was about nine months old.

She won't walk in the walker, but will push it herself and walk with it. Or she will walk with the chairs. We have the kind with casters on the legs. (Melanie)

She may move from one piece of furniture to another if she's able to reach the second item with one hand while she safely keeps her other hand on the first support. She might love to have you arrange your living room furniture so she can cruise all around the room. To do this, set the pieces of furniture close together so that she can reach from one to the other.

Danette is walking. At about eight months, she started walking around or to the furniture. She took her first steps three or four weeks later. For a couple of weeks, she just took a few steps, then she started walking all over the place. (Caroline)

Walking at nine months is unusual. The average age to start walking is between twelve and fourteen months. Some children wait a couple of months longer.

Your toddler requires even more constant supervision than she did when she was crawling. She will run outside to explore whatever is happening. By herself, she would run into a busy street. What can you do about this? *Supervise her!* Try to be tolerant. Remember how curious she is and how impossible it is for her to control her own actions at this age.

Baby's increased activities are often a worry:

I worry about Maelynn getting hurt, but I try not to be over-protective. I worry a little, of course, but I try not to overdo it. I worry about her falling down, but when she falls, I say, "Oh, oh, you fell." I don't make a big scene out of it.

I have an aunt who says, "Oh, did you get hurt? Oh no!" and this scares her kids more. So I try to stay real calm so she won't get scared. I've watched my cousins—after they fall, they'll keep playing until their mother screams, then they start crying. I'm learning a lot from them because I don't want Maelynn to be like them. (Joleen, 17 - Maelynn, 9½ months)

Your baby continues to like water play. Now that she is older, this can be a problem if there is a pool nearby. A child can drown in a couple of inches of water. Always be with her when she's playing in water, whether it's in a tiny pool or in a big pool, or even in a bathtub or a pail of water.

The purpose of giving a child a bath is to get her clean. Right? Yes—to you. But to your child, a bath is simply water play.

Robin loves to sit in the bathtub. She'll sit there for hours with me beside her. When I look down, all the water is splashed out. She kicks and throws it out. (Melinda)

Heidi loves baths. She likes to get all soapy. She even likes having her hair

*washed. I pour a glass of water over her head and she loves it.
(Jenny)*

Sometimes she'll want to do it herself. Give her a washcloth or bath
mitt to use while you're washing her. Let her help dry herself with her
own towel.

Trying to keep an exploring toddler soap-and-water clean at all
times can upset her. It may also turn her into a child who is afraid of
getting dirty—which limits drastically the amount of exploring she
can do.

Buy or make the toughest and simplest clothes possible for your little toddler. Make sure she doesn't feel guilty if she gets herself and
her clothes dirty. This is *not* a stay-clean stage!

CLEANLINESS VERSUS HYGIENE

Penelope Leach, author of *Your Baby and Child from Birth to Age
Five*, explains the difference between cleanliness and hygiene. While
overconcern about cleanliness or neatness is not good for an exploring
baby, good hygiene is vital to her health.

Leach writes (page 230), "You will get the balance between the two
about right if you are exceedingly fussy about food and excreta and
not very fussy about the cleanliness of anything else."

She explains that good hygiene is a matter of protecting your child
from an overdose of harmful bacteria. While there are bacteria
everywhere, most of them are harmless. The body can cope with
them. The body can also cope with a few "bad" bacteria. But if these
bad ones have a good breeding place, they multiply very rapidly. And
that's dangerous for baby. Good breeding grounds are food and
excreta.

Cooked food must be kept covered and cold or hot, never warm. If
a tiny bite of cream pie falls under the table and you miss it when you
clean, bacteria will start multiplying. If baby picks that tiny piece of
pie up several hours later and stuffs it in her mouth, it may make her
very sick.

Be extra careful about cleanliness in the bathroom, too. Be sure you
always wash your hands after you change her diaper. Wash her hands
for her if she explores her own body while you change her. Mop up
toilet accidents and burped-up milk quickly.

Always clean up pet feces immediately. This may mean inspecting
your yard every morning, even several times a day, if your toddler
plays there. Children can get pin worms from handling pet feces.

OUTDOOR PLAY

Most children this age love to play outdoors. If you don't have a grassy yard, is there a park nearby? Of course, being outside when you're one year old means lots of supervision from mother or another caregiver.

> *Dale loves being outside, and he likes the park a lot. We go every Sunday because his father plays baseball. We're constantly chasing after him. (Arlene)*

> *Heidi loves to go to the park. I take her there every once in awhile, together with her ten-month-old cousin.*
> *She notices little bugs on the ground, little ants. She'll put her face down close to them, make her little noises, and show me. She has a little bugcatcher toy. When I put a bug in it, she picks it up and looks at it. Then I let the bug go.*
> *I take her for a walk every evening. I teach her things on the way. We stop every day and look at two dogs and some parakeets behind a fence down the street. One day the owner showed us his birds. She was thrilled. (Jenny)*

A child doesn't need shoes until she starts walking outside. When you buy them, be sure they fit well and aren't too big. There should be about one-half inch of space between her big toe and the end of her shoe.

You will have to replace her shoes often because her feet will grow so quickly. As long as they fit well, it's all right to buy the cheapest brand you can find.

MORE LANGUAGE DEVELOPMENT

If you have talked to baby ever since he was born, and you've given him lots of learning experiences, he'll be working hard learning to talk by the end of his first year. He won't be saying many words yet, but he'll try.

> *Heidi's a lot of fun at this age. She'll point at something and grunt, "Truck," "Tree," "Birds." First step,*

she grunts, wants me to say the word. Next step, she'll be talking.
She notices the airplanes and helicopters in the air. She points
at those and makes her noises. She knows her eyes, nose, mouth,
tongue, hair. One problem—there's a lot of cussing in the house
and I don't want her to pick that up. (Jenny)

Reading to your child, as mentioned before, is an important part of
his language development.

Heidi loves picture books. I read to her. She has books in her toy
box. She looks at them, then shows me and grunts that she wants
me to read to her. It's really amazing how she wants to talk so
bad. (Jenny)

Peggy Daly Pizzo describes in *How Babies Learn to Talk* a research
project which studied the effect reading to a child has on that child's
language development.

Researchers studied a group of mothers who read to their babies 15
to 20 minutes each day. They read from simple, inexpensive children's
books, pointed at the pictures, and talked about them. They used the
books as the basis for talking with their infants.

Language development of these children was compared with a
carefully matched group of children who weren't in the study and
whose mothers did not read to them consistently. By the time they
were 17 months old, the children whose mothers had read to them had
better speaking abilities than did the other group of children. The
research continued until the children were 2½ years old. The read-to
children continued to speak better than did those whose mothers did
not read to them.

I read to Danette, especially Dr. Suess. Jim has a bunch of
books he's buying, Snow White and other Disney books, but I
like Dr. Suess best. I think reading to her gives her a head start in
her education.
I enjoy sitting and reading with her. I read mostly at night, but
a lot of times in the afternoon, too, we'll read a book. Often I sit
in my rocking chair, she sits on my lap, and we read. (Caroline)

As your child begins to say words, he may especially like his own
"Book of (his name)'s Words." Use light cardboard for the pages.
The cardboard in panty hose packages works well. Punch holes in the
pages and tie them together with yarn. Find pictures to represent the

words he is saying. "Ma-ma,"
"Da-da," "Bye," and "Dog" may be
his first understandable words. Put a
picture of each in the book, then read it
with him. He may be "reading" to you
soon.

The pictures are the important thing.
Don't get hung up on teaching your
child to read for several years yet. But
you can count on him learning to read
with less struggle later if he enjoys
books with you now.

Watching television may increase a
child's vocabulary. Many children mimic
TV commercials delightfully. But speaking ability develops best in one-to-one
exchanges—Mother or Daddy talking
directly to baby, and baby responding. Television doesn't wait for that
important response. Neither does television always, or often, concentrate on things familiar to baby.

By the end of this stage, your child may be talking in "sentences."
His version of a sentence, however, is generally one word such as
"Hi." If he says "Up," he means "Pick me up." But don't expect
sentences complete with a noun, a verb, and an object. Most children
don't speak in real sentences until after their second birthday.

DEPENDENT ON MOTHER

Toward the end of her first year, she may seem very dependent on
mother. A nine-to-fifteen-month-old baby generally wants to stay pretty close to Mother. She can't bear to see you leave. She follows you
all day long. When you take her to visit a friend, she may spend the
entire time in your arms. Only babies with good attachment to their
mothers act this way. It's entirely normal, and if she needs you, she
needs you.

If a stranger comes in, baby may make friends after a few minutes.
If the new person insists, however, on talking to and grabbing baby
immediately, it won't work well. Let baby take her time. She will cling
to mother for a few minutes, gradually giving the other person her attention.

Alice is real open with most people unless they want to pick her up

right away. But when she gets used to them, she'll go to them.
(Melanie)

This clinging-to-mother stage makes it hard to leave the baby. It's not a good idea to leave while she's sleeping. When she wakes up to find a baby sitter instead of Mother, she may be very unhappy and frightened. It's far better to hire the sitter to come to your home a half-hour before you leave. Then baby has a better chance to adjust to the situation.

If she does cry as you leave, your sitter may report that she started playing happily by the time your car was out of sight.

Playing peek-a-boo with baby from early infancy may help her understand that if you go away, you come back. But it takes time to understand the important idea that, if they leave, Mother and Daddy really do come back.

LET HIM HELP

Trying to copy what you do is important to a toddler. At nine months, he explores everything for the joy of exploring. Almost everything is new to him. But at fifteen months, he wants to follow adults' examples. While earlier he banged with a spoon, now he will stir with it like Mommy does.

Alice likes to try to write, perhaps because I've been writing a lot of letters this year and she likes to watch me. She knows keys go in the ignition, and she'll try to do that. (Melanie)

Baby loves to do what you do. Let him "help" you as much as possible as you do your work. While you're cooking, set him in his highchair near you. Are you baking a pie or making tortillas? Let him have a little piece of dough so he can work along with you. If you're stirring something, give him a small pan and a spoon so he can stir, too. If you have plastic dishes, let him help you set the table.

He can have his own dustcloth while you're cleaning the living room. Don't use a treated dustcloth, however. He might put it in his mouth. Be careful, of course, that cleaning supplies are completely out of his reach. Nearly all of them are extremely dangerous for small children.

He'll like a toy broom to use as you use yours. Sponges make good toys at bathtime or during water play at any time. Get them in a variety of colors and sizes.

Letting him help you clean the bathroom is not a good idea. You would be encouraging him to play in the toilet, and you don't want that.

Toward the end of this stage, he'll start learning to undress himself. If you choose clothes with big buttons or, even better, with zippers, you'll make it easier for him. Wide sleeves with big armholes and wide-necked garments will also help. While he'll learn to unbutton his clothes fairly soon, don't expect him to be able to button up for a long time yet, perhaps not for several years.

Alice takes off her socks and shoes. She'll put her shirt on. She likes to play peek-a-boo with it. If I'm putting a shirt on, she'll pick up anything around, maybe a nightgown, and put her head through the hole. Then she laughs. (Melanie)

PLAYING TOGETHER

She'll love playing with you. Because she likes to imitate, she may enjoy playing follow-the-leader. Keep it simple at first. Clap your hands, put a hat on your head, and wave your arms.

I'm enjoying Danette more as the months go by—she gets better and better! I go crazy with her new toys. We sit on the rug and play all kinds of games. I bounce her up and down on the bed.

We go outside and I chase her all over. Jim and I hold her hands and run with her. (Caroline)

Some of our learning, whatever our age, occurs through touch. A great deal of babies' and toddlers' learning happens this way. Help your toddler learn by playing a matching textures guessing game.

Choose items with specific "feel" such as sandpaper squares, pieces of felt, fur, corduroy, and silk fabric, nails, pebbles, raw macaroni. You'll think of many more. Put two of each item in a big paper sack. Take turns with your toddler in pulling out an object. Then each of you finds the mate to the item you took out. No looking permitted, of course.

Sounds interest your toddler, just as they have since she was an infant. Wind chimes outside her bedroom window are pleasant for her.

Records, radio, music boxes, and bells will intrigue her. "Singing" with you is great fun.

Dance with baby. Before she is standing or walking, she'll love dancing in your arms. Later she'll entertain you by dancing by herself.

Danette likes music. She likes to sing. I hold her and dance with her a lot. I'm crazy with her. (Caroline)

Alice likes to dance. I play a lot of tapes, and she likes to put them in. I don't down her for that. I don't spank her hand. I let her help me. (Melanie)

Let her make her own "music" with a drum made from an empty oatmeal box. Tape the lid on the box, then give her a wooden spoon to use as a drum stick. Show her how to play her drum.

Your toddler may enjoy showing off. Her sense of humor may be developing nicely.

Alice makes faces at me, sniffles her nose, laughs. If she is doing something people like and they laugh, she grins real big. Lots of times when she does something we like, we clap. Then she starts clapping herself. (Melanie)

Early in this stage, baby will love to pull a toy on a string. When she's crawling, sometimes she'll go backward so she can watch the toy as she pulls the string. If the toy makes a noise as she pulls it, so much the better.

A favorite activity is emptying things. Your toddler will empty dresser drawers, kitchen cupboards, bookshelves, trash cans, whatever she can reach. As soon as you put things back, she'll be ready to take them out again.

Dale doesn't know what "No" means. I try to keep him out of cupboards. I put rubber bands on them. But the drawers he pulls right out and takes clothes out.

I tell him "No" and set him down, but he just goes right back and does it again. (Arlene)

Alice gets in the kitchen trash can and takes things out. She gets in the cupboards and plays with the pots and Tupperware. (Melanie)

Giving her a dresser drawer, a kitchen cupboard, and a bookshelf that are "hers" may help. Don't expect her to be satisfied only with emptying her toys, however. She'll like that kitchen cupboard a lot more if she can empty it of your pans and plastic containers. Of course you'll be sure all cleaning materials have been safely put away.

It may also help to give her a variety of containers to empty. Perhaps her toys can be kept in small boxes or baskets. Giving her many opportunities to empty things "legally" should help her learn not to empty and re-empty everything else in the house.

I'll fill a can or a box with a bunch of stuff. Danette likes to take one thing out at a time, play with it for awhile, then take something else out and play with it. (Caroline)

PROVIDING TOYS

One-year-olds like giant snap-lock rings and beads. They're also ready for big wooden or plastic blocks. They play with them mostly by putting them in and dumping them out of containers. Your toddler may be able to balance one block on top of another soon.

Balls are still the best toys for your child. Get him several in a variety of sizes from small ones (but too big to be swallowed) to big beach balls. He will love a simple game of catch with you.

Felt toys aren't good because the dye in the fabric usually isn't colorfast. Check your child's stuffed toys to be sure the eyes and ears are firmly attached. Does the animal have a bell around its neck or even a ribbon on which baby could choke? You need to take off any part of that toy that he could pull off.

A round cereal box makes a fine tunnel. Take the bottom off, then show baby how to push a car through his tunnel. He'll watch for his car at the other end. Or you can tie a string to the car, put the string through the tunnel, and let him pull the car through.

You can also make a cardboard hill for his car. Just fold the cardboard to set at a slant on the floor. Then show baby how to put the car at the top of the hill and let it roll down.

Your child may be ready to fingerpaint by the time he is a year old. Of course, he will taste and examine the paint first. Then he may paint a little.

You can make a safe (from a tasting standpoint—it still makes a mess!) fingerpaint by mixing two tablespoons of cornstarch into two tablespoons of cold water. Then add one cup boiling water and stir again.

For color, use food coloring or powdered fruit drink. Soy sauce added to the starch base will make the paint brown. One tablespoon of prepared mustard to two tablespoons of the base makes a canary yellow paint.

Finger painting takes some preparation. After you have made the different colors of paint, refrigerate in a covered container any you think you won't need today. Put old clothes on your child and lots of newspapers on the floor. A small chair and table with lots of working space would be ideal, but a highchair will do. Almost any kind of plain paper is all right for finger painting—brown wrapping paper, paper bags, cardboard from shirt and panty hose packages. Tape the paper down to the table or tray before baby starts painting.

After all this preparation, he may do more tasting than painting. You can show him how to use the paint on the paper. He may find the whole thing a bit weird, but he'll probably have a ball.

INTERACTING WITH OTHERS

Busy as she is, your toddler will often show her affection for you and for others.

Robin is really lovable. She gives kisses and hugs—and she spits at you if she really likes you! (Melinda)

Alice likes babies smaller than she is. She kisses them. I say "Kiss Mama," and she will. (Melanie)

Between nine and fifteen months, she likes to be around other children. She may play by herself, but she'll enjoy watching the others. Sometimes she may try to join their fun.

Dale likes being around the kids here. When we go for a walk, he sees little kids and says "Hi-hi." They just look at him and think he's a baby, I guess. (Arlene)

Don't expect a toddler to share her toys with another child for a long time yet. She's still too busy learning about herself and her world to be able to understand why Johnnie, just because he's a guest, should play with her ball.

Heidi is very stingy with her toys and books. She's at that age. (Jenny)

Do you have an older child? If he is more than three years older than the baby, he probably spends most of the time playing with children his age. When he does interact with the baby, he is probably quite gentle usually, and treats the baby like the baby she is.

A brother or sister not yet three, however, is apt to show resentment and dislike for the baby. This stage is particularly difficult because the baby will constantly get into her brother's or sister's toys. She'll generally be a nuisance to your older toddler. The closer together the children are in age, the more hostile your older child may be.

When Sylvia was first born, Crystal didn't like her too well and would hit her. I let her help with the baby and didn't make her feel she was being thrown out. I explained that Sylvia was her baby, too. Now if anybody makes Sylvia cry, Crystal will protect her. When her little cousin hits Sylvia, Crystal hits him. (Carrie)

As you supervise the two, remember that the older child, if he is under three, needs you almost as much as does the little one. You will wonder at times how you can stretch your caring and your attention far enough for both. Sometimes it helps if you know that fusses between your two are normal. A one-year-old and a two-year-old can't be expected to get along beautifully all the time, or even much of the time.

WHAT ABOUT TELEVISION?

Guard against using the television as a baby sitter. At this age, your child probably won't be especially interested in watching it anyway.

Shelly doesn't like TV. She would rather be doing something else. I don't watch TV myself so I don't think of it. I don't like kids watching TV all the time—my cousin, who is 16, does that. He even leaves it on when he goes to bed. (Dixie, 18 - Shelly, 17 months)

If your child is sitting in front of the television, he isn't exploring

his world except in a very passive sense. He's not using his big muscles
as he would be if he were out running and jumping. Unless mother is
watching with him, he isn't even interacting with her.

"TV is passive learning. Children learn far more from active learning experiences. In fact, TV can be addictive. Kids who get 'hooked'
on it will sit in front of the television for hours, not moving at all,"
commented Sally McCullough, Infant Center teacher.

*My cousins come down here once in awhile, and it seems like
the whole entire week they watch TV. I don't like it. I don't like
kids being so obsessed with TV they won't even go outside.*

*I think it's OK for a short time in the morning when I'm get-
ting ready for school. Marty watches cartoons for awhile. He
probably can't understand them, but he looks like he really
knows what is happening. He especially likes to put the TV on
and off. (Yumiko, 16 - Marty, 21 months)*

Later, you may have trouble getting your child away from the
television set, especially if you encourage him to watch TV now. Give
your toddler plenty of opportunities for active play. Then push books,
not TV, during his quiet moments.

*Marty has always had books. Almost every time we go in the
grocery store, he grabs one and we buy it. Mostly he likes the pictures. He names off what is there. Often, he won't even let me
read a page before he turns it himself. (Yumiko)*

LESS SLEEP NEEDED NOW

Your child needs less sleep as she grows older. By her first birthday, she'll probably need only one nap per day. Some babies want to nap in the morning. Then they get fussy by mid-afternoon. But if you put her down for a second nap, she's awake later and later in the evening.

If you would like to have her in bed at a "decent" hour at night, try keeping her awake a little longer in the morning. Then feed her a light lunch, perhaps at 10:30 A.M., before her nap. When she wakes two hours or so later, give her another light lunch. She may last until early supper, then go to bed for the night.

The morning nap can gradually be pushed to a later time. Before long, she may be able to wait until noon for lunch, then have her nap. This is important to a lot of parents. Much as they love her, they like having their evenings free of the constant child care they experience all day long.

> Danette used to go to bed at 7:00, but lately she's started going at 8:00. I give her supper. She plays for quite awhile, then at 8 o'clock I give her a bottle. After she drinks her milk, she kisses me good night, and I put her to bed.
>
> She's very very good about sleeping. She'll go to bed at 8:00, wake up next morning at 6:30. She has a bottle, then plays until 8:00 or 8:30. Then she wants her breakfast.
>
> A couple of months ago she started fussing at bedtime. I wanted her to go to bed at a certain time, so I would put her in her crib. She would cry, but I would leave her in her crib for perhaps ten minutes. That seemed like a long time, but she would get tired and would go to sleep. After about two nights, she just started going to sleep. (Caroline)

Many active toddlers are *not* "very very good about sleeping." Probably at least half put up some fuss about going to bed, especially if other family members are still up.

Many parents prefer to have their small children in bed two or three hours before they go to sleep themselves. Most often a time between 6 P.M. and 8 P.M. is chosen. However, a different schedule may work better for some parents.

One young mother reported putting her toddler to bed regularly at 11 P.M. The mother, a college student, usually studied another couple of hours before she went to bed. She had to get up by 8 A.M. to go to her classes. Her daughter usually woke up at 10 A.M. Since her

grandmother cared for her in her own home, the schedule worked
beautifully for everyone.

While in a few cases, 11 P.M. can be a fine bedtime for a small
child, an earlier hour works better for most families. Most important,
however, is that the child have a regular bedtime. You can't keep her
up until 10:00 tonight, then expect her to lie down and go right to
sleep at 8 o'clock tomorrow night.

As outlined in Chapter Seven, following the same routine every
night helps most children accept bedtime. Unless bathtime is a
boisterous play session, bathing her before she goes to bed may relax
her.

Help her find the blanket or teddy bear that is part of the going-to-
bed ritual. Read her a story. Then feed her that last bottle of milk as
you rock and sing or croon to her. It may take half an hour for her to
unwind, to relax enough to go to sleep.

If she insists on taking her bottle to bed, remember the problem
caused by milk dripping on her teeth all night. The milk film can
cause serious tooth decay. So if she insists on a bottle, you should insist on putting water in it, not milk.

COPING WITH ILLNESS

In earlier chapters we talked about fever. Fever is one of the early
signs of illness in a baby, and you shouldn't ignore it. What can you
do about fever at home? Give the baby Tylenol as recommended by
your doctor.

Cooling baths are another way to bring fever down. But if baby
shivers while you are bathing him, it
is too cold. A good way to do this is
to put a towel in lukewarm water.
Then wrap the baby in the wet towel.
It helps bring his temperature down,
and he's less apt to shiver.

Lukewarm water is the best thing
to use. Don't use alcohol. Corrine
Ray, Los Angeles Poison Control
Center, strongly advises against using
alcohol because the fumes can be
dangerous for baby to breathe.

It's also important to give your
child liquids when he has a fever.
Some babies who have sore throats

that are causing the fever don't want to do a lot of sucking.

That one throat infection Lynn had was terrible. I took her to the doctor, and they gave me penicillin to give her. About a week later I took her back to school.

She was really sick—she couldn't keep anything down. She couldn't suck out of her bottle because her throat was so sore. She cried a lot. We'd go to sleep, and she would wake up 15 minutes later. Her crying got on my nerves, but if I picked her up, she would quit crying. (Sheryl Ann, 17 - Lynn, 7 months)

A way to encourage your child to take lots of liquids is to give him popsicles. If a little piece breaks off in his mouth, it will melt quickly and he can swallow it. This much sugar won't hurt him.

Popsicles are also good for babies and toddlers if they have a lot of nausea and vomiting. Sucking on a popsicle will often help. Orange and other fruit juices, of course, can be frozen to make your own popsicles if you don't want to buy the sugary ones. Besides being cold and making him feel better, homemade juicesicles are nutritious.

When your child has an ear infection, call the doctor. While Tylenol can take away some of the pain and the fever, it doesn't kill the germs causing the infection in the ear. Only prescription medication can do that, so you need to take baby to the doctor. Most doctors, when you say "Ear infection," say "Bring him in." There's a real danger of permanent hearing loss if an ear infection is not treated promptly.

Jonita had an ear infection which made her congestion problem even worse. Yes, I used to prop bottles. My mom probably does. (Ellen, 17 - Jonita, 6½ months)

As discussed in Chapter Three, most infants' ear infections are caused by propped bottles.

Before you call your doctor, make some notes about your baby's condition. Then you'll be able to describe his symptoms more accurately. Is he coughing? For how long? Has he lost his appetite? Does he have diarrhea? What is his temperature? Has he been exposed to any diseases? Has he received all of the immunizations he should have had by this time?

If your doctor prescribes medication for your baby, be sure to ask if you should give baby all the medicine that is in the bottle, or if you give it only for a certain number of days. Most antibiotics (penicillin, Ampicillin, Ilison) need to be used until they are all gone. However, decongestants such as Actifed and Dimetapp are to be used only when symptoms of congestion are present—when he has a stuffy, runny nose.

Most children catch a cold occasionally during their first two years. Colds are most contagious in the first couple of days, sometimes before the carrier knows he is sick. Therefore, it's impossible to protect your child completely from getting colds.

Neither you nor your doctor can "cure" your child's cold because there is no known cure. But you can help him to be more comfortable. If he has a fever or headache, Tylenol may help. If he has a runny or stuffy nose, decongestant medicine may make him feel better. If his nose becomes sore, a little cream or ointment on the area may be soothing.

If he's coughing, your doctor may recommend cough medicine. A cold-water vaporizer will help him breathe more easily if he has a stuffy nose. The old-fashioned steam vaporizers are dangerous, and they don't work as well.

If he doesn't want to eat, don't worry. When he's feeling better, he'll be hungry again. Encourage him to drink juice, water, clear soups, even a little weak tea.

How often your child has a cold depends on two things: the number of people with colds to whom he is exposed, and his own resistance. If he is in good health generally, eats nutritious meals instead of junk foods, and gets plenty of rest, he is much less apt to get sick.

Stuffy noses are also often caused by allergies. Allergies are caused generally by reactions to foods, plants, animals, or pollutants. A large percentage of allergies in children under two seem to be caused by food. Therefore, doctors generally recommend changes in diet for babies with these symptoms.

A lot of allergies disappear in time as baby becomes more adjusted to life on the outside. Therefore, most doctors don't start serious allergy testing until a child is much older, usually school age.

Diarrhea that lasts more than 24 hours is best treated by giving the baby clear liquids and nothing else for 24 hours. Liquids you should give him include Pedialyte (non-prescription liquid you buy in the drug store), clear water, weak tea, and water mixed with apple juice (one tablespoon apple juice to eight ounces of water). Offer no solid foods, and feed him liquids as often as he will take them. If, after 24 hours, the diarrhea hasn't stopped, call the doctor.

Sometimes diarrhea appears suddenly:

Jay has had diarrhea. We were in a restaurant one time. The

*minute I put him in the highchair, he started grunting. Suddenly
it was running all down the highchair. I about died. I got napkins
and picked him up and took him to the restroom. I put him in
the sink and washed his bottom. The bus boy cleaned up the
highchair. (Bev, 17 - Jay, 8 months)*

If your baby has something like conjunctivitis (pink eye) or im-
petigo, you shouldn't have him around other children. You should
take the same precautions during the first day or two he has a cold.

If you know a friend's child has one of these conditions, keep your
baby away from him. Of course, later when your child is out in the
neighborhood playing, he will pick up an illness occasionally because
you can't control your neighbor's child. These generally aren't serious
diseases. Mainly they're an annoyance to both you and your child that
you avoid if you can.

*The little girl next door had an eye infection, and now all the
kids in the apartment complex are getting it. She also passed
ringworm around to all the kids.*

*I know they can't afford a doctor, but I wish she would keep
her child in when she's sick. We don't know how to say it to her.
I don't think it's fair to the other mothers and children. (Louise,
19 - Mark, 5½ months, and Meghan, 23 months)*

MAJOR TASKS FOR PARENTS

As the parent of a nine-to-fifteen-month-old child, you have three
major tasks, according to Dr. Burton White. First, you need to design
your child's world so that she can satisfy her curiosity without getting
hurt and without causing damage to your home. See Chapter Eight,
"Child-Proofing Helps Baby and Parents."

Your second job is to react to your child when she wants you. She
may want your help because she is frustrated at something she can't
do herself. She may have hurt herself slightly and needs comforting.
Or she may be excited and want you to share her excitement. Your
assistance, comfort, and enthusiasm are very important to her.

It's crucial to your child's learning that you respond promptly to
her needs and to her interests. If you are talking on the phone, it's
better to say, "I'm talking on the phone. I'll be with you in a
minute," than it is to ignore her. Of course, you'll need to carry
through on your promise and be with her "in a minute."

According to Dr. White, mother should stop to see what the child wants. Then she usually should provide what is needed. Next she talks briefly at the child's listening level about the event. Once you have assisted or comforted and talked to your child, your next step is to leave her alone. Let her get back to doing her own thing.

Your child learns a lot from an interchange like this. She learns to use another person, you, as a resource when she can't handle a situation herself. She learns that someone thinks her discomfort, excitement, or problem is important, which means *she* is important. Her language learning also gets a boost each time this happens.

Your third major responsibility with your child, according to Dr. White, is to carry out your role as authority. This will be discussed in greater detail in Chapter Ten.

Being firm is often necessary. Don't say "No" constantly, or you'll destroy some of your child's curiosity. But when you do say "No," mean what you say. If you say "No," then you laugh because she really does look pretty funny sitting in the middle of the dining table playing in the sugar bowl, is she going to take you seriously? Instead, say "No," get her down from the table, and put the sugar bowl away.

The important thing is to see that she carries out your requests. At this age, this generally means removing your child from the situation or distracting her. Ideally, you won't say "No" a second time because you'll already have taken care of the problem.

Loving, caring for, and guiding your child throughout her early life is an exciting challenge. Your baby has become a "real" person, a child who is on her way to becoming a self-sufficient individual. You are an important part of her growth.

Chapter Ten
Babies, Toddlers, and Discipline

What word do you pair with "discipline"? Perhaps you say "punishment." But discipline comes from the same root word as disciple, one who is taught. That's what discipline is all about—teaching your child to cope with the world he lives in.

You want him to get along with other people, to respect their rights. You don't want him to damage or destroy the things in his surroundings. Most of all, you probably want him to have as satisfying a life as possible. You want him to learn to be self-disciplined.

Discipline is the essential foundation for all of this learning. A child who grows up without firm, loving discipline is the spoiled child, the child who thinks only of himself and what he wants. He hasn't learned to care about other people's feelings

Or he may care about other people, but he doesn't know what is important to them. He has been cheated. He doesn't know what will offend someone and what will not.

If you, his parent, don't discipline him, you're denying him the chance to learn how to behave with others. Discipline is learning to live within our cultural values.

IMPORTANCE OF DISCIPLINE

Providing discipline for your child is an extremely important part of your parenting task. It is probably the hardest part of raising kids. Disciplining her means you care about her and you are concerned with her behavior. Discipline is one expression of love.

A child without limits may feel fearful of her power. Consistent limits help her feel safe and free to explore because someone is watching and caring.

If people don't learn what their limits are, they are always pushing. They don't know which limits are firm, and which ones will give. This is a big problem throughout life for some people. You don't want your child to carry such a burden.

She will learn about limits through discipline. Note, however, the word is discipline, *not* punishment. Punishment should not be a big part of disciplining babies and toddlers.

Discipline means she has to learn from her mistakes. But you can't hit a kid every time she does something wrong. The way I see it, if you're going to hit a kid, she's just going to do it again to get back at you. I think you tell her what you want, and she won't do it again. (Melinda, 16 - Robin, 9 months)

WHAT ABOUT SPOILING?

Lots of people worry about spoiling a child. By spoiling they usually mean raising a child who whines, insists on having her own way all the time, and is generally disagreeable.

Some people even worry about spoiling a new baby. But you can't! A hungry infant can't wait for food, for comfort. As we've said so often in the book, the baby only learns the world is not to be trusted if she is left alone in her misery.

Discipline for an infant means meeting her needs. No more and no less. Meeting her needs supports her developing trust in people around her. This trust is basic to becoming a well-adjusted, caring human being. It's the foundation for self-discipline which is the eventual goal.

Meeting your baby's needs is a hard job. Perhaps you are prepared to get up at night those first two months. You know a tiny infant needs care and attention when she cries. Although caring for her is a hard and exhausting task, you try to meet her needs. You probably don't think much about spoiling her at first.

The tendency to worry about spoiling her comes a little later. When she's awake more during the day at about four months, for instance, you may start wondering about this "danger." Perhaps those around you are telling you you're already ruining her by going to her each time she cries.

It may be hard to believe, but if you continue to answer her cries and, in addition, play with her regularly, you'll probably find she takes less of your time and energy than she would if you left her to cry for awhile.

For at least six months, she isn't going to cry "just for attention" unless she needs that attention. Research data shows that babies whose cries are answered quickly actually cry less than babies who are left to cry it out.

Gradually, however, you need to stop treating your child as a baby. She is becoming a person who needs a different kind of discipline than she needed as an infant. Satisfying most of her needs for food, warmth, cleanliness, and companionship are no longer enough. When she's moving around, she must have some consistent limits. When she starts walking, there will be more, although she's not ready for the same kind of discipline her preschool brother needs.

FIRM GUIDANCE PLUS FREEDOM

She needs firm guidance, yes, but at the same time she needs a terrific amount of freedom to explore. What looks like defiance from a toddler is often a simple lack of understanding what you want her to do.

Most toddlers are "good" if they happen to feel like doing what you want them to do or not doing what you don't want them to do. Discipline works best at this stage if you can help her want to do what she must do.

If you want her to pick up her toys, don't order, "Pick up your toys right now." Instead, make it a game. You might suggest she put her toys in her wagon. Tell her you'll help her haul them to the toy shelves.

You'll be able to think of lots of other ways to get her to want to do what you want her to do. This is so much more important than setting out to prove to her that she "must" obey you. A battle of wills results in lots of frustration for both of you and little else.

There will be plenty of times, no matter how hard you try to make being "good" easy for her, that she will have to do as you say whether or not she wants to do so. Firm limits are necessary for your child's safety and welfare and to protect the rights of others.

You certainly won't make a game of keeping her out of a busy street. You'll always do whatever is necessary to keep her away from an unsupervised swimming pool.

> *We live in an apartment, and they have a pool there in the adult section. Henry can walk over there, and sometimes the gate is open. So when he does that, I spank him. He understands me pretty much. (Olivia, 20 - Henry, 23 months)*

As discussed later in this chapter, spanking a toddler usually doesn't accomplish much, and can cause extra problems. However, if a child is almost never spanked, a sudden swat on her diapered bottom may startle her enough to have some effect. Save it for the big problems— a method of keeping her out of busy streets and swimming pool areas. And remember, it will work only if it's done very seldom.

Eventually your toddler will understand wrong from right. She'll be able to take responsibility for her own actions. Your understanding and help during her difficult toddler stage will build a good foundation for all her future behavior.

Henry gets on our nerves. He always wants to go outside and play, and then he stays out real late. Sometimes if he really gets on it, I spank him. But most of the time I give him what he wants so he'll be quiet for awhile. (Olivia)

But giving him what he wants in order to keep him quiet is not helping Henry learn what his limits are. A parent can't hope to have a child who is happy every minute of his life because of her efforts. Sometimes there are things you have to do because you love him and you help him through the difficult things. You help him grow. You have to teach him.

If your ten-month-old is chewing on the electric cord, pick her up, take her away, and give her something else to play with. If she cries, don't let it throw you. She can't play with that cord.

When you decide it is a "No," it's important that it's always there. There can't be an "OK this time." If it's "No," it has to be "No," like a wall. You can push at it forever, but it's still there.

REWARDS ARE IMPORTANT

Learning happens more because of rewards than because of punishment. Your infant finds that if he smiles, you smile back. So he smiles more often because he is being rewarded for smiling.

During your baby's first year, you need most of the discipline yourself. It is you who must stop the wrong kind of behavior. If he puts something dangerous or dirty in his mouth, it is up to you to take it out. During these early months, the responsibility to "do" something is yours, not your baby's.

The goal of good discipline is gradually to transfer this responsibility for his own actions over to your child, to teach him self-discipline.

During the second half of his first year, discipline gets a little more complicated. The complications increase throughout toddlerhood. But the word still means teaching, not punishing. Hitting your child is not a good way to discipline for the simple reason that it doesn't work very well.

Babies, toddlers, and most other people love and need attention. If he gets a lot of positive attention, he'll probably continue doing those positive things that draw the attention he craves. If he seems to get attention mostly through being naughty, he's more apt to be naughty.

Spend time with him when he is behaving well. Make absolutely sure he doesn't need to be naughty in order to get attention.

Rewards for a toddler need not and should not be candy or a toy. If you like something he is doing, a smiling comment is a powerful reward. Your approval means a great deal to him.

EACH CHILD IS DIFFERENT

Each child is completely different from all other children. This makes parenting a terrific challenge. No one has ever reared a child identical to yours.

Respect for your particular child and her needs is an excellent starting point for discipline. Your expectations need to be related to her particular level of social and intellectual as well as her physical development. An appropriate expectation for one child may not be right for her friend.

If all children were alike, or even if most children were, perhaps a brilliant blueprint for discipline could be written. But since children aren't alike, you need to become an expert on your child. No one else will be that expert.

> *Remember that every child is different. What is right for one may not be right for another. We really need to listen to them. I mean REALLY listen, not just hear the words. (Thelma, 20 - Janeen, 18 months, and Melissa, 4 years)*

Is she a quiet child who doesn't get into much trouble? If you raise your voice, does she burst into tears? Or is she a superactive baby who at six months was crawling to the coffee table and knocking things over?

Some kids are terribly active and may give you a lot of discipline problems. Others may be easy to control. Obviously discipline methods must vary with the child.

Discipline begins with your relationship with your child. You have been developing this relationship ever since she was born. If you have a good relationship, she wants to please you just as you want to please her. You want to do things to make her feel good. She wants to do things to make you feel good.

"Discipline needn't be such a bugbear if you think of it as helping a child to help herself . . . to help her learn to live and play happily with others, to explore safely, to cope with feelings, to know what she can do, to develop interests," writes Trish Gribben in *Pajamas Don't Matter* (page 32). As you set limits for your child, you want to allow for the joy of learning. You don't want to be too restrictive.

MUST CHILDREN BE HIT (SPANKED)?

Spanking/hitting doesn't seem like such a good idea if we think about Ms. Gribben's comment. Hitting a child won't make him be good. There's no way you can force him to eat or to urinate on the toilet, for example.

Yes, hitting him can sometimes make him stop doing something. But that is only part of the solution. He needs to know what he should do.

Lately Antonio has been something else. Yesterday at the welfare office they had a little water faucet and he kept running over there. I know I brought him back at least six times. I grab his arm and say, "Don't do that," and five minutes later he does it again.

I try to refrain from spanking. It has to be something really bad to do that. I just don't think spanking is a good way to discipline. I don't think it's any more effective than saying, "No, we don't do that." (Becky, 18 - Antonio, 26 months)

People disagree a great deal on whether to spank or not to spank a child.

I remember I used to give in to Kelton a lot. My girl friend always put me down because I wouldn't spank him.

I think you can do more without a lot of spanking. I'd try to talk him into doing things. (Erin, 23 - Wayne, 9 months, and Kelton, 7 years.)

Some parents spank to teach, and some parents spank because they're angry. We knew a couple who had a little girl who sat on their white quilt and got chocolate on it. She had chocolate on her pants and didn't know it, and her dad spanked her. I think that was abusing her because she didn't even know she had chocolate on her clothes. (Ginny, 17 - Juan, 4 months)

Hitting a child is not a good punishment for several reasons. First, a baby or toddler will seldom understand why you hit him. Even if he knows why, he also sees that hitting people is all right. It must be—Mother or Daddy hit him.

I think some people use spanking too much. I have a lot of friends, and when we were growing up, I was fairly good. But I had friends who were getting the belt every other day for what they did.

I think that just made them more spiteful. They would tell me how they hated their fathers because they would hit them. (Yumiko, 16 - Marty, 21 months)

Punishment depends on fear for effectiveness. It can interfere with learning because none of us learns as well if we're afraid. Punishment too often gives a child the feeling of failure.

Harsh punishment can be emotionally scarring. As Yumiko commented, some children seek revenge. Others become guilty and humiliated victims, people who are afraid to do anything for fear of failure. Punishment makes you want to be more careful not to get caught.

Another reason not to use hitting as punishment is the real danger of getting out of control. Physical child abuse is a tragic reality for many families in the United States. More than a million children are abused each year, and about 2,000 die from child abuse. If a parent decides that hitting is a good method of punishment, that parent may be more apt to hit too hard than would the parent who doesn't believe in hitting in the first place.

My mom said once I was doing something really terrible. She spanked me, and she got to the point where she knew she had to stop. She realized that she would hurt me. At that moment she knew how anybody could be a child abuser. You just have to make yourself stop.

If you start hitting a little bit and it doesn't work, you're going to start hitting harder. If the kid doesn't get hit very much, it will work better. (Yumiko)

Because we're talking about babies and toddlers, however, this debate surely isn't necessary. There should be almost no need to spank a child under two. You should be able to handle a toddler by arranging his life so he has only the absolutely necessary restrictions. You should be able to stop his activities when necessary by either removing him from the scene or helping him do what he must do.

I try to stop DeeDee and Leon before they are really in trouble. Then I don't have to spank so much. I don't like spanking. (Tamera, 21 - Leon, 20 months, and DeeDee, 4½ years)

Many parents probably resort to an occasional swat on a diapered bottom. Their child survives nicely, but the fact remains—that swat probably didn't accomplish much.

Felipe does something bad, like getting in the refrigerator over and over in the middle of the night. Sometimes I'll spank him. He'll cry about five minutes, then go right back to the refrigerator. But if I tell him to go to bed, and in the morning he can have Cheerios, he'll go back to bed without a spanking. (Roseanna, 15 - Felipe, 2 years.)

If you find you're spanking your toddler a great deal, is it possible she doesn't get much of your attention otherwise? How much time each day do you spend playing with her, giving her your full attention?

USE "NO" SPARINGLY

"No" is still an important word in discipline. It is such a valuable word that it must not be "spent" too freely. Your goal, when you say "No," is to get your baby to react, to stop doing whatever it is that you don't like. If she hears "No" every two minutes all day long, the word is not going to be very impressive. But if a few times a day she hears "No," and she hears a different, I-mean-it tone of voice, she will learn to react, to obey. And that's the goal you're working so hard to achieve.

Don't go overboard and think "No" is a bad word. Obviously, it's a very necessary word. But use it sparingly.

It's important for you to be consistent. Know where you stand. Let your child know that you know. If you threaten, follow through on your threat.

If the forbidden activity is touching the hot stove, you'll have no trouble in being consistent. You'll always react in the same way—you'll stop her before she gets hurt.

On the other hand, if you don't

think the forbidden activity is important enough to make you follow through, don't say "No" in the first place. Test yourself. For one day, make a note of every time you say "No" to your child. Also jot down the reasons you said "No."

At the end of the day, analyze your record. Did you say "No" a lot of times? Each time, did you see to it that your child stopped whatever it was you wanted stopped? Were there situations for which you said "No" today, but yesterday you thought weren't important, or even funny? Your research may show interesting results.

Sometimes a creeping baby will go toward a forbidden object saying "No-no" as she does so. She may check to make sure Mother is watching. If she is, she continues right ahead. Sometimes she doesn't remember. Sometimes she can't control the urge to do the forbidden. And sometimes she may be testing her mother. Is this a way to get Mother's attention?

If Marty is doing something I don't want him to do and I say "No," he will look at me with his hand moving toward the object I told him not to touch. He will look at me as if he is daring me . . . as if he is saying, "Yeah, Mom, you're going to tell me what to do?" (Yumiko)

Marty has a nice game going between himself and his mother. If he does this, he knows he will get Mother's attention. He may even be laughing while he does it.

Research done by Dr. Mary D. Ainsworth of The Johns Hopkins University showed that the baby with a lot of freedom to investigate her house was better able to control her own behavior than was the baby whose mother constantly told her what not to do and who stopped her exploring. Babies who were told "No" a lot actually got into more trouble than did babies whose caregivers child-proofed the house so they could explore a lot.

Right now I just pick Robin up and move her if she gets into something I don't want her to have. I put her in another corner of the house, or I take the item away and put it on a high shelf. (Melinda)

Arranging your own time schedule so you have extra time for deal-ing with your toddler is one very effective step to good discipline. If you think about it, you may realize that your toddler's tantrums are apt to come at the worst times—when you're trying to get to school on time or you must get dinner on the table for your family. Could it be because you're rushing too much to respond to your child's needs? Sometimes an extra ten minutes lets you and your toddler do what you feel you have to do without both of you feeling frantic.

Shelly drives me nuts sometimes. When I'm in a rush to do something, I have to get her ready in a hurry. Sometimes she starts crying, and I get really mad. (Dixie, 18 - Shelly, 17 months)

If it's time to get ready for school and your child "refuses" to let you dress her, you don't need to hit or scream at her. You can try to distract her by giving her a toy or a picture book to look at while you get her dressed.

If that doesn't work, you can say, "I have to dress you now so we can go to school." Then, if she continues to yell and jump up and down, hold her firmly and dress her. Be firm, but gentle and friendly. You'll probably get her dressed faster this way than you would if you hit her or yelled at her.

Remember, be sure she knows you love and respect her even if you don't like what she is doing. Don't ever attack her personality. Attack what she is doing, but not her.

Children are neither good nor bad. They are busy little people. Sometimes they do things that please us. Sometimes they do not. It is not them, but the things they do that are good or bad.

POSITIVE APPROACH WORKS BEST

You want to be able to say "No" to your baby when necessary, and you want him to react by stopping whatever he is doing. You already know that you'll get better results if you use "No" only occasionally.

But this doesn't mean you let baby do whatever he wants to do the rest of the time. When you distract him from an unwanted activity by giving him something else to play with, you can often do so without using the word "No" at all. "Here's your ball. Can you roll it to me?" works better than saying, "No, don't do that" to a nine-month-old baby.

When you're telling your child what you want or don't want him to do, be sure to get his attention first. Stoop down so you have eye-to-eye contact with him as you talk to him.

You'll get further with your toddler if you give positive, not negative commands. Instead of saying, "Don't touch the ash tray," try "Leave the ash tray on the table." Instead of "Stop pulling the cat's tail," say "Let's pet kitty gently."

Give him a choice whenever you can. "It's time for your bath. Do you want it in the tub or in the shower?" may get his cooperation faster than ordering, "Take your bath now." "Do you want lunch outside or in your high chair?" may make him more willing to leave his morning play than will a command, "Come to lunch right now."

When you want him to do something, tell him ahead of time. It will help him learn to anticipate and plan ahead. He'll be able to complete his present activities and be ready for the next happening. No one enjoys being suddenly picked up and carried off without a word of warning.

"You need to . . . " and "You may not . . . " are two phrases that often work with toddlers. You aren't threatening, but you're giving necessary directions. The directions are often needed. The threats generally don't help.

Reinforcing good behavior is an important part of discipline. If, when your child is playing quietly, you ignore him, his behavior is not being reinforced. Instead, join him in his play or talk about what he is doing—or just sit quietly with him and watch him play.

Turning on the TV gives your toddler lots of reinforcement. All by himself, he has caused light, action, sound. What a feeling of power he must have.

> *What really makes me mad now is Todd will stand on the TV cart and turn the knob up full blast. I take him and swat him on the butt and say "No." And I told myself before I had him, "I'm not going to hit him . . . " (Jill)*

Perhaps Jill could remove the knobs from the TV, or she could simply unplug it. If Todd can't turn it on, Jill won't need to punish him for doing so.

If she doesn't want to do that, she might find it best not to react at all when he turns it on. Most toddlers don't want to watch much TV. If he has a chance to turn it on and off enough, the newness will wear off. If Mother doesn't react, it won't be as exciting.

BEING YELLED AT HURTS HIM

Too often people use tactics they don't want their child to copy. They're rude to their children. They yell, they use bad language, and they make horrible threats.

People think child abuse is beating your kid. But it's not just that. It's also yelling at them. That's what really hurts the kid because they don't know what you're saying and they do it again, and they get hit for it. You yell and they don't understand. They get frustrated and you get frustrated. They start getting into trouble more and more often. (Roseanna)

Yelling is frightening to a child, and it is hard on his self-esteem. Poor self-esteem is a nasty stumbling block not only to good behavior, but to learning as well.

If he feels he isn't a very good person, he won't act very good. That's not what you want for your child.

We are our children's models. If we want our children to respect other people, we have to show respect for them.

If we just remember to treat them as "small people," like being polite to them. Yelling at them all the time can be just as wrong as abusing them physically. (Thelma)

Have clearcut rules or guidelines for him to follow. But don't have too many of them. Always be consistent about enforcing the rules you do set up. If you can't be consistent, you shouldn't have the rule.

When your baby is crawling all over the house and exploring everything he possibly can, you aren't always going to be patient, of course. There will be times when you yell at him. He'll be frightened when you do, but, hopefully, it will be over within a few minutes. You'll be ready to talk and play with him again.

Just remember that he has no idea why you suddenly screamed at him. He can't possibly understand that grabbing the ash tray one more time was the last straw. You couldn't take any more without yelling, but he doesn't realize why. Of course, it's important that this doesn't happen very often.

I try. I'm better now. There for awhile I was losing patience and I'd yell at Carlos, tell him to shut up. I have a temper, but I can take more than I could before. (Renette, 16 - Carlos, 6 months)

How you feel about yourself influences how you discipline your child. If your life is going well today, you probably aren't wanting to take your frustrations out on your child.

If he spills his milk on the floor when you're rested and feeling really good, how do you react? What if he spills his milk right after your husband calls to say he's working late again and you can't go out tonight? Or you've just learned your boy friend is leaving town? Is there a difference in how you respond to your toddler's messiness? If there is, you're normal.

If I'm sick or get a headache, it isn't Marty's fault that he is acting normal. If I don't feel like running around watching him, sometimes I go take a bath. He will take it with me or sit there next to the bathtub with his toys. That relaxes both of us. (Yumiko)

Realizing this happens and not feeling guilty about it is a good place to start. Sometimes, even with a toddler, it's best simply to tell him you're upset today. Assure him it's not his fault. Then hug him an extra time.

Sometimes Meghan will do things that bother me a lot, and I know I have to get her away from me for a little while. The best thing I've found is just to walk off. There's always a day when your nerves are on edge and you have to get out for awhile. I thought it was just me, but I know it isn't. Once I pushed her away and she fell and bit her tongue. I felt so bad. I hugged her and said, "Mommy is feeling bad today." She seemed to understand. (Louise, 19 - Mark, 5½ months, and Meghan, 23 months)

All parents get upset with their kids, even their babies. But if it gets to the point where you're yelling at and hitting your child because of your own frustrations, think about getting help. See Chapter Fourteen, page 269.

CONSTANT SUPERVISION NEEDED

When baby learns to stand sometime in the second half of his first year, he will want to practice his new skill. So he will try to pull himself up by hanging on to almost anything. A sturdy coffee table, couch, and some of the chairs may be fine supports. But he will also try to pull himself up by grabbing the unsteady lamp or the tablecloth.

You'll warn him of these dangers. Then he will go right back to try again. Someone may tell you he should be punished. After all, he isn't "minding" you.

But at this stage in his life, he forgets, or he simply can't control his strong impulse to grab whatever is handy in his repeated attempts to stand.

If you can remove the tablecloth, do so. If the unsteady lamp can be banished from the living room for a few months, banish it. This is the best approach to discipline at this age.

But maybe these are items that, for whatever reason, must stay. Then each time baby starts to pull on the tablecloth, you need to move him away from it at once. Show him a safe place to pull himself to standing. There should be many such places in your home. Tell him "No" as you take him away from the tablecloth.

Neither hitting, spanking, nor a raised voice is a good solution to this problem. Pulling to stand is a developmental need, something he must accomplish. If you spank him each time he goes toward that tablecloth, he may eventually tune you out. He may seem not to mind being spanked. Or he may become afraid. He doesn't understand why

you hit him. If you tell him, he still won't understand at this age.

Imagine how you would feel: You are just learning the wonderful new skill of standing. In your eagerness to perfect this skill, you want to practice. But when you attempt to practice, your mother, the most important person in your world, hits you. How would you feel?

Consistency is the key once again. If it's really important to you, or to the people living with you, keep that tablecloth on the table. Your child will eventually mature enough to understand he must not pull on it. But he won't learn by being hit. His learning depends on a lot of patient teaching from you.

For awhile, you must be his inner control. You must set his limits, and help him go along with those limits. Nagging and punishing a baby for forgetting your rules doesn't make sense. He first must mature enough to be able to follow those rules. Each time he grabs the tablecloth, patiently take him away from it to an area where pulling to stand is safe.

Perhaps you're wondering, "Why so much concern about a tablecloth?" Most of us probably don't leave one hanging down where a toddler can pull it off the table.

True. But many families have other things around which are just as appealing to a toddler. The important thing to realize is that adults, *not the toddler,* must take the responsibility for dealing with these situations.

If you choose not to child-proof your home, or for some reason you can't do so, you must be willing to spend an enormous amount of time helping your child cope with his surroundings.

SCRIBBLING TODDLERS

Scribbling is described in Chapter Eleven as the art of the toddler. What about scribbling on the walls? How would you react if your toddler practiced her art on the living room wall?

Surely none of us wants scribbling done directly on our walls. We may have a bulletin board or other way of displaying baby's art work, but we certainly don't want it on the walls or furniture.

Supervision is the key. A toddler who is drawing or painting needs supervision. It's that simple. No one under two should be left in a room by herself for long. If you know she has a pencil or a crayon in her hand, you'll be even more determined not to leave her alone.

She can work beside you while you cook and clean up your kitchen. If you're studying, arrange a place beside you where she may write, too. The best place for her to scribble is in her highchair. Until she's

older, you may decide to let
her have crayons and pencils
only while she's sitting in her
chair.

If you're right there, you'll
be able to notice any signs
that she is about ready to
write in the wrong place. If
you see her walk away from
her paper, crayon in hand,
you have two choices. You
either bring her back to her
paper to color some more, or
you take the crayon in ex-
change for another toy. You
might say, "If you want to
write, you must write on the paper. If you're through writing, Mommy will take the crayon. Here's your tennis ball."

Because she likes you and because you're giving her the attention
she wants so badly, she usually won't try to make an issue of wall-
writing. But if you're ignoring her, she knows she can get your attention quickly by scribbling on that wall.

MEALS CAN BE A HASSLE

Mealtime is torture for some parents of babies and toddlers. An infant can, and often does, disrupt a meal by seeming to demand
breastfeeding or a bottle just as the family is ready to sit down to
dinner.

A few months later she presents a different problem. If she's eating
table food, it seems sensible to feed her while the family eats. This is a
good social time for her, too.

But what happens when she has learned the power of saying
"No"? Especially if her mother is determined she'll eat, she may
decide not to bother at all. Almost all toddlers play with their food to
some extent, but some children appear to do little else.

When she's about a year old, she starts needing less food. Soon
after, "No" becomes her key word. Mother may be worried that she
isn't eating enough. If she coaxes the toddler to eat, her "No" will be
more definite than ever. Besides, she probably gets a lot of attention
for that "No." This really reinforces her negative behavior.

Worrying about a toddler's eating, watching her spit her food out,

or seeing her dump her milk on the floor doesn't add much enjoyment
to the family meal. But there are some positive things you can do.

You can place newspapers around her chair to take care of the
mess. You can give her mostly finger food she can handle herself.
And most important, you needn't be at all worried about her starving
to death. She'll eat if she's hungry. If you can be casual about her
eating, mealtime should never turn into a serious discipline problem.

If you insist she eat when she doesn't want to, if you slap her for
spilling her milk, or yell at her for playing with her food, mealtime
will be miserable for everyone.

Giving her a few Cheerios may keep her busy for several minutes
while the rest of you eat in peace.

Do you want your child to say "Thank you" and "Please" at appropriate times? The best way is not to order her to say these magic
words or even to ask her to repeat them. She's not a parrot. But
remember how much she likes to mimic you. If she hears you using
these words, she'll learn to use them, too.

NOT READY TO SHARE

Toddlers aren't ready to share their toys. They're too busy learning
what is "mine" to understand about sharing.

> *I have a nephew who is 2½. Robin beats him up, pulls his hair,
> bites him, takes his toys away. He does the same thing back to
> her. Or he cries and says, "Robin hit me." (Melinda)*

Toddlers often explore playmates as they would objects. They taste,
pull, and push. Robin is demonstrating this fact.

> *Robin's stingy. She'll have all her toys laid out, and she won't
> even want to play with them. But if somebody else comes, she's
> ornery and won't share at all. (Melinda)*

When another toddler visits, have him bring a toy or two of his
own. He won't want to share either. If it's possible to have two each
of several toys, it will help keep the peace.

WHAT ABOUT BITING?

Sometimes two little ones play side by side, pretty much ignoring
each other. At other times, they may play together. Partly because

they aren't ready yet to share toys, there will be bickering. Suddenly one child is crying, and you see teeth marks on his arm. What should you do?

Some people say, "Bite her back so she'll know what it feels like." But please don't. Biting back only shows her that you bite, too, so it must be all right. It also shows her she can't really trust Mother because Mother bit her. In fact, she may not understand at all why you're suddenly biting her.

A child who bites (most do at one time or another) usually can't express herself well in words. Until she learns to talk, she has to get her point across some other way. She didn't like what that little boy did, so she bit him.

Naturally you won't allow biting. Tell her firmly that biting Jimmie hurt him, and you do not want her to do that. The first time may be the last time, so don't be too horrified. Be sure she knows you still love her a lot, you just don't like biting.

If she bites a child again, remove her from the play area. Tell her she can't be with the other children if she's going to bite.

If you have a child who bites time after time, be doubly sure she gets plenty of good attention at other times. Does she bite when she's tired or hungry? You can encourage her to get more rest. Maybe she needs a mid-afternoon glass of milk and a piece of fruit. And sometimes when the situation becomes too exciting and too stressful for her, perhaps she needs a quieter place to play.

DISCIPLINE CHAIR APPROACH

Jim Mead, director of *For Kids Sake, Inc.,* Brea, California, recommends the "discipline chair" or "time-out" method of discipline for children who are about two years old or older. You need a chair and a kitchen timer. If/When it's necessary to punish your child, set him in a chair near you. Don't put him in another room. Don't even make him sit in the corner of the room. You aren't banishing him.

Set the timer for a few minutes. For a toddler, try just one or two minutes. One minute of sitting still is a long time for an active toddler. If he won't sit there, hold him gently on the chair. When the timer goes off, he's free.

Using the timer takes you off the hook. He can't get down until it dings. That's simple, something he can understand. He can't beg the timer to hurry up. He knows the timer isn't going to keep him there longer than promised.

Mead stresses the individuality of each little kid. What "works" with one child may not with another. But he insists the time-out chair works remarkably well with most children.

SUPERMARKET DISCIPLINE

When you're in a supermarket, keep your toddler beside you or in the basket. If he runs down the aisle, don't expect him to come back when you call him. He's not ready yet to follow rules given from a distance. Instead, go after him. Take his hand or gently pick him up.

Has your toddler ever thrown a tantrum at the supermarket? If so, what did you do? Did you react in the same way you would have if you had been at home? Or did you feel you "had" to punish him because of what other people might think if you didn't?

It's a temptation to change the rules when people are watching. We all want to be considered "good" parents. Even if we know it doesn't help to scold or hit a toddler in the middle of a tantrum, we may feel people around us think we should. Or we may do the opposite—give him the cookie, whatever started the tantrum—anything to turn off the embarrassing yelling.

Try not to worry about what other people are thinking. Treat your child's supermarket tantrum in the same way you handle an at-home tantrum. Be kind and loving, but don't give in to his demands.

Remember the magic word. If you can be *consistent* with him, even in the middle of a crowded supermarket, you have learned a marvelous lesson in discipline.

EXTENDED-FAMILY DISCIPLINE

Since it's so important for crawlers and toddlers to receive consistent discipline, you need to share your ideas on discipline with the other people who care for your child. If Grandma lets her play with the pans in the cupboard and you don't, she's going to be confused.

My mother lets Alice get away with more, and she does more with her. She'll hit at Mom and throw things at her because she can get away with it. She doesn't do those things with me. She's no bad baby. (Melanie, 15 - Alice, 13 months)

It's hard living at home. They spoil Janet. I didn't want that to happen, but it's happening. My mom lets her get into everything. During the day I tell her "No." Then when I come home after my mom has taken care of her, she's spoiled rotten. (Candi, 16 - Janet, 18 months)

You need to work out an arrangement with your child's other caretakers, an arrangement that you can all accept.

Sometimes this is a difficult goal just for mother and father. If one parent was brought up by parents who spanked a lot and the other wasn't, it may be hard for them to agree on discipline methods for their child. When this is the situation, they need to do a lot of discussing in an effort to compromise. Children learn early to play one parent against the other, certainly not an aid to good discipline.

An even harder situation involves young parents still living with their own parents. Older brothers and sisters, even younger siblings, decide they'll help discipline the baby.

When I tell Antonio "No," he may do it again, but it will be a little while. But if I spank him, he'll run to my mom and cry, then go right back and do what I told him not to do. The bad thing is if I do say "No," he cries, and my brother and sister baby him. (Becky)

An extended family can be bliss for a toddler if it means more people to love her and to care about her. It can also cause a lot of confusion if Grandma slaps her hand for touching the ash tray, 8-year-old Aunt Susan hits her for grabbing her doll, and 14-year-old Uncle Joe laughs at whatever she's doing.

If a young mother doesn't want to resort to hitting as a method of disciplining her toddler, she may get a lot of static from her extended family.

It's changing now that Shelly is older and has her own personality. When she does something wrong, my mother and sisters hit her hand. Or when she does something, they'll tell me, "Hit her," and I'll say, "Why?" I don't think that's right when she didn't know what she was doing wrong.

If she does something wrong, I want to tell her what it is. I don't want to hit her hand like they tell me to. They think I'm being too soft, and that she'll walk all over me later on. (Dixie)

If the young parent tries to explain, she may feel she gets nowhere. If she is still an adolescent, she and her parents may still have problems to work out concerning her own growing up. To her parents, she may appear to be an immature teenager who needs their help. And that help may extend to telling her how to raise her child.

She has her own child, yet she is dependent on her parents. It is, indeed, a dilemma for many young parents.

> *I can't tell her I learned this in school because she would say, "Well, what do they know? I've been a mother." I can't treat Shelly like I want to because I live with them. There are more things I would like to do with discipline, but I can't because there are too many people around. (Dixie)*

> *My brothers slap him around because he's a boy, and I tell them not to. Then when he's with kids, he hits them, and they say that's all right because he's a boy. (Laurette, 17 - Derek, 18 months)*

It's a difficult situation, one that each family must work out together. If young parents are careful to take the full responsibility of child care, they are more apt to have their own parents' cooperation in the way they want their toddler disciplined. If grandma babysits a lot, and if grandpa is providing for the young family financially, they will, of course, feel quite involved in the rearing of their grandchild. Discipline is one of the most important aspects of that rearing.

But if your parents know you are eager to take this responsibility for rearing your child, and you are doing the best you can to cope with it, they're far more likely to go along with your wishes on discipline.

Discipline is not easy. It is an extremely hard part of raising children. It takes an unbelievable amount of common sense and maturity. It also takes a deep desire to help your child learn self-discipline as the first step toward becoming a responsible adult.

Above all, good discipline demands an unending supply of love.

Chapter Eleven

Fifteen Months-Two Years: Your Little Runabout

Todd is so busy. I wonder how he got all that energy. I'll put little crackers in a container, and give him a second container with it. He'll put the crackers back and forth from one to the other. You can see how his little mind works—he'll try to put half on this side and half on the other.

It's unbelievable how much he knows—I guess more than I really give him credit for.

He's a lot of fun and a lot of work. The older he gets, the more work he is. Before, I could just hold him. I didn't have to be constantly getting up and running after him. Every day he gets more of a mind of his own. He'll tell me "No" when he's doing something I don't want him to do. (Jill, 18 - Todd, 16 months)

Marty hates the word "No." If I say "No," he wants to do the opposite. He's very active. I say anything, and he picks it up, sometimes in sentences.

He likes clothes—he likes to put his training pants on and off. He likes hats. He likes dolls. He's even starting to learn to swim. (Yumiko, 16 - Marty, 21 months)

Derek is kind of bratty now. He'll stick his tongue out at you. He wants to explore, and I let him touch everything. We don't have much out here that he could hurt or could hurt him. (Laurette, 17 - Derek, 18 months)

The runabout stage in a child's life is one of the most difficult for his parents—and for himself. He is trying to move away from being a dependent baby. So far, he has relied on other people for almost everything. Now he wants to be an independent person who makes many of his own decisions and who is rather self-reliant. To develop properly, he needs to take this step, hard as it is on those around him.

Infants are OK, but with toddlers, you have to kind of know what you're doing. And you have to take it one day at a time. (Roseanna, 15 - Felipe, 2 years)

TODDLERS, LIKE TEENAGERS, STRUGGLE FOR INDEPENDENCE

The toddler's "negative stage" has been compared to the beginning of puberty. At that time, as you may remember, young people struggle toward becoming adults who make their own decisions. No longer does the adolescent want her parents to "run her life." A great deal of friction occurs in many families because of the parents' desire to stay in control of their teenager's life while the teenager insists on taking over that control. It's often a difficult time for everyone.

Your toddler probably has similar feelings. No, she doesn't want the family car tonight, but she does want to feel she is in control of what she eats, when/whether she uses the bathroom, and how long she plays outside.

Henry is a handful. He doesn't really mess things up and break things, but he climbs, gets into everything. I'm constantly having to watch him while I'm doing everything else. It gets very hectic.

Every time I tell him to do something, he says "No." Sometimes I put him in the bedroom and shut the door. He'll bang on the door and cry, and that gets on my nerves. When I get really uptight, I let Marvin take care of him and I get out of the house. (Olivia, 20 - Henry, 23 months)

Teenagers and their parents are ahead if they can each give a little. Perhaps she can't have the family car whenever she wants it, but she can use it for errands and an occasional date. Perhaps she can't stay out as late as she wants, but maybe she and her parents can arrive at a reasonable compromise.

The consequences of treating adolescents either too strictly or too loosely may be severe. They still need parental support, but they also need to be able to take responsibility for their own actions. Teenagers who either lose control of themselves or have never learned to take control of their lives can end up in serious difficulties. They not only may have trouble with other people, but with the law as well.

Parents and toddlers, too, need to adjust to each others' wishes. Your toddler also needs to feel she has some control over her life.

TEMPER TANTRUMS

Unlike teenagers, your toddler doesn't have to worry about "outside" law. But losing control—in the form of frequent tantrums—can be pretty frightening for him. He desperately wants to do things his way. At the same time, he needs your firm guidance badly.

Temper tantrums happen because of frustration. During this stage, your child will have a lot of negative feelings. He wants so badly to do everything himself. But when he tries to put his clothes on, it's a struggle. Or he tries to put a big can into a little one, and it doesn't work. Yet he doesn't want you to help him.

These and many more happenings add up to a lot of frustration. But he can't talk it out. He doesn't know that many words yet. So he screams. His screaming may turn into a real out-of-control temper tantrum.

When Shelly gets really mad, she holds her breath, and I'm afraid she might pass out one of these days. She started when she was ten months old. She turns purple. I blow in her face and she breathes again. Sometimes I scold her. Then I start hugging her because I know she's so upset. (Dixie, 18 - Shelly, 17 months)

I ignore Leon when he has a tantrum. I turn around and act like he isn't there. My husband will say, "Stop that," and try to give him a swat, but I would rather have his tantrums ignored. (Tamara, 21 - Leon, 20 months, and DeeDee, 4½ years)

What should you do?
First, what should you *not* do? Don't spank or otherwise punish

your already upset child. If he is having a "real" tantrum, he's lost control of his own actions. If he's "just" screaming, hitting him won't help.

But don't give in to him either. If he's screaming because you said he couldn't have a piece of candy, don't stop the screaming by handing over the candy.

If you do, what happens next time he wants candy? Of course, you have another screaming session.

> *When Felipe is really really tired or when he doesn't have his way, he may have a tantrum, but hardly ever with me. It's more apt to be with my mom. He knows he can get away with it with Grandma, that he can have his own way. (Roseanna)*

Sometimes it's best to ignore a temper tantrum. If you can't do that because you can't stand the screaming, pick him up calmly and take him to his room.

> *If Meghan is mad, she screams, drops to the floor, has a tantrum. But she does this much less than she used to. I either ignore it or I set her in the corner. I say, "Now if you want to throw a fit, you can sit there while you do it." (Louise, 19 - Meghan, 23 months)*

An even better approach may be holding him gently. Feeling the security of your arms may have a calming effect. After all, he is a very upset little child, and he needs to know you still love him—even though you won't give in to his demands.

MOST IMPORTANT STAGE IN LIFE

Helping your toddler develop well is perhaps the greatest challenge you will ever face. Dr. Burton White considers this period, together with the nine-to-fifteen-month stage, the most important learning period in a person's entire life. How your toddler develops socially and intellectually now is the basis for all of her future development in these areas. Her growth in language and curiosity during this time is also of vital importance.

While parenting during this stage has many difficult times, you will also find lots of enjoyment in a well-developing toddler. You will find you are no longer living with a baby but, rather, with a young and very interesting person.

Meghan is motivated to figure things out. She plays with everything. She loves things that are not toys, especially her father's tools and hammers. Of course she only plays with them when Daddy is right beside her. She loves to play with keys, to unlock the doors like Mommy and Daddy. She likes to play out-side with the kids, but she comes in every once in awhile to check on me. (Louise)

Janet likes to go shopping. When I get ready to leave and she hears keys or sees me get my jacket, she grabs her coat. She loves new shoes, puts her foot up to show you.

I always have to keep an eye on her. I lost her at the Broadway store one day. I cried. I couldn't imagine where she was. Finally a lady brought her over to me. Janet wasn't even upset, just me. Since then, I bought a stroller, and I can keep track of her a little easier. (Candi, 16 - Janet, 18 months)

Marty explores everything. He opens doors, closets, drawers, pulls all his clothes out. I just go in there and pick them up and make him help. It's not that drastic when a kid pulls his clothes out of his drawer. When he's old enough, he'll fold them up himself. Now he helps. . . he hands them to me. If he spills milk, he'll usually grab a napkin and try to mop it up.

*He climbs up on his dresser. He gets his toes caught in the
drawer pulls and uses them like a ladder. He can get out of his
crib now, too. (Yumiko)*

According to Dr. White, your toddler needs to develop in three major directions. First, as you know, she needs to feel close to her main
caregiver, usually her mother. Second, she needs to explore her world.
Third, she needs to practice using her body, particularly in gross
motor (big muscle) activities. It's especially important that each of
these three areas develop.

If her interest in Mother is allowed to become the only important
thing in her life, she has a problem. And, of course, if she doesn't feel
close to anyone, she has an even bigger problem.

If a child has the equipment and space to practice motor skills—
running, jumping, throwing—but is not allowed to explore and to
continue to satisfy her curiosity, she won't develop as well as she
should.

Your important task is to give her plenty of opportunities to
develop in all three areas.

"TERRIBLE TWO'S" NOT SO TERRIBLE

Often, people speak of the "Terrible Two's" as if extreme negative
behavior suddenly turns up after a child's second birthday. Dr. White
and others believe, however, that this negative attitude sometimes
starts as early as 13 or 14 months.

At least by the time he is 17 months old, your child will undoubtedly enter this difficult phase.

He will often want his own way, no matter what. No longer can
you distract him by offering a substitute for the forbidden activity. If
he sees that you disapprove of whatever he is doing, he may be even
more determined to continue doing it. He will often be hard to
live with.

Two thoughts may comfort you. First, this happens to just about
every child. His negative actions certainly do *not* mean you are a poor
parent or a terrible person. Second, his extreme negative behavior will
probably go away, or at least become much less intense, within a few
months. Perhaps by his second birthday, you will find living with him
is a little easier.

Verna Hildebrand, author of *Parenting and Teaching Young
Children* (1980), points out (page 244), "Becoming independent is a
long uphill struggle from infancy to adulthood. Adults may find

children difficult at this age. But they should remember that being a
toddler is even more difficult than caring for one. Toddlers need all
the help they can get."

You still need to be firm about the things that matter. But give him
choices whenever possible. Don't say, "Come to lunch right this
minute." Instead, a few minutes before lunch is ready, ask, "Do you
want to wash your own hands for lunch, or shall I help you?" At
bedtime you might say, "Which book do you want me to read
tonight?" During this negative stage, don't ever say, "Do you want
lunch?" or "Do you want to go to bed?" unless you can handle
"No" for your answer.

Avoid showing your power when possible. Don't order him to do
something unless it's really necessary. If it is necessary, then of course
you insist that he go along with your wishes.

Routines, not only for bedtime, but also for meals, naps, baths, and
dressing, may help. Let him do it himself as much as possible. At
times, he will insist on doing it himself when you know he can't
possibly succeed. He may get terribly frustrated, but still won't let you
help him. You need far more tact in dealing with a toddler than with
the most temperamental spouse or employer in existence.

How much should you help your child? He needs to continue to be
able to call on you as his resource for help when he needs it. But
sometimes a child of this age seems not to want to work things out for
himself. If he always wants Mother to help him put the puzzle
together, either it's too hard for him, or he isn't learning to be as independent as he should be.

Use your best judgment. Help him when you think he needs you—if
he wants you to or will let you. Guide him toward more independence
when you think this is advisable.

If Marty doesn't know how to put something together, he'll get
help. If he wants to read a book, he brings it to me. He pulls legs
off his plastic doll and brings it to me. But he is pretty independ-
ent. Sometimes if I walk up and try to help him, he seems to be
saying, "Mom, I can do it, leave me alone." (Yumiko)

Competent as your toddler is, you still need to supervise water play,
whether in the bathtub or outdoors. He will continue to enjoy this
kind of play, especially if you join him. He may even be able to blow
soap bubbles soon.

I bought Derek a little pool, and I've been sitting in it with him. He pours water on me and laughs. (Laurette)

ACTIVE PLAY IS IMPORTANT

Running, climbing, jumping, swinging, and generally leaping about
are all necessary for your toddler's development. Playground equipment can be exciting for her if it's not too elaborate and hard to use. If
she can climb it herself—and if she wants to—she's probably safe.
Don't help her much, and don't urge her to play on something about
which she feels fearful.

> *When I take Meghan to the park, she climbs. At first, she*
> *wanted me to come get her down from each thing, but I thought*
> *she should learn a little independence. So I sort of closed my eyes*
> *and didn't help her for awhile. It seemed mean, but I thought if*
> *I'm there to do it, she'll expect Mommy to help her all the time.*
> *But she is very independent outside and even in the house.*
> *(Louise)*

Toddlers generally love to swing. Do you have a tree or something
else to use for hanging a swing? An old tire on a strong rope makes a
great swing.

If you have your own house, you might put a couple of strong
hooks in the rafters above a
playspace. Securely tie a thick
soft rope to the hooks. Put a
big knot at the other end.
Your child can hold on to it
and try to straddle it. Later,
when she is older, you might
even want to put a rope ladder on it for her. This could
be a good project for
Grandpa.

If you don't have stairs in
your home, find some occasionally so she can practice
going up and down. Other-
wise, she is apt to fall when
she suddenly is at the top of
a flight of stairs and has had
no practice in going down safely.

Shelly is good at stairs now. She used to fall. She climbs them on her knees, then comes down on her butt. At first, it was a problem. When she was real quiet, I'd know she was going upstairs. I let her go, but I was right behind her. (Dixie)

Twice in one day Marty fell down the front steps and hurt himself. But he's learning. He goes down backwards now. (Yumiko)

A board about eight inches wide and six feet long makes a good "toy." Your toddler can use it for a balancing board. Putting one foot directly in front of the other is a hard task for toddlers. She can practice on the board. She can also practice this skill on the lines of your floor tiles.

Walking the plank is even more fun if you set it up on two piles of magazines. Later, your child will be able to walk up it when one end is on the chair, the other end on the floor. If you supervise, the board can even be used for a see-saw by putting it across a sturdy box.

She'll enjoy riding toys although she may not be ready for a tricycle until she is at least two. Best is a low kiddie car in which she can sit and push herself along with her feet. You need to look for one that is simply built and won't spread her legs too far apart. Remember that toddlers have short legs. Some plastic models are built too wide.

She is learning to throw balls now. By the time she is two, she may be able to throw overhand more or less in your direction. She can kick a ball, too. Sometimes the dog joins the game:

We play ball. I throw the ball, the dog picks it up and brings it to me, puts it down. Todd then picks it up and he throws it.

We always play chase in the house. I act like I'm a monster and I'm going to get him. (Jill)

Sean throws a big ball and kicks it. He's been playing with it for about two weeks. He did have a smaller one that he would throw around and kick, too. (Ginger, 18 - Sean, 17 months)

A tennis ball can provide a lot of fun for a toddler. She can have a wonderful time throwing it and watching it bounce. It's easier for her to handle than is a bigger ball. Perhaps best of all, she can't knock a lamp over, put out a window, or hurt another child with a tennis ball.

Acrobatics are fun for toddlers. Is there any way you can let her play on a mattress? Jumping on your bed can be pretty destructive even if you remove the bedspread and your child takes her shoes off. But if you have an old mattress or foam rubber pad you can put on the floor, she'll love playing on it.

Shelly is very active. She'll watch people do something, then try to copy them. My cousin does gymnastics, and she tries to do what he does. (Dixie)

PLAY SPACE, PLAY TIME NEEDED

Even if you must cope with a crowded apartment, try to make play space for your toddler. It's still best if this space can be part of the kitchen or living room close to you rather than in a room away from everyone.

If you or older brothers and sisters need protection from him, perhaps it's time to set up that playpen after all—but not for the toddler. A four-year-old could color peacefully in the playpen while your toddler plays in the same room, but outside the pen.

You might even decide to set up your sewing machine or typewriter inside the pen. You could be sociably near your toddler, but get a lot more done without his "help."

Organizing your child's play materials is important. If he can't find part of the toy he wants, he won't play well. Does he seem to have lots of toys that he doesn't use? Are some of them broken? Are there parts missing? Are they hard to find at the bottom of a deep toy box? Are they hidden behind storage doors?

Perhaps you can get a few open shelves. Cement blocks and boards, if not stacked too high, make good shelving. Make sure they are stable so your toddler can't push them down. Help him keep his big toys on the bottom shelf, his others where he can reach them.

It's wise to have only a few toys readily available, the toys he is really interested in at the time. When you bring his other toys out again, they may seem new and interesting. Besides, if you leave everything out, a child this age will simply throw them all over the floor. You may even want him to use the more complicated stacking toys only at times when you can play with him.

One mother in a small apartment with little storage space placed several hooks high on the wall. On each hook she hung a pillowcase of toys. They came down for play one at a time. The apartment was less of a disaster area, and her child's play undoubtedly was more satisfying to him. He wasn't confused by seeing all his toys dumped out at once.

Above all, play with your child regularly. Hopefully, you will do this because you want to. Of course your work and activities take a lot of time, and they—and you—are very important. But if he has to whine and beg to get your attention, the ten minutes of play you finally give him won't be much fun for either of you.

Make the most of whatever time you can give your child. Be sure to give him your full attention. Follow his lead—does he want to roll a ball back and forth? Then play ball with him. Tomorrow he may decide to let you help him build a tower with his blocks, or perhaps he'll be ready to fingerpaint. Always talk to him about whatever you are doing together.

I love this age when Derek is running around. It makes me feel good that I can teach him something. After dinner he starts winding up again, so I usually take him for a walk. He wants to know what everything is. By the time we get back, he's pretty calm again. (Laurette)

A follow-the-leader game is easy to organize right in your living room. You be the leader first, and crawl under the table, around a chair, through a big box you've placed there, and over the big ball beside the box. Next time, let your child be the leader.

You can make your own bowling game. Use two-quart milk cartons for the bowling pins. You may need to put blocks inside them to give them enough stability to stand up. Then show your youngster how to roll a ball toward the "pins" to try to knock them over.

Throwing newspaper balls is fun for a toddler and remarkably safe for your house. Crumple newspaper into a ball and hold it together with a little tape. Make several and offer them to your child.

If he is naming small objects such as a ball, a car, a spoon, and a doll, make him a feel-box. A box in which small appliances are shipped is usually sturdy enough for this game. Cut a hole in the side big enough for your child's hand.

Show him the little items one at a time. Let him handle and examine them. Then put each one inside the box. Ask him to put his hand in the box and pick up an item. Then, without taking it out or

looking at it, ask him to tell
you what it is.

If this seems too easy for
him, try some plastic knives,
forks, and spoons. Can he
tell them apart by the way
they feel?

You may notice your tod-
dler is beginning to sort items
into groups. This is a start
toward making sense out of
his world by classifying
things and people into
groups. He has already
classified people into those he
knows and trusts and those

he doesn't. He certainly classifies toys into "mine" and, more slowly,
"yours."

When you purchase toys for him, a good set of small objects is a
good buy. Be sure none of the parts are so small that he can put them
in his mouth. Perhaps you'll choose a city street scene or a barn with
animals and people. You'll find he begins playing by classifying—
dividing the people from the animals, for example.

Soon he will be creating scenes and using his imagination. He'll
make the cars go fast, the dogs chase one another, and the policemen
stop traffic.

PLAN FOR INDOOR PLAY

Scribbling has been called the art of the toddler. Put a piece of sturdy drawing paper in front of your child. First, you put a mark on the
paper with an oversized kindergarten crayon. Then hand the crayon to
her saying, "Now you color." She will love it. She will also need
supervision unless you want the scribbling extended to your walls, furniture, and telephone book.

Scribbling is how she learns to draw. Instead of teaching her to
draw later, show her how to scribble during her second year. Her
scribbling will turn into drawing a year or so later.

Putting out big sheets of paper for painting and scribbling is important. You don't have to buy paper. Just put out big paper bags that
have been cut open.

It's time to make or buy a few simple puzzles for your child. Paste a picture on cardboard, then cut it in three pieces. Can she fit them together? If she does it quickly, perhaps she's ready for a harder task. If so, cut the same puzzle into five or six pieces. Can she still put it together?

She can probably place a circle and a square in a formboard. She may be ready for the commercial post office toy with holes of different shapes and matching blocks to drop into the holes.

You can make a stacking toy for your child. Use various sizes of cans such as juice, tomato paste, and soup cans. Go around each can a second time with a can opener. Then feel it to see if any sharp edges remain. If it's still sharp, throw it away and try another can.

Your child will like the designs on the cans, but if you want something fancier, cover them with glued-on fabric. Putting fur on one, silk on another, and vinyl on the third adds nice touching experience to the stacking game.

She may be able to "string beads" now. The beads can be empty spools, big buttons with large holes, empty tape rollers, even hair rollers. Dip about two inches of the end of some cord in white glue. Let it dry, and it will be stiff enough for your toddler to stick it through the holes. The cord should be no longer than ten inches. You don't want to run the risk of her wrapping the cord around her neck.

A few months ago, your child probably learned to stack one block on top of another. Now she can make a higher stack, a tower of blocks. Or she may stack cans of food, one on top of the other.

She will enjoy rearranging all kinds of objects around the house. She may take everything out of your kitchen cupboard and line the items up on the floor. She may balk at putting them away. If the job seems too much for her, ask her to help you put them back. Or make a game of seeing if she can put them away as fast as you put lunch on the table.

> *Lance climbs right into the cupboads with the pots and pans. Then he puts them inside each other. He can play in the lower cupboards although I rubberbanded one that I don't want him into. (Celia)*

> *Sean explores a lot. He gets into cupboards, everything you let him get into. He gets out the pans and bangs them together. He also bangs the cupboard doors back and forth. (Ginger)*

> *Felipe loves the drawers. He gets his clothes out, his shoes, his socks. He takes them out and puts his shoes on. Then he takes them off and puts another pair on.*
> *Each time he goes to the bathroom, he takes everything out of the drawers. It used to bother me, but he doesn't get into them as much as he did. I didn't spank him, but I'd tell him to pick them up, and he'd cry. (Roseanna)*

LET HIM "HELP"

Toddlers generally love to "help" with housework. If he can have a small broom, he'll sweep right along with you. Mopping the floor is his idea of real play.

When you're cooking, you can think of ways to involve him. Let him add the seasonings—premeasured by you, of course. If you're baking, he can sift ingredients and help you stir the mixture.

If you can figure a way to let him help you wash dishes without having a nervous breakdown yourself, he'll love it. If you have two sinks, he can use one to wash plastic spoons, cups, plates, and pans. You'll probably be ahead if you put a lot of newspapers on the floor before he starts washing dishes. Then his spills can be rolled up and thrown away.

He can be a real help at times. With a little direction, he can usually put his toys away. If he's tired, however, he'll need your assistance.

Felipe says "No" when I tell him to pick up his toys. Sometimes he picks them up, sometimes he sits there and stares at me. If I take the cart and wheel it around, he'll pick them up and put them in it. (Roseanna)

He can follow your simple request, "Bring me the dustcloth." He can help you make the beds, especially his own. He will love to mimic you.

Henry will open the drawer and get a can opener. Then he'll get a can and give it to me. Or he'll try to open the can himself. He likes to do what I do. He can even unlock the front door himself. (Olivia)

HER IMAGINATION DEVELOPS

Often children in this age group have a marvelous time pretending. They love to dress up in Mother's or Daddy's clothes. Putting on your shoes may be a favorite activity for her. Different kinds of hats will fascinate her. Save some of your old clothes for her dress-up play.

Leon pretends he is a dog, a cat, a bird flying. Sometimes he rides a horse (on the arm of the couch). He and DeeDee will go in the bedroom and pretend they're in outer space. They will sit and talk and talk. He understands her and she understands him. (Tamara)

*Antonio plays house with his cowboys, soldiers, and boats. He
loves motorcycles—the little ones and the real ones. We went by
the shop yesterday, and he wanted to get on one.*

*He will tell his doll "No" which is what I tell him. Or he'll
say, "Behave yourself." (Becky, 18 - Antonio, 26 months)*

Soon your child may involve you in her make-believe play. If she
invites you to feed her teddy bear, do so. Your participation is good
for her, and besides, you'll have fun, too.

*Janis does a lot of acting. I got sample diapers in the mail the
other day. She went in and got them and said, "These are for
me. The mailman sent them for me." She asked me to put them
on her, so I did. Then she pretended she was a baby and crawled
around.*

*She likes music a lot, punk rock. She used to like Rock
Lobster. She sees my brother pretend like he's playing a guitar, so
she does it, too.*

*She picks up everything. She tries to play baseball. She'll hit it
and do the running. She always slides into base. She's a real
character. (Darla, 17 - Janis, 2 years)*

*Sean's a show-off in the stores. They have this thing in the In-
fant Center called Jack-in-the-Box. In the store he plays Jack-in-
the-Box. He puts his head down, says the words, then comes up
and claps his hands while everybody watches. (Ginger)*

Dolls are important to almost all children. Most parents now seem
to understand boys need dolls as much as girls do. After all, if playing
with dolls is early practice toward being a parent, it must be as important for boys as for girls. Most men, as well as most women, will
become parents.

*Janet has two dolls, a little boy doll and a bear doll, Frankie
and Henry. She takes them in the tub with her. She calls them her
babies and takes them to bed. (Candi)*

Marty rocks his "bacobaby." (Yumiko)

Most toddlers love music. She may turn the radio on so she'll have
music for her dancing. Dance with her if she asks you. You'll both enjoy it.

Janet rolls her eyes and makes us laugh. She dances up a storm. I dance a lot and she watches me. (Candi)

She'd like to have her own musical instrument such as a drum, cymbals, or musical triangle. You can make her a drum from a one-pound coffee can. Two pan lids make cymbals.

TODDLERS AND TALKING

You've been helping your child learn to speak ever since he was born. You've talked to him, named things and people, read to him. He may be saying quite a few words by now.

Felipe talks quite a bit. He says names, "Rock-a-bye baby," "Book," a lot of things. (Roseanna)

Sean knows his body parts—nose, eyes, mouth, ears, hands, feet, legs. He just learned his arms yesterday. He answers the telephone. He says, "Who's this?" and then keeps talking. (Ginger)

Todd is starting to say two words together—"Go bye-bye." (Jill)

Now that he is beginning to say a few words, there are two more ways you can help him.

First, don't correct his speech. When you talk to him, pronounce words correctly and clearly. But if he says "pitty" for "pretty," don't worry about it. He will learn faster if you don't criticize.

Second, your child may not bother talking if he sees no need to do so. If he points at the refrigerator, do you immediately hand him a cup of juice? If he gestures for a cracker, do you give it to him right now? Instead, try encouraging him to say the word when possible. Don't frustrate him, of course, by waiting more than a few seconds. Above all, remember that children start talking at different ages.

*Shelly pulls at me to get attention. She says "Bottle" and
"Eat." If she wants something, she calls it out. She has been doing that for about two months. (Dixie)*

*Marty will be sitting there jabbering. He'll sound like he knows
what he's talking about, but I can't understand what he's saying.
(Yumiko)* (As his mother took him off to the bedroom to change
him, he was saying. "Bye, Jeannie. Bye, Jeannie.")

While most children can name familiar things and occasionally
speak in two-word phrases toward the end of the second year, your
perfectly bright two-year-old may say scarcely a word. Don't worry
about it. Continue talking to him about the things you're doing with
him. You can begin to talk about what happened yesterday and your
plans for tomorrow now because he is beginning to understand the
idea of time. Use simple, clear, slow speech.

READ TO YOUR CHILD

If you have been reading to your child, he probably is talking more
than he would have otherwise.

*I read to Shelly. I think that helps her learn to talk. I started
reading to her when she was about ten months old. I would read
to her before she went to bed or when neither she nor I was doing
anything.*
*I don't like to read unless it's what I want to read. But when I
read to Shelly, I know what I'm getting out of it. I enjoy it. And
she starts mumbling as though she's reading. That's how she
learned the names of doggie, etc. She turns the pages, but doesn't
tear them up. She just wants to turn them. (Dixie)*

*Antonio talks constantly. He has a memory like you wouldn't
believe. He remembers everything. He was talking sentences
before he ever turned two.*
*For awhile I was reading to him when he was about 1½. I had
time before I started to school, and I read to him quite a bit.
(Becky)*

*Sean takes a book and opens it up and seems to be reading—
jabbering. I have read to him a lot. He likes to point at the pictures, and he listens when I read to him. (Ginger)*

Felipe brings his books to me and says "Here," and I'll read to him. He likes to look at them by himself, too. He'll get them all out and just look at them. He likes to do a lot of things on his own. I think he's ripped only one page. (Roseanna)

When you choose books for your toddler, you'll want those with bright, simple pictures. At this age, her favorites will probably be books with pictures of things and people she already knows about.

If her grandparents live with or near you, a book about a child playing with Gramps will interest her. Books about dogs and cats are good. She may especially like stories with pictures of babies.

As she grows older, of course, you won't limit her books to stories about familiar things. The rhythm of Mother Goose rhymes will appeal to her. Fairy tales, stories about animals, people, and places she has never seen are an important part of her education. Provide lots of variety in her books, because books can widen her knowledge of and interest in many different things.

Books about familiar topics, however, are more likely to keep a toddler's interest.

CHOOSE NON-SEXIST BOOKS

Books can play an important part in a child's learning about himself and his world. Don't let his books show a slanted, sexist pic-

ture of that world. Too often, children's picture books portray all mothers in the kitchen cooking dinner and all fathers out earning the living.

Children's picture books sometimes suggest through illustrations and through words that little girls stay clean, play quietly, and cry occasionally. Little boys, however, are expected to play roughly and get dirty. But they aren't supposed to cry.

A horrible example of such a book, *I'm Glad I'm a Boy, I'm Glad I'm a Girl,* was published in 1970 by Simon and Schuster. It included such statements as "Boys have trucks. Girls have dolls . . . Boys are doctors. Girls are nurses. Boys invent things. Girls use what boys invent. Boys are policemen. Girls are metermaids."

This book is, fortunately, out of print. But books still on the market may carry a similar message. They may indicate you can do some things and not others simply because you are a boy or you are a girl.

Look for books that show boys and girls, men and women, as human beings with lots of different abilities and interests. Don't choose stories and illustrations that suggest that your child must limit his/her interests because of his/her sex.

You want your daughter to be glad she's a girl. You want your son to be glad he's a boy. But an athlete, a doctor, or a police officer can be glad she's a woman. A nurse, a dancer, or a preschool teacher can be glad he's a man. Books can help your child realize the wonderful opportunities open to boys and girls, to men and to women. Choose those books carefully.

Chapter Twelve

Toddler Routines

Most toddlers continue taking a fairly long afternoon nap. Some, however, may not want to nap. It's best to put her to bed anyway, together with her favorite stuffed toy and some books. Tell her you understand she doesn't want to sleep, but that she needs to rest for an hour. Chances are she will go to sleep. If she doesn't, an hour of quiet play will refresh her for the rest of the day.

SLEEP/REST STILL IMPORTANT

Your toddler will be less cranky if she eats and sleeps, or at least rests, at regular times. You also need time for yourself. Her daytime naps help both of you.

When toddlers hit the "I'll do it myself" stage, complete with lots of "No," bedtime may once again become a problem:

Bedtime is a hassle. Henry won't go to bed before I do, and he won't go in his crib. For the last couple of months, he has been in bed with me. If I put him in his crib, he cries and climbs out of it. He goes to sleep with me, then I put him in his crib.

He has his bath after he eats dinner. I put his pajamas on him and get him ready for bed. Then he wants to go outside, and he gets all dirty again.

He goes to bed when we do, but at 6:30 in the morning he doesn't want to get up. Today I brought him to school asleep. I

*couldn't wake him up. He used to go to
bed earlier. I think the change was when
he quit taking a bottle and started playing
outside. (Olivia, 20 - Henry, 23 months)*

Parents often start a bedtime ritual when
their child is six or eight months old. They
find it helps their child settle down to sleep
without a lot of fussing. If this isn't working
as well now, the solution may be an even more
complicated bedtime ritual.

Six months ago, perhaps you read to her,
rocked her a few minutes, and put her to bed
with her teddy bear. Now she has to have a
drink before she kisses you, not after. She
may want the same story every night. Perhaps
she has to tell each toy "Night-night." Whatever her routine, woe to
you if you upset it!

This ritual, if she feels she is in charge, can be a good compromise.
You get what you want when she goes to bed without a huge fuss. Of
course, you each give up something, too. You take the time to go
through the ritual with her, and she goes to bed. So don't try to get
out of that bedtime story once in awhile because you're tired. It's important to her.

> *Derek used to drive me up the wall when he wouldn't go to
> sleep. He is really active. He has this one blanket that he has to
> have to go to bed. He's had it all his life. Everybody calls him
> Linus. He takes his blanket and his bottle to bed. I've been want-
> ing to wean him.*
>
> *I'll say, "Where's your blanket?" and he'll go get it. He'll get a
> diaper for me, and I'll clap. Then he'll lie down so I can change
> him. (Laurette, 17 - Derek, 18 months)*

Roseanna's and Yumiko's bedtime rituals with their children don't
follow this pattern, but they work because each child follows his own
routine:

> *Felipe broke his crib so he sleeps on the sofa. At night he turns
> off the TV or stereo, then comes over and lies down. We have to
> give him a bath before he goes to bed or he won't go to sleep at
> all. He has to have one of his dolls with him, too. He goes to bed*

between 8:00 and 8:30.

I never put him in bed with me because I knew he would get used to it. Sometimes he'll go to sleep at the foot of our bed (with his own blanket) when he gets cold. By morning he'll be back in his own bed. (Roseanna, 15 - Felipe, 2 years)

Bedtime isn't as easy as it was when Marty was in the Infant Center. I think he got tireder there. He really wants to be with me, so he won't just lie down on his bed and go to sleep. Instead, he lies on my bed with me or on the couch. I don't like to let him cry.

I don't think it's so bad that he wants to be around me while he goes to sleep. If he slept with me, it would be different. He falls to sleep on the couch a lot at night watching TV with me. That seems to be the easiest way. Even with my mom, he does the same thing.

When he was first born, I used to put him in bed with me a little, but he has never really slept with me. I would rather he didn't get used to it. (Yumiko, 16 - Marty, 21 months)

Double-diaper your child at night. Otherwise, she'll probably soak right through the diaper onto her nightclothes and bedding.

SOLVING BEDTIME PROBLEMS

If your child already has a problem going to bed, the solution may not be easy. One young mother, whose husband recently joined the Navy, moved in with her parents-in-law for two months. She then decided she and her daughter would be better off in their own home. But Esperanza's child didn't adapt to coming back home as well as she had hoped:

Juanita is a crybaby now. She is really spoiled because I've been at Ruben's mother's house. She got a lot of attention there. When I came back home, I couldn't give her that much attention because I have to do a lot of things here. She won't stay in her crib to take a nap. She just screams. I either take her out and set her in here, or I leave her in there and she screams.

Here she used to sleep three or four hours for her naps. Over there she would sleep only 45 minutes or so. Before, she was always real happy, but now she isn't. She has really changed and I don't understand why.

When Juanita was four months old, I got real attached to her because Ruben was gone. I always had her by me, and I spent my whole time with her.

She hates that crib now, but I hate to put her on my bed. She sleeps with me a lot. When Ruben comes home, I guess I'll have to let her sleep with us.

I should start getting her used to the crib and let her cry. She takes a bottle when she goes to bed. She drinks her bottle, then wriggles around for thirty minutes before she settles down to sleep. (Esperanza, 17 - Juanita, 1 year)

Juanita has had more change than she likes in her first year of living. First, Daddy was home. Then he left. Then Juanita and Mother moved in with a family consisting of Grandma, Grandpa, and several young aunts and uncles. Now she's back in the apartment with her mother and her other grandma who is gone most of the time.

She's not sure what's going on in her world. First, she needs a terrific amount of love from Mother. But Mother is lonely and unhappy because Daddy is gone. It's a difficult situation any way you look at it.

But if Esperanza really wants Juanita to sleep in her crib, perhaps she should insist—and insist over and over again—that she sleep there. At the same time, she needs to try extra hard to help Juanita feel secure again.

If a baby cries when she's put to bed, it's probably because she doesn't want to be there. She doesn't want to be there because she doesn't want to be alone. She would far rather stay out in the living room with mother. She may feel a bit deserted when she's in bed by herself and Mother has shut the door firmly behind her.

One "solution" often tried when baby cries is to get her up again, hoping that in time she will quiet down enough to go to sleep. But with this method, she gets to be up with you. She learns that if she cries, she can get up. Why would she go to bed tomorrow night without fussing?

The opposite "solution" is to shut the door even more firmly and leave her alone to cry. A few minutes of crying won't hurt her. If she's tired enough, she'll go to sleep, exactly what you want.

But some babies will cry and cry for a couple of hours if left alone. They may fall asleep from exhaustion, but they're not apt to sleep well after such an ordeal. This is the kind of crying Esperanza described. Her solution was to let Juanita sleep with her on her bed. But that wasn't the solution Esperanza wanted.

A sensible approach could be a combination of the first two methods. When she cries, go in to see her. Tell her "Good night," pat her back a minute, then walk out. If she continues crying, repeat the process five minutes later. Continue going back in to reassure her every five minutes until she goes to sleep.

She may cry for another hour, but she knows you haven't left her because she's seen you every five minutes. She also knows she won't be brought back into the living room after bedtime. This method, according to Penelope Leach, author of *Your Baby and Child from Birth to Age Five,* will almost always work. Within a week at the most, your toddler should be much more accepting of her bedtime.

Why make such a fuss? Why not let her go to bed when she's ready? As mentioned before, most toddlers will let themselves become utterly exhausted before they will give in to sleep. A tired toddler is often a miserable toddler.

Helping her learn to eat and sleep at regular hours is almost certain to improve her disposition. In fact, the "spoiled" toddler who whines a lot and is generally demanding may improve a great deal if she is put on a reasonable time schedule.

SHOULD CHILD SLEEP WITH PARENT?

"Should" you sleep with your child? Most child development experts in our culture say "No." Tina Thevenin, author of *The Family Bed,* believes otherwise. In her book, she stresses the advantages of letting small children sleep with their parents. Apparently there is room for disagreement.

However, having her child sleep with her was described as a "problem" by several of the young mothers interviewed.

> *One thing I did that I wish I hadn't was letting Heidi sleep with me. When she was little, a newborn, I took her to bed with me. She didn't like her crib very much. She would sleep with me all night, but my mom would say, "You have to put her in that crib or she won't ever sleep in it." She was right. At about five months, I put her in her crib and let her sleep by herself. When she would wake up, I would get her a bottle and go back to my bed. Dennis feels pretty strong about not wanting Heidi to sleep with us.*
>
> *I have a suggestion for mothers of newborns. If they breastfeed and have the child in bed with them, they should, after they feed him, put him in his own bed. (Jenny, 18 - Heidi, 13½ months)*

Sometimes a mother feels she has no choice but to sleep with her baby. There's no room otherwise.

> *Gary wakes up about three times each night. I give him a bottle and change him. He sleeps with me.*
>
> *I had no choice. I didn't want him to, but we moved here when he was about 1½ months old, and there was no place for the crib. I had to store it away, so he slept with me. Then a month ago my sister moved out, and there was room for the crib. I put it up the other day, but he won't sleep in it.*
>
> *He is really attached to me at night. He won't go to sleep until I do. I hope he outgrows it. (Jan, 15 - Gary, 1 year)*

It might have been better to put Gary to bed on his mother's bed each evening, then move him out in the living room when the rest of the family went to bed. Perhaps his crib mattress could have been set up on the living room floor each night. If he rolled off, he wouldn't have been hurt.

But since he has already formed such a strong habit of sleeping with his mother, she still has two choices. She can continue letting him sleep with her. Perhaps he will eventually outgrow it, as she hopes. The danger here is that his mother may suddenly decide at a later time that she doesn't want him in bed with her. It may be even harder to get him to sleep elsewhere then.

A better solution is to insist he sleep in his crib now. She could follow the check-on-him-every-five-minutes routine described above. It will be difficult both for her and for Gary, but it might be worth the effort.

Brigette found a fairly simple solution to a similar problem:

> *Rudy has slept with me at least three-fourths of his life. It got to the point where he wouldn't go to sleep until I was in bed with him. I would lie down with him for about an hour until he was asleep. I strongly recommend you not sleep with your kids— except when they're sick, of course.*
>
> *Now I'll be marrying John, and I don't want Rudy to think John is kicking him out of my bed. A friend suggested I get him a new bed and make a big deal of it. She said I should do this long before my wedding. Then when I got married, it would be all done. So I bought Rudy a youth bed. He was thrilled, and it worked. He goes to sleep by himself in his own bed now. (Brigette, 22 - Rudy, 3, and Joy, 4)*

A crisis in a child's life may cause sleep problems. Bedtime became more difficult for Helen after her parents split up. Rosemarie described the situation:

> *Bedtime is a problem. Helen doesn't want to go to bed without me. Sometimes she will lie down on the couch. I try to go to bed by 9 P.M. She would go into her own room and her own bed before we split. Now she wakes up at 2 A.M. and gets in bed with me. But it is getting better.*
>
> *I don't like her to sleep with me, and I don't think it's good for Helen. I don't want her to be too dependent on me. If she wakes up, I try to force myself to get out of bed and take her to her own room. I sit with her and help her get to sleep in there.*
>
> *I don't really think it's bad. But if I were to get married again next year and put her out of my bed, she would think, "Oh my gosh, Mom doesn't love me, she has someone else." If I can convince her now, it won't be such a shock. When we lived with my parents, she was always in our room, but in her crib. I have never*

had a problem with it until our separation, so I feel at terms with it. (Rosemarie, 19 - Helen, 3 years)

Rosemarie understands that Helen needs extra mothering since her father moved out. Rosemarie is wise to think ahead to the problems that might arise if she let Helen sleep with her. It's hard to find the energy to take her back to her own bed, but she feels it's worth the effort.

Your toddler may have a nightmare occasionally. He'll go to bed and to sleep. A little later, you hear him screaming. When you go in, he may be kicking, moving frantically. He needs you to reassure him that you're there, that it was only a bad dream.

Go in and talk to him for a minute. Perhaps he would like a drink of water. When he calms down and isn't afraid anymore, tell him "Good night" and go back to bed.

Occasionally young mothers spoke of giving their year-old children several bottles during the night. If he had a bottle at bedtime, he doesn't need the extra food. Again, remember the danger of tooth decay if your child sleeps with a bottle of milk.

If he wakes, instead of handing him a bottle, offer him a cup of water. Tell him "Good night" and walk away. If he continues crying, try the every-five-minute routine for a week. You'll be exhausted, but if he starts sleeping through the night, think how much better you'll feel the next week.

MEALTIME FOR TODDLERS

Many adults consider eating an enjoyable pastime. Some of us enjoy it too much!

But for many small children, mealtime becomes a hassle, a fight with Mother and Dad. "Eat your meat right now." "Just one more bite of green beans." "No dessert for you until you finish your carrots!"

A toddler's mealtime doesn't have to be a bad experience for everyone. Toddlers have the same kinds of food needs as the rest of us. They need nutritious foods from the Basic Four food groups. They also need a relaxed, friendly atmosphere at mealtime. Both needs are important.

By now, your child can probably eat her meals with you. With a little planning, most of your food should be suitable for her. Cut meat, fish, and vegetables into finger-sized cubes. If you are frying food for your family, it would be better for your toddler if you could broil or dry-fry her food in a non-stick pan. Serve her food before you add the spices or the rich sauce. Foods to avoid completely at this age include popcorn and nuts.

Convenience foods such as canned soups are not as nutritious as foods you prepare yourself. Soups and other dehydrated meals usually contain more salt than your child should have. These foods also contain a variety of preservatives, colorings, and artificial flavorings. It's all right to serve them occasionally, but a steady diet of already-prepared foods is not especially good for any of us.

Give her small helpings of food. Don't worry if she doesn't seem to eat much. She doesn't need as much as she did six months ago when she was growing so much faster than she is now. She needs twenty ounces of milk daily. Like the rest of us, she also needs some fruits and vegetables, bread and cereal, and protein foods.

If she doesn't drink enough milk, put it in puddings and soups. Does she like cheese? Let cheese take the place of some of her milk.

While most toddlers insist on feeding themselves, you may find she occasionally insists just as strongly that you feed her. That's all right. She may not be feeling well, or she may simply be tired of feeding herself all the time.

Allow plenty of time for your toddler to eat. Rushing through a meal is not her style. She'll eat many foods with her fingers, but by her second birthday, she'll be able to handle a spoon quite well.

Heidi drinks out of a cup and eats with a spoon very well. She eats what we eat, all table foods. (Jenny)

Alice eats what we eat now—except she can't handle some of the meat like pork chops because she has only eight teeth. (Melanie, 15 - Alice, 13 months)

COPING WITH MESSINESS

Learning to use a spoon is hard work and takes a lot of practice. He has to try. If mother insists on neatness at the table, he'll be discouraged. While he's learning, it's impossible for him to be neat.

When Derek eats and he's through, he's through. You'd better get him down fast—or he'll throw his food and jump out of his highchair! (Laurette)

Marty eats everything that we eat. But sometimes he plays with his food and that bothers me. (Yumiko)

When he eats a cracker, he may first gum it. Then he'll rub the resulting mess all over his face and into his hair. There is no reason to let him sit on the couch while he makes this mess, of course. But his highchair can be cleaned up. He is fairly easily washed, although he may not appreciate your efforts. If you give him a second washcloth to use on himself while you clean him up, it may help. Try not to let the mess upset you.

If you really want to see a mess, offer your toddler some spaghetti with sauce. When he was about two years old, our oldest son's favorite food was spaghetti. Judging from a photo from that era, the spaghetti he didn't eat he usually worked into his hair.

Some parents are so horrified at the mess their toddler makes while eating that they don't want anyone else around at mealtime. That's OK. Because of the mess, some people feed toddlers before the rest of the family eats. This is undoubtedly better than scolding the child for his absolutely normal messiness throughout dinner.

If you realize how normal this messiness is, and that it will happen at this age, you can probably handle it without too much frustration. Put a thick layer of newspapers on the floor under his chair to catch the spills. Roll them up after dinner and throw them away. Then you have only your toddler and his chair to clean.

By now, your child will probably be drinking most of his milk from a cup. If you fill it only one-fourth full, the inevitable spilling will be less of a disaster. You can refill it—one-fourth full—as often as he wants it. Be sure you encourage him to drink plenty of milk.

TODDLER NEEDS LESS FOOD

If your family meals are nutritionally balanced, your toddler, assuming she eats a little of most things, should have a balanced diet. She needs the same Basic Four foods the rest of us need. The difference is that her servings are smaller than those for adults.

Remember that your toddler's appetite is much less this year than last. She's not growing nearly as fast as she did those first twelve months.

It is during this stage that many mothers decide their toddlers are "terrible eaters." "She just doesn't eat a thing," they say. But if you overfeed her now, remember, she is apt to become a fat adult. You don't want your child to spend her life fighting unhealthy, unattractive fat.

Don't try to force or even coax her to eat. Offer small servings of nutritious food. Don't offer sweets at all. If she seems to need one in-between-meal snack, make it part of her daily food plan. Carrots, orange juice, graham crackers, milk, and apple are examples of good snack foods that won't pave the way for your lovely child to become a fat adult.

Sean snacks a lot—plums, grapes, nectarines, peaches. He doesn't eat much candy and other sweets. I won't let him. He doesn't need any candy because of his teeth, and because it would spoil his appetite. (Ginger, 18 - Sean, 17 months)

If she doesn't want to eat any lunch at all, try not to show any emotion as you take her food away. She won't starve by suppertime. Just don't tide her over with a handful of cookies a couple of hours later. If she eats it all and asks for more, give it to her in the same way, without an emotional reaction. Whether she eats all of her food or not is not what makes her a "good girl."

Meghan was not a good eater. She wouldn't touch anything. All she wanted was a glass of milk constantly, and it really worried me. I told the doctor about it. She laughed and said, "Oh, I can tell you're going through the fun stage."

"What can I do about it?" I asked. She said to give Meghan vitamins with iron, and that seemed to help her appetite. She also told me to quit fussing about it.

I try to avoid candy, although I do treat them once in awhile. But I don't like to give them too many sweets. Sometimes when Meghan

*doesn't want to eat, I think it's because she's too busy to bother. She
does love pizza. (Louise, 19 - Mark, 5½ months, and Meghan, 23
months)*

If your child doesn't eat a wide variety of foods, don't be upset.
Continue offering her the variety of foods the rest of your family is
eating. You say she won't eat any vegetables at all? What about raw
ones? She can get even more vitamins from raw vegetables than from
cooked ones.

Until she's two, however,
don't give her raw carrot sticks
or other hard-to-chew foods. If
she likes raw vegetables, grate
her carrots and potatoes for her.

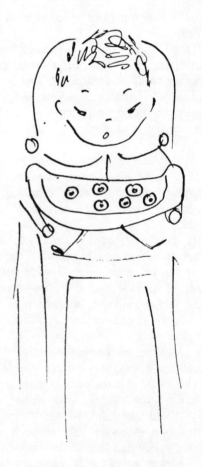

*Henry doesn't eat his dinner.
He doesn't eat any kind of meat
except bologna and weiners, but
he will take one bite out of a
hamburger.*

*He won't eat at all some-
times, then comes back for
cookies. Or at night he'll open
the refrigerator and get the
cheese and bologna. He loves
fruits, sometimes vegetables.
(Olivia)*

If you have a picky eater
already, think about what she
does like. If the only meat she'll
eat this month is hot dogs, feed
her hot dogs. She'll get some
protein. Chicken and fish are
better for her than hot dogs, but
hot dogs are better than
nothing.

OUTLAW JUNK FOOD

Keep the junk food away
from your picky eater. If he

isn't hungry enough for meals, he certainly doesn't need a coke, potato chips, or even cookies an hour later. While one or two oatmeal cookies provide a little nutrition, a handful of sugary snacks won't do much for him except ruin his appetite for more nutritious foods.

But avoid telling him he can have his dessert only if he eats his vegetables. You don't want him to think his dessert tastes better than the rest of his dinner. In a well-planned meal, dessert is not junk food. If it's offered at all, it is as nutritious as the rest of his dinner.

If you are in your own home, or if the people you live with are willing, don't keep junk food there at all. If you don't have candy and cookies in the cupboard or soft drinks in the refrigerator, your toddler can't have them while he's at home. The occasional sweet he gets from the outside world won't matter that much as long as you aren't providing them, too. But sometimes Grandma can cause a problem:

DeeDee's eating habits are terrible, and I'm trying to get her to eat more fresh fruits and vegetables instead of candy.

My mom likes to take DeeDee for one day a week. She used to take her out and buy her a coke and Lifesavers. Then when I took her to the dentist, she had five cavities—$125. So that was it. I told Mom if she ever feeds DeeDee candy again, she has to pay the dental bills! (Tamera, 21 - Leon, 20 months, and DeeDee, 4½ years)

I tried not to give Felipe cokes and sweets. But when he is with Grandma, he controls her, and he gets them. Now he opens the refrigerator and grabs, but he likes a lot of fruits, especially oranges. The only kind of cereal I give him is Cheerios. He likes meats. I give him popsicles when I get home from school and I have to clean house. (Roseanna)

If you have a toddler who already appears overweight, don't put him on a reducing diet. Do, however, guide his eating so that he gains weight more slowly. Make a list of the food he eats in a three-day period. You may be surprised at the amount of high-calorie food he consumes.

Don't cut out the meat, vegetables, milk, fruit, and cereal, his Basic Four foods. Get serious about not having junk food in the house. If he drinks more than a quart of milk a day, try diluting it with water. Most doctors don't recommend skim or low-fat milk for children under two.

Encourage your overweight toddler to get more exercise. Do you take walks, but push him in his stroller? Get him to walk with you. Is he outdoors enough? It may take real effort on your part to get him to a park if you don't have a yard, but it may well be worth the effort.

You have three basic responsibilities connected with feeding your child. First, you need to offer him the nutritious food he needs. Second, help him learn that mealtime is a pleasant, sociable time. It's not a period of coaxing him to eat, or a time to argue with the rest of the family. And third, help him stay at a healthy weight.

WHAT ABOUT WEANING?

Sometime in the second year of life, your child should be mostly weaned from taking her bottle. Occasionally she may want a bottle at night. If she does, put water in it, not milk.

> *It wasn't too hard to wean Sean. When I was taking him off it, whenever he would see a bottle, he'd want it. I'd give him one at night, but I finally got him to quit. (Ginger)*

Some people want their child to be weaned from the bottle sometime during the first year. That's OK if she gives up her bottle voluntarily. But there is nothing wrong with your child having a bottle into the second year if she seems to need it and wants the sucking.

> *Antonio was almost two, and off and on at night he would still have his bottle. He would wake up twice at night to have it. Finally one day I had had it. I said, "You won't get any more bottles," and I threw them in the trash. He cried three or four nights, but no problems since then. (Becky, 18 - Antonio, 26 months)*

There is nothing wrong with going to bed with a *bottle*—that's just fine. It's a nice comforting thing, and all of us like to be comfortable when we go to bed. But it is not good to have milk in that bottle. The toddler, who doesn't need food throughout the night, gets used to having it.

> *Felipe was about 1½ when I gave him his bottles and told him to throw them in the trash, and he did. I would give him a cup of water when he woke up. He'd get mad, but he'd go back to sleep. (Roseanna)*

If your toddler wants a bottle at bedtime, put water in the bottle. Give her a cup of milk just before she goes to bed.

> *Alice will take two or three naps during the day. She's attached to her bottle. At night she has to go to sleep with the bottle, but she doesn't care what's in it. I'm starting to give her water at night. If I give her milk in a cup and water in the bottle, she'll quit demanding the bottle so much. (Melanie)*

As you give your baby a bottle of milk, hold her in your lap while you feed her. A child under two will let you know when she's ready to give up the bottle. She will drink a little, then look away or start to play. Two things need to happen at that time: she has to get enough milk, and you have to be comfortable that she is telling you she doesn't need the sucking experience any longer.

CARE FOR TODDLERS' TEETH

Your toddler may have had no trouble cutting his early teeth. But his first and second molars, cut during his second year, can be a different matter. He may be quite miserable and irritable when these molars are coming through his gums.

You can't do a lot to help, but give him something cold to bite on. He may like to play with ice cubes. Even rubbing his gums with your finger may help, if only to let him know you're trying to do something for him.

If he seems to be in a lot of pain, it may not be his teeth. If he keeps putting his hand up to the side of his face, perhaps he has an earache. Check with his doctor.

Your toddler needs his own toothbrush. You should be brushing his teeth as soon as three or four teeth have erupted. Now he will want to help, but be sure his teeth are brushed thoroughly at least twice a day.

> *Heidi doesn't get any candy at all. I'm protecting those teeth. I'm starting to brush them now. (Jenny)*

The easiest way to show him how to brush is to stand him in front of you with the back of his head against you. Brace his head against one hand and brush with the other. Show him how to brush the upper teeth down and the lower teeth up, the way they grow. You'll need to supervise his brushing for several years yet.

SHARING TODDLER CARE

Keeping up with a superactive toddler is hard. If two parents can share the supervision task, everyone will be better off. Mother won't get so exhausted, Daddy will enjoy his child more if he is involved, and Baby, of course, will be most pleased of all.

> *Norm is much more involved with Lance than he was with Laurel. With Laurel, he didn't know what to do. I think it's harder for guys because so often girls baby-sit and know what to do with babies. With Lance, he helps when he can, mostly by playing with him. (Celia, 21 - Lance, 18 months, and Laurel, 4 years)*

> *Jim spends a lot of time with Danette. He comes home, and the three of us go outside and play. It's surprising how much time he spends with her. He helps with feeding and changing. He started that about two months ago. (Caroline, 18 - Danette, 10 months)*

Other fathers are less involved:

> *Once in awhile Ed helps me, but not really very much. When we go places like to the park, he is always chasing after Dale, but he doesn't do much at home. (Arlene, 17 - Dale, 11½ months)*

> *Dennis isn't too much help, perhaps because of the problems we've had. He thinks the baby is just mine. His mom helps me a lot, and my mom did when I lived at home. You can get very irritable if you don't have anybody to help you. If we want to go out, sometimes we take Heidi. We make a bed for her in the car while we go to the drive-in. (Jenny)*

Sometimes if Mother wants more help, she needs to insist a little:

> *Curt works twelve hours a day so he doesn't have much time*

for the kids. It puts quite a strain on us.

*I decided recently that if I want to go shopping Sunday after-
noon or at night, I'll go. I tell Curt the kids are bathed and fed
and ready for bed. He doesn't complain.*

*For a long time, he wouldn't get involved. But with the two, I
decided I couldn't do it all, and he's finding he likes it. DeeDee
and Leon run and greet him at the door now, and he thinks that's
neat. (Tamera)*

Many single parents cope well. But sometimes it gets especially hard
if you're alone:

*It's hard being a single parent. We were living together for
awhile, and I miss the emotional support.*

*When I get really uptight, I put Juanita in the crib and let her
cry. There's nothing I can do unless I hold her all day, and then
I'm more upset.*

*I don't read to her because she's too hyper. We sometimes play
patty-cake and peek-a-boo. I run and hide in the house and she
looks for me.*

*I had to quit school this summer because she had bronchitis
and she was teething. I couldn't leave her in the Infant Center.
When school starts, I hope to go back. (Esperanza)*

Young parents, married as well as single, often have mixed feelings
about living with their own parents. During the toddler stage, when
baby is into everything, feelings may get especially tense. Most young
mothers interviewed, however, seemed to feel a need for family help.

*My mother will watch Robin once a week so I can go out. I've
learned one thing. If you have any problems, don't hide them
from your mom. Mothers understand more than I thought they
did. (Melinda, 16 - Robin, 9 months)*

*My little sister will say, "Mother, Melanie won't let me give
Alice any candy." I do let them give her animal cookies, but she
wanted to give Alice some chocolates. Alice has bad teeth
already. So my mother says, "That's Melanie's baby—you let her
be."*

*The only time my mother has a lot of say-so is when Alice is
sick and I don't know what she needs. Mom helps me a lot.
(Melanie)*

Sometimes Marge (Dennis' mother) will tell me what clothes to put on Heidi. I just ignore her. This morning we left for school. I thought it would be kind of cold, so I put a sweater on her. Marge asked me why.

I like Heidi to go in the grocery store with long pants on because I know it will be a little chilly. Marge asks me why. I suppose I'm being too protective. (Jenny)

Most of these young mothers are eager to take as much parenting responsibility as possible. They appreciate the help they receive from their families, but they want to be independent as soon as possible.

I don't want Maelynn to get close to my mom or my sister so she would rather go to them than to me. I have a cousin like that—he'd rather go to my grandmother or my aunt instead of his mother. I don't like that, and I'm trying to get Maelynn not to do that. So I talk to her a lot, and I usually take care of her when I'm here. When she's sick, she stays with my mom or my sister. (Joleen, 17 - Maelynn, 9½ months)

DON'T RUSH TOILET TRAINING

First of all, "toilet training" should not even be discussed in a book limited to parenting children under two. Most children aren't ready to use the toilet until after their second birthday. But we'll talk about it briefly.

"Toilet training" is a strange term. Nobody has to be "trained" to urinate or defecate. It's something we all do. Babies are born with this ability. They don't need to be "trained."

In our culture, of course, "toilet training" means training the child to urinate and defecate in the toilet instead of in his diapers. While he's being "trained," he wears "training" pants, and he's not supposed to have "accidents" in those training pants.

There's another strange use of a word. An "accident" is something that should not have happened, that could possibly have been prevented. Urinating is no accident!

Imagine you're a toddler. Your mother puts diapers on you for months. She changes them when you get them wet or messy. Then one day she puts another kind of panty on you, and suddenly it's an "accident" if you get those panties wet or dirty. Confusing.

Attempts at early toilet training must seem very strange to a child. If you have to "train" him, he may not be ready to use the toilet.

You'll save yourself and your child a lot of effort if you cheerfully diaper him until he decides he wants to use the bathroom. This will seldom happen before he is two, and sometimes it's quite a bit later:

> *Helen is still in diapers. She always says, "Mom, I'm not ready yet." We have worked at it. We have even tried bribing her. She says, "Mom, when I'm ready, I'll let you know."*
>
> *I tried when she was 1½ or 2, but it didn't work so I decided to wait. I knew she would be ready by the time she was 2½, but she wasn't. She'll let me know when she's ready. (Rosemarie)*

> *Toilet training? With DeeDee I waited until she was about 27 months old, and it only took a week after I quit putting diapers on her. She never wet the bed, and she never had any serious accidents.*
>
> *My mom thought I waited too long with her. I would let her go in and sit down on the toilet, but she didn't do anything. I did that for about six months until she learned what the word "potty" meant. My mom helped me a lot with her. (Tamera)*

The best possible way to teach your toddler you want him to use the toilet is to let him watch other people use it. He'll get the idea.

> *I was up one morning, and I was in there brushing my teeth. Rudy came in and he pulled his pants down and he wet. He has done it himself. He was about 22 months old.*
>
> *He has always gone to the bathroom with other guys, my brother and little kids that run around here.*
>
> *I kept diapers on him at night for awhile, and he would wet. As soon as I took them off him, he would wait until morning. I was so thrilled when he went to the toilet that I called everyone and said, "Guess what, Rudy used the toilet!" (Brigette)*

RENT-A-KID METHOD

Jim Mead, founder of *For Kids Sake, Inc.,* a parent support group in Brea, California, advocates the

Rent-A-Kid technique. Wait until your child seems ready to start urinating in the toilet, then rent a child for the weekend. The child must be the same sex as yours, and s/he must agree to take your toddler with her/him every single time s/he goes to the bathroom. Mead says your toddler will be using the bathroom him/herself by Sunday night.

Of course, if you can do it without too much embarrassment, the ideal way to teach your child how to use the toilet is through modeling. You show him how.

If you encourage your child to sit on his little potty chair while you're on the big toilet, he'll probably get the idea faster. After all, he wants to mimic you when you're washing dishes and raking the yard. Mimicking you while you're on the toilet may also appeal to him. Most important, instead of putting pressure on your child to use the toilet, you're modeling for him the method you want him to learn.

Mead realizes that some parents won't be comfortable sharing the bathroom regularly with their child. That's why he developed the Rent-A-Kid method.

He stresses the importance of getting a small potty chair for your child. "What do you think a little kid thinks about if you put him up on the big toilet?" he asked. "He thinks about how high he is and how afraid he is of falling in. The little seat close to the floor makes him feel more secure."

Mead is especially interested in toilet training ideas because he says efforts at toilet training result in more child abuse than does any other aspect of child rearing. Parents get all worked up about it.

But this is one battle the child always wins. There is no way a parent can make a child urinate in a particular place. This is one area the child is in control, a very infuriating situation for many parents.

Mead makes two more suggestions on the subject. Let your child color a bull's eye on the inside piece of a paper toilet seat cover. Let him drop the bull's eye in the toilet, then see if he can urinate in the "eye."

Freezing colored ice cubes is Mead's other suggestion. Drop several in the toilet. If your child, boy or girl, urinates on them, the ice will crackle and pop as the warm urine melts it. Fun!

When I was potty training Melissa, I made it fun for her, like a game. I even gave her treats when she used the potty.

I didn't try to force her. When she didn't get to the potty in time, I changed her and didn't scold her. It was a slow process, but it worked. (Thelma, 20 - Melissa, 4, and Bobby, 18 months)

Making urinating fun for the child is more important for the parent than for the child himself, explains Mead. If the parent can join in a little silliness with the child, s/he is less likely to get so angry that s/he hurts him. Mead has seen far too many children physically abused by their parents because they weren't using the bathroom in the way their parents wanted.

Get your child a potty to set on the floor or, if you don't think it will frighten her, a child's seat on the big toilet. Explain what it is, and that when she's ready, she will use it instead of getting her diapers wet.

I have tried toilet training with Meghan, but I've heard that you aren't going to potty train that child until she is ready. One time Meghan tinkled in the potty and I thought, "Oh, she's ready." But it was completely by accident. And she isn't ready yet.

Sometimes she sits on the potty, but she doesn't do anything. I tried 1½ days without diapers, but she wasn't ready for it at all. (Louise)

If this happens to you, relax. Forget about "training" your child. But be alert to any signs that she is ready.

If you have decided it's time to train your child, are you ready? This is an important part of the whole procedure. Do you have time? Can you stay in there with her? Can you praise her successes? Ignore her failures?

If your parents are having out-of-town company, can you handle puddles on the floor? Sometimes people try to toilet train their child right before going to see Grandma. That's not a very good reason or a very good time.

When you think she's ready and you're ready, put training pants on her for two or three days. She can get them down easier and faster than diapers.

I just started introducing the toilet to Troy slowly, perhaps from laziness. I was afraid he might be the only child in kindergarten that wore diapers. I would take him to the bathroom and try to get him familiar with it, but I wasn't pushing too hard. You can't make them go if they don't want to. The baby sitter would take him every couple of hours and just set him on it.

Then I took the diapers away, and didn't put diapers on him at all. For three days it was kind of a mess—I put plastic pants over

his training pants. Then he just started using the toilet.
Other people were really worried. They'd say, "Oh, he's 2½
and not potty trained?" and I decided maybe I should push it a
little. (Rebecca, 20 - Troy, 2½ years)

If your child piddles on the floor, don't scold her. Just clean it up.
If after two or three days, she still piddles on the floor regularly, it
must not be time for the training pants. Put diapers on her again
without showing any disapproval. If she's not ready, she's not ready.
That doesn't mean she's bad.

If you get discouraged, check out the kindergarten class down the
street. You'll probably not find a single child in diapers.

Chapter Thirteen

You May Have Problems

They have all these shows about young girls getting pregnant, and none of them ever work out. But it can work. I was very fortunate. (Celia, 21 - Lance, 18 months, and Laurel, 4 years)

Laurel was born three months after Celia graduated from high school. Nine months later she and Laurel's father were married. He had a good job, and within two years, they bought a house. Lance was born when Laurel was 2½.

Many young mothers who feel good about themselves and their babies are quoted in this book. Most of them don't think parenting is easy. They agree with a lot of older parents that taking care of a baby or toddler is a challenging and difficult task.

But most of the young women quoted so far are coping remarkably well. They love their children and generally are taking good care of them.

Sixty-one young mothers were interviewed intensively. Others shared through letters and telephone conversations. As with all human beings, each had problems as well as joy in her life.

Sometimes when I'm crying, I hold Sharon, and she somehow gives me security. When I'm really tired, I look at her and think it's worthwhile. Sometimes I want to quit school because it's so much work, but I don't because of her. (Rachel, 16 - Sharon, 4 months)

It wouldn't be honest to ignore the problems. Parenting is more than knowing what to expect of a child at different stages and using good sense and love in caring for that child. Mothers and fathers are more than "just" parents. Each one has her/his own life to deal with, too. Each one is an individual with problems, pain, and joy apart from the very important role of parenting a child.

NEVER ENOUGH MONEY

Money is often a problem. If the young mother depends on welfare payments (AFDC—Aid to Families with Dependent Children), there is never enough money.

Sometimes I run out of money. There is no way I can rely on welfare. They let you work, and you can have one-third of your earnings, so I work part-time. My mom watches the kids when I work.

My cousin said, "I'm going to get pregnant and get on welfare." I told her she was crazy.

When you move into a new place here in California, it costs about $1000. They won't rent to you unless you're 18, and your parent has to sign for you even then. My girl friend lives with me. She says every time she wants a child, she'll take care of one of mine. (Leslie, 20 - Kerry, 4 months, and Amy, 27 months)

A young mother, recently laid off the job she had held for two years, reported:

Prices have gone up terribly. Clothing is very expensive. It's hard because I'm unemployed. Little shoes cost so much, almost as much as mine. I spent $82 yesterday for Jeremiah and got almost nothing. I've been trying to save and get enough money for an apartment, but then rents go up again. (Dolores, 19 - Jeremiah, 3½ years)

Even if the parent is working, the money often doesn't stretch nearly far enough:

Wayne made good money, but we still had money problems.

He was in control of the money and I had no say-so over it. He said he was doing the work so he would manage the money—as if taking care of the baby weren't work. I had to ask him if I wanted to write a check. (Janette, 18 - Myles, 7 months. Janette has filed for divorce.)

Finding money for a divorce sometimes seems impossible:

We were together only a year, and we've been separated for three years. Yet my divorce won't be final for another six months. Carl had been promising me for three years that he would file because I couldn't afford to. But he never did, and now I'm working, so I filed. It'll be a relief to have that done. (Brigette, 22 - Rudy, 3 years, and Joy, 4 years)

HEAVY EXPENSE OF MOVING OUT

Living with your own parents is often difficult when you have a child yourself. Wanting to move into a place of one's own is certainly an understandable goal. But if you have never lived on your own, if your parents have always paid the bills, you may not realize how expensive it is to keep an apartment.

I plan to move out in three months when Holly (friend with a baby) turns 18. I'm 16. Hopefully I can get $350 from welfare. An apartment will be $250 a month, and I'll split that with Holly. Then we can go half on the groceries, and Robin will be eating table food by then. We should be able to make it. (Melinda, 16 - Robin, 9 months)

First, it is doubtful that Melinda will be able to receive welfare if she moves out at age 16. If she can get money on her own, she and Holly may still have trouble renting an apartment. Apartment owners often choose not to rent to young single mothers and their children, especially if they must rely on welfare for their income.

I don't want to stay here because I don't get along very well with my parents. But to get an apartment costs $1000 to move in the door. I can't possibly do it on welfare.

Most places I call won't even accept children. I don't know what I'm going to do. Maybe I can find a roommate, but that's hard when you have a child. I wish I could have waited about six more years. Myles isn't a toy. (Janette)

I want to move into another house—more than anything for the space. Art and I are in the same room. There are six people in this small house. Besides, I want to be on my own, more independent. (Margie, 19 - Art, 3 years)

In some areas of the United States, apartments may rent for less than they do in California. However, in these areas AFDC payments are usually considerably lower.

Getting along on welfare takes extremely careful money management. Roseanna is determined to finish high school, so she copes with her welfare income:

I'm a pretty good money manager because I have to be. When I get my check, I pay my bills first, then I buy groceries, usually $20 a week. I buy meat first, then vegetables, then canned food. I usually use fresh vegetables because they're a lot cheaper. The only thing I buy that's junk is popsicles. (Roseanna, 15 - Felipe, 2 years)

Even if both husband and wife are working, they may have heavy financial problems:

We had credit, and we got deeper and deeper in debt. When we finally wrote it down in black and white, we had $1600 debts each month, but we brought in only $1100. So we wrote letters, trying to be rational. That didn't help. They picked up all our furniture, and we filed for bankruptcy a year ago.

It was hard on the kids when the furniture went. We had no

*refrigerator. We slept on the floor on a mattress and ate out of
an icebox. How do you explain that to kids?*

*After filing for bankruptcy, your credit is ruined for seven to
ten years. You have to have a co-signer or have a lot of collateral
in order to get credit.*

*We scrimp from week to week. We're just not money managers
at all. What we're trying now is Glen has the checkbook. He
keeps it so I can't write checks.*

*The worst thing you can do is to file for bankruptcy. I would
sell everything in my house before I'd do that again. I would go
to a finance counselor, but Glen won't go. He thinks we should
be able to manage it ourselves—but we're not.*

*It's just hard. The important thing is to manage your money. I
think we should be teaching money management in the schools.
(Mitzi, 22 - Vaughn, 2 years, and Selene, 5 years)*

Whatever your income, you might think about Mitzi's last comment. Sometimes a class in money management can help a person plan
how best to budget her income.

If you think you're heading for financial trouble, get help. Don't
coast along until you have the big money problems facing Mitzi, Glen,
and their children.

You may be able to find a non-profit group offering credit counseling in your community. Be careful of credit counselors who charge big
fees.

Look under "Debt Counseling" or a similar heading in your phone
directory. Try to find someone who, at little or no charge, will help
you work out a plan to budget your income. With professional help
plus lots of effort on your part, you may be able to pull out of seemingly hopeless money problems.

MORE ON THREE-GENERATION LIVING

Living with your parents when you have a child of your own has
been discussed in several preceding chapters. Of the sixty-one mothers
interviewed, forty-two were living either with their own parents or
their parents-in-law at the time of the interview. Fifty-six had lived
with parents for some time after the birth of their babies. Only five
had lived entirely separate from parents since becoming parents
themselves.

Nearly all of these young mothers saw good points in three-
generation living. They also described problems brought about by lack

of independence for themselves. They found it very difficult to play
the role of somebody's child at the same time they were working hard
at being somebody else's parent.

*I had the support of my parents when I needed them. When I
was sick, they were there. They helped out on expenses. It was
good because it helped us get a start financially. But it was also
as if the three of us didn't have our own life. "Where are you going? What time will you get home?"*

*You can take only so much of being married and, at the same
time, being treated like a child again. We lived with them for a
year. (Rosemarie, 19 - Helen, 3 years)*

*My parents have been good about everything. They don't put
much pressure on me. My mom is such a big help. If they weren't
like this, I probably wouldn't even be in college now. They want
me to get my education, too.*

*Sometimes it gets frustrating, but somehow it kind of evens
out. My dad will say you shouldn't do this or that. I'm not one
to keep my mouth shut, but we haven't gotten into any big
arguments yet. Mostly my dad is kidding so it doesn't bother him
too much.*

*I imagine sometimes it will be hard. I've read where single
parents living with their parents get very upset and just leave. I
really respect my mom and dad for what they've done for me.
(Jill, 18 - Todd, 16 months)*

Of course there are advantages in living with your family. Janis is learning to talk quicker because everybody is talking to her. She's real athletic and into sports already. She counts, knows most of her alphabet, her colors. She learns a lot because everybody teaches her.

But she's spoiled. My mom—if I scold Janis, she will baby her. She'll run to Mom.

I have four sisters and brothers living here. Three step-sisters come over every weekend. Janis tries to play with everybody, and then she gets too rough with kids her own age. (Darla, 17 - Janis, 2 years)

What I can't stand is when we walk in and we already have eaten, and they tell me to set Derek down and feed him. I say he has eaten, and she says, "What?" I say "Hot dogs," and she says that's not good for him.

Or she tells me it's too hot to have him in the water. They make me feel like I'm doing everything wrong. I don't know everything, but they don't know everything either. If I say "Black," they say "White."

But this is their house, I'm still underage, and we all have to adjust. I get real up-tight when they're on my case, but not at Derek. (Laurette, 17 - Derek, 18 months)

My mom doesn't bug me, but she's making me feel like I don't know what I'm doing, like I'm a little kid or something. For example, Shelly never got used to the crib.

She's in a room with my cousin, and they keep coming in and out, turning on the light, and waking her. So I pick her up and take her in where I sleep, but my mom says I'll have problems later on. I tell her I can't help it, that I have to get some sleep so I can go to school. She'll sleep there for about two hours, but not the whole night.

If Shelly had the room by herself, I would let her alone. (Dixie, 18 - Shelly, 17 months)

It's all right sometimes, but other times it can be bad. I'll want to go out and want them to keep the baby. My sister will say "Yes," but when I go out the door, she will say "No." Then my mom says she never got to go anyplace when she had me.

The other day she got mad and said I couldn't go out that night. I just stayed home because arguing with all seven of us living here is bad. (Sheryl Ann, 17 - Lynn, 7 months)

A surprising number of young parents talked about their concern because Grandma thinks the baby should have candy and other foods his mother doesn't think are good for him.

Janis doesn't like to eat a whole lot, or even at all sometimes. So my mom will resort to sweet cereal so she'll eat. But I know if you wait until she's hungry she'll eat what we have. They give her ice cream and candy, and she's going to get cavities too soon. Mother says, "She needs something in her stomach," but all it is is sugar. (Darla)

Shelly doesn't snack a lot except when she sees somebody eating something. She has very little candy. First of all, she makes a mess, and besides, I don't want her to get cavities. I don't give her soft drinks either, just orange juice or apple juice.
Everybody tells me, "You're so mean, you don't give her any candy. When she gets older, she's going to see all that candy and eat it all."
Even my mother tells me I'm so mean. She makes herself sound like she knows more than I do. She used to always give candy to Shelly behind my back. One time they were eating chocolates, and I told Shelly she couldn't have any. Then she walked by me, and she had chocolate all over her mouth.
It makes me feel bad. I feel like telling them to mind their own business, but I can't do that. Mom's beginning to do more of that, and it's getting to me. It's building up, and I know I'll wind up telling her something I shouldn't. (Dixie)

It's better if you don't fight with your parents because you'll end up needing their support. If you have to go some place, you'll have to have somebody you can trust with the baby. I figure, just don't fight with them, stay on their good side. I needed their help a lot. (Charmaine, 17 - Kevin, 34 months)

IS MARRIAGE A SOLUTION?

When a teenager discovers she is pregnant, the "solution," according to some people, is to get married. In the past, this was often the choice. "Shotgun" (forced) weddings occurred frequently.
Today, single parenting is not as unthinkable as it used to be.

Some young mothers have no choice. Boy friends have been known to leave town when they learn of girl friends' pregnancies.

Other young couples choose not to get married. Perhaps they realize that's not what they really want. Or maybe they plan to be married later when each has matured a bit more.

Some teenage couples, of course, marry before conception occurs. Others decide to marry when pregnancy is diagnosed. Some young marriages are the beginning of a satisfying long-term family relationship. Some of the young mothers quoted in this book are happily married.

But about 60 percent of teenage marriages end in divorce within five years. Couples who marry while they are in their teens are more likely to break up than are couples who marry when they are older.

Rosemarie feels she was rushed into marriage by her parents:

I got married because I was pregnant. My parents forced us into it. It was the wrong reason, but my mom seemed to think it was the solution. We told them on Monday night that I was pregnant. By Saturday, we were in Las Vegas getting married.

We were both back in school on Monday morning. We were living with my parents—stayed with them that whole first year. That was a hard way to start a marriage. They were very supportive—actually helped us financially for awhile. But they treated us like the high school kids we were. They wanted to know where we were going if we went out, what time we'd be back, the whole thing.

We graduated from high school a year after Helen was born. We both found jobs, and my mother-in-law took care of Helen. We rented a little apartment not far from my folks' house. But moving out didn't solve our problems. We were fighting more and more.

Then one day Dick hit me, and that did it. My father used to knock us around when I was little, and I vowed then that when I grew up, nobody was going to hit me. I had warned Dick I'd leave if he ever hit me. So I did.

I knew I could support myself and Helen, so I wasn't afraid to leave. I started the divorce papers. I saw it all the way through, and I don't really have any regrets.

I have custody, and when Dick wants to take Helen for the day, he takes her. At first he wanted custody and was going to fight for it, but he gave up about a week before we went to court.

He doesn't see her that often. His theory is if he doesn't have her, he doesn't want to see her much. He takes her out once a month, and he wants me to go with them, but I don't like to because we fight. If I don't go, he doesn't want to take Helen.

To be perfectly honest, right after my divorce, I didn't know how we would survive. But I didn't have a choice. I couldn't live with him. Now I'm trying to put my life back together, and I'm adjusting pretty well.

Helen and I are living with my sister and her husband and their baby. We couldn't afford a decent apartment by ourselves, so I split living expenses with them. I couldn't handle living with my parents now because they would try to take over. Being with my sister is a little different because we're peers.

I've been out of high school two years now, and this fall I'm going back to school to take accounting. I've decided that no matter how long it takes me, I'll get my degree. (Rosemarie)

REBECCA'S STORY

Rebecca, too, rushed into marriage, then found two years later that she had made a mistake. She and Jack have separated, and she has filed for divorce.

We fell right into the old pattern, and what they say is true. Getting married because of pregnancy gives you a strike against you. You don't have time to adjust to each other. You should listen to what other people say because sometimes they know.

I thought getting married was the right thing to do because we were talking about it anyway. We just did it earlier because I was pregnant. But I wasn't prepared at 17 to make decisions for the rest of my life.

It worked out fine for Jack. He was 23, so he was out looking for a wife. He was ready to settle down to being the little family man not doing anything. I thought I was, but I wasn't. Not that I didn't enjoy it, but it just wasn't working out. I got the father treatment—as if I were the child.

I thought I was happy being the mother, staying home with the apron on, but I found out I wasn't. I realized I had missed something, that I had gone from 17 to 30, skipped an important stage in my life. I think it's important that even though my husband thought he gave me independence, it's not the same as doing it myself. I think it's an important stage I need to go through.

Jack thinks there has to be blame, that this is just a cop-out.

*He thinks I should be able to tell him exactly what he did wrong.
He says, "Haven't I always given you anything you ever
wanted?" But I say there is more to life than buying me a new
dress when I want it.*

*He was working hard, and we were just paying bills and not
taking time for our relationship. He wants to change now, but I
don't want to do that. I realize what I did a lot was making his
needs my needs. I didn't pay attention to my own needs.*

*I'll be damned if he's going to tell me what I can do and what
I can't do. I have a whole life ahead of me.*

*Going to that marriage counselor helped a lot. He talked to me
more than he did to Jack because Jack doesn't think he has any
problems. He's satisfied to go to work, come home and eat, have
sex once in awhile, and sleep.*

*I don't know what I'm looking for in life, but I'm looking for
more than that. He's very satisfied, can't understand why I have
these problems.*

*The marriage counselor would ask me questions, and I would
say, "I don't know." He would say, "Why don't you know?"
He made me realize I did have thoughts and feelings about
things, that I was important.*

*It isn't that I don't care about Jack, but we can't be close
again. I have to worry about my own problems. I have money
problems and he doesn't, but I would rather be poor and happy.*

*I'm relieved now that we've separated because I find out there
aren't going to be as many problems as I thought there would be.
It's not easy, and it doesn't make it any easier when you're only
20. But I have no doubt that I will survive.*

*I saw a change in Troy's behavior after we split and I started
feeling better about myself. I think it's wrong to stay together for
the sake of the kids. They'll survive. I think it's much more important for me to be happy and single with Troy rather than to
be married and unhappy. You have to feel good about yourself
before you can feel good about anyone else anyway. (Rebecca,
20 - Troy, 2½ years)*

MARRIAGE CAN WORK

Tamera hadn't planned to marry so soon. But she loves her children
and her husband, and she's satisfied with her life now. She knows that
if she starts preparing herself soon, she can still have the career she
wanted. It will be a little delayed, but it will happen.

Early marriage—it's hard. Sometimes I wish I had waited. There are a lot of things I missed out on. But I wouldn't give my kids up for anything because right now they are my whole life.

I figure that since I didn't get to do a lot of things when I was a teenager, I'll be quite young when they're in their teens. Then I can be independent and do things I want to do but can't now.

This September Curt and I are going to start taking night classes at college. I may take accounting. I won't rush right into it, but over a little while I'll start getting my education. Then I can get a good-paying job when the kids are older. Then when they are teenagers, I can go out and have my career, and it won't interfere with them. Curt thinks that is super-fantastic. (Tamera, 21 - Leon, 20 months, and DeeDee, 4½ years)

If you are married already, you're probably trying hard to make it work. Good luck and best wishes!

If you aren't married, consider this suggestion: If you have any doubts at all, if anyone can talk you out of getting married, then don't do it. But if you both are absolutely certain marriage to each other is right for both of you, get married. Then work hard together to make your marriage a happy and satisfying long-term relationship.

SPEAKING OF FATHERS

Some couples stay together throughout pregnancy, but don't get married. Many break up after the baby is born.

Kimberly and Tom followed this pattern. So did Yumiko and Marc. Kimberly and Yumiko each wanted her baby's father to be deeply involved in parenting. Each was disappointed.

We'd been going together about four years. Oh, we'd argue and break up, but we always got back together. I moved in with Tom when I was about four months pregnant. I went back to my

mother once, but I was back with Tom in two days. He was charming when he wasn't mad.

We took a prepared childbirth class together, and he coached me during labor and delivery. But Karl cried a lot when we got home and Tom was no help at all. Karl was awake crying most of the night, and Tom never spent more than 15 minutes trying to help me.

At first I thought he was having a hard time adjusting to the responsibility of being a father. Then I realized he really wasn't taking any responsibility. We had an argument once, and I suddenly wondered, "Why is he so upset? He doesn't help take care of the baby anyway."

The only time he would hold Karl was when he was happy—which wasn't very often those first weeks. He didn't buy him food. My mom gave us a crib and a little swing, and I got the rest of his stuff at my shower.

Tom said he couldn't help with him because I was breast-feeding—but Karl had colic and breastfeeding didn't help. I even bought some formula so Tom could feed him, but he still wouldn't.

Finally he started staying out late with his friends, and I couldn't take it any longer. We had a huge argument one night, and I took Karl and moved back with my mother.

I just want to start my life over and not worry about Tom. At first I didn't think I'd want to go out with anyone, but I'm getting over that. I'm starting where I was before.

My friends accept the fact that I have a baby. When I meet a guy, I tell him right away. If it makes a difference to him, he's not worth knowing anyhow.

It's taken me four years to do this—and I think Karl finally made the difference. Karl being here meant I wasn't just thinking of myself. I know he senses emotions, that how I'm feeling affects him. When I was unhappy, he was, too.

I'm just glad I didn't marry Tom. My family wanted me to. That would have been a terrible mistake. (Kimberly, 17 - Karl, 2 months)

Yumiko and Marc attended different high schools. Marc was working, but he saw Yumiko nearly every day during her pregnancy. For another year they remained close. He spent nearly every evening with Yumiko and Marty. Sometimes Yumiko's mother would baby-sit Marty so they could go out.

As the months went by, Yumiko, 15, realized she was growing up
faster than Marc. They started fighting and finally split. Yumiko is seeing another man now. She described Marc's relationship with Marty:

> *Marc doesn't take much responsibility for Marty. I used to*
> *push him when we were together. I'd say, "You're a father now.*
> *You should do this."*
>
> *Now he doesn't come to see him very often. Several times he*
> *has called and said he was coming over to take Marty somewhere,*
> *and then he didn't show up. That was disappointing for Marty. I*
> *don't feel there is any big reason for Marty to go over there. I*
> *don't think it hurts him, but he doesn't need it.*
>
> *I think Marc feels he doesn't have to worry about seeing Marty*
> *because he'll always have some legal rights. But I don't like the*
> *idea of him showing up when Marty is five and saying, "Hello,*
> *I'm your daddy." I think it's unfair to a kid for daddy to show*
> *up just whenever he feels like it.*
>
> *Sometimes I feel like saying, "Go do your own thing, Marc.*
> *Don't even come over here." I can't do that, but I would think*
> *he could stop by here at least once a week. Marty was used to*
> *seeing him every day. He calls Marc "Daddy," but he doesn't*
> *really know what that means. (Yumiko, 16 - Marty, 21 months)*

REPEAT PREGNANCIES OCCUR

A lot of teenagers who have had one child have another within one
or two years. A study reported by the United States Department of
Health, Education, and Welfare (October, 1979) states that 44 percent
of teenage mothers are pregnant again within a year after the first
birth, and 70 percent pregnant within the second year.

Often this second pregnancy is not planned. It may, in fact, create
real hardship for the young mother:

> *I wish I had had them at least a year further apart. It's hard*
> *because Crystal still needs a lot of attention, and Sylvia needs so*
> *much, too, with feeding, changing, bathing, and everything else.*
> *They need so much, and their father takes a lot of time, too. It's*
> *hard trying to divide myself three ways.*
>
> *I used to be able to do what I wanted, but no more. I know*
> *I've missed a lot—I feel like I went from a child to being a*
> *mother—and that's actually what I did. (Carrie, 18 - Sylvia, 14*
> *months, and Crystal, 31 months)*

*I didn't want Kerry—it was a total accident. I was on the pill,
but I ran out and was going to wait until after my period. This
pregnancy upset me terribly. Amy was the only one I wanted. I
don't like having two kids.*

*I thought about abortion, but I knew deep down I wouldn't do
it. Her father's mom said, "But that's my first grandchild," and
my mom said, "You won't be welcome in this family if you do
that." That's my whole family. (Leslie)*

Many of the young mothers commented that one child is enough at
this point in their lives.

*I could have another one, but I would like Felipe to be in
school first. I want to move and have enough money to think
about another one. Nowadays, it's so expensive. A pair of shoes
for a little kid costs a fortune—it's terrible! (Roseanna)*

*Girls often think they're completely in love right away, and
their boy friends think they should stay home. It's like playing
the part, then realizing later that's not what they want. A lot of
girls I know don't go on birth control—at least they end up getting pregnant again. I think they just don't worry about it.*

*They may use birth control for awhile, then they go off it.
They don't take it seriously. They don't seem to think it will happen again. Being 17 and having two kids a year apart seems in-
sane to me. There are so many things you still have to learn to
know what you want. To end up having to teach two kids is too
much.*

*If you want to be an independent person, you can't depend on
the man to use birth control. Independence is important to me—it
always has been. If you use birth control yourself, you know for
sure. (Darla)*

*Once you're pregnant, it's up to you if you have an abortion or
keep it. I don't put anybody down for an abortion, because if
you know you won't be happy with that child, it will be even
more tragic.*

*But after she has her baby, every girl should find a birth con-
trol method. I think if I get pregnant again, it will be because I
want to. If you're in a relationship with one person, both of you
should take the responsibility.*

With one child, I can go ahead and do what I want. With two

or three children and no husband, you're really limited. I
wouldn't want another child until I'm married. (Shirley,
20 - Virginia, 4 years)

WHAT ARE YOUR OPTIONS?

If you aren't pregnant now, you have three options as far as
pregnancy is concerned.

One is obvious. If you don't have sex, you won't get pregnant. The
majority of high school students still choose this method. When you
see statistics stating that 35 percent of all girls under 18 have had sex-
ual intercourse, that means that 65 percent have not.

Your second option is to use birth control if you are having sex. If
you don't want a baby, this is essential.

Lots of teenagers think, "It won't happen to me. I won't get pregnant." But one couple in 25 will become pregnant at the time of *first*
intercourse. Of the couples having intercourse twelve times, *one-half*
will become pregnant.

Would you ride in a car if you knew that one-half of those who
take twelve rides will have a serious accident? If you aren't ready to
have a baby, or if you already have one and aren't ready for another,
an unplanned pregnancy is certainly a "serious accident."

Your third option is to get pregnant. If you're having sex and you
don't use birth control, this is the option you apparently have chosen.

If you are pregnant now, you still have two options other than raising the child yourself. You can get an abortion, or you can release
your child for adoption.

Releasing her child for adoption used to be the accepted "solution"
for a pregnant teenager who was not married. Today, however, only
eight percent of unmarried pregnant adolescents choose adoption for
their child. Yet this could be the most loving, caring decision a birth
mother could make.

For more information on adoption and for personal accounts of
young mothers who chose this option recently, see *Pregnant Too
Soon: Adoption Is an Option* by Lindsay.

Chapter Fourteen

Sometimes Parents Feel Trapped

It would not be facing reality to ignore the fact that some (many?) teenage parents feel they have missed an important part of their growing-up years. They sometimes feel trapped into taking the responsibilities of parenthood before they are ready.

It's hard being a mother. I can't do a lot of things I want to do because I have to take care of Mona. To me, it's hard raising kids. I thought it would be easy. Sometimes it gets on my nerves and I feel like hitting her. So I give her a bottle instead and tell her to shut up. I can't stand it when she cries and cries.

Layne and I got married before Mona was born, and we've been by ourselves ever since. It's hard. Too many bills, and I have to get a job because Layne doesn't make that much. (Ellie, 17 - Mona, 11 months)

NO MORE KIDS

I would never have any more kids.

Seventeen is too young. I have my own life I have to take care of, and I don't know which way to go.

I have to get back on welfare because we're separated, and he isn't paying child support. I plan to go to cosmetology school.

Even my parents say they're going to take Myles away from me because I like to go out. But that's natural, I'm young. But they

263

think I should stay home all the time. When I go places, my mom
takes care of him or I take him with me.

  It's hard to take him shopping. Sometimes I just leave my
basket in the store and walk out with him.

  It's hard to get friends with a baby, and it's hard to get a boy
friend. Sometimes I feel like sitting down and crying. I meet a
guy, tell him I have a kid, and he says goodbye. (Janette,
18 - Myles, 7 months)

  I gave up all my childhood to marry Charles and have a baby.

  Being grown-up is a lot of responsibility. Like now, it seems all
I have is responsibility. I don't have any fun. My soap opera and
smoking are the only entertainment I have. I used to drink, but I
completely gave that up.

  If I had known what I know now, I probably would have had
an abortion with Hilda.

  If I could advise anybody, I would tell them to wait until they
have done what they wanted to do. I feel like I'm sacrificing for
the kids. It seems like I don't ever have the joy of it, I just have
the cleaning. Charles has the joy because he comes home from
work and plays with them, but I
don't have any real joy.

  Sometimes I go in the
bathroom and shut the door.
When Charles comes home, he
asks what I'm doing shut up in a
little box, and I tell him that's
my privacy. I would rather have
them older. (Colleen, 18 - Ruby,
7 months, and Hilda, 21 months)

Maria is a single mother who is very
unhappy with her situation.

  It makes it hard being the
father and mother at the same
time. It would help to have a
father around, but there is
nothing I can do about it. When
Pedro grows up, I don't know
what I'll tell him. His father
never knew I was pregnant. I put

"unknown" on the birth certificate.
My big brother is around, and he holds him. I think that will help.
If I'm going shopping, I have to take the stroller. Yesterday we were walking around in the Mall and I saw this guy. He looked at me and seemed to be thinking, "She has a baby!" He was somebody who would have spoken to me at school. He just looked the other way. I looked at the baby and thought, "Why did I have you?"
I look in the mirror and I don't like what I see.
My mom wanted me to get out of the house and go roller-skating with my sisters, so I went. But I felt like an old lady. I used to go all the time.
I wish I could do things like I used to, but it's too late now. I want to be on my own, but I can't until I turn 18. I wish I could have my own place with my baby, but I can't. (Maria, 17 - Pedro, 2 months)

At this time, Maria lives with her mother, brothers, and sisters.
Sometimes being with family is the best possible situation. Feeling trapped is hard to live with, but the support which a family can give often makes it possible to weather the ups and downs of being a teen parent.

I think it would be awfully hard for somebody to handle all I have that didn't have support, mental support, from family and friends. If they were going to just walk away and do it on their own, I would probably say, "You can't do it."
In that case, I think adoption would be a better option. Even with a lot of financial support, it's hard.
Hold your head up high. If somebody doesn't like it, too bad. You can't let what people say and think get you down because then you would be down all the time. You really have to grow and be a strong person.
It was hard for me to go back to my school. It was a private school, and hard for me to get back in anyhow. I knew there were kids that were saying things about me. I was the first girl to get pregnant, leave, and then go back. Others had just gotten pregnant and dropped out.
I don't regret the situation I'm in. I like being a young mother. In fact, I always wanted to be a young mother—but not this young! (Margie, 19 - Art, 3 years)

CHILDREN MAY SUFFER

Child abuse may be physical, mental, or emotional. It can happen in any family, rich as well as poor, and to children whose parents are older as well as those with teenage parents. Parents who were themselves abused as children are more apt to mistreat their children than are parents who didn't go through such trauma.

But all of us get up-tight with our children. All of us at some point have trouble controlling feelings which could lead to abuse.

Sometimes if you're just staying at home, you've had it, and you shouldn't feel bad. You feel like you're going crazy and no one else is like this. When I feel like that, I try—it doesn't always work—to sit down and read for awhile. I always try to relax when the baby is asleep, at least an hour when I do nothing except watch TV or read.

Sometimes if things are building up and I get in a fight with Norm, I just have to pull myself together and calm myself down. It isn't easy. You have to remember you aren't really bad for sometimes not liking your kids. (Celia, 21 - Lance, 18 months, and Laurel, 4 years.)

Joanne's son was born when she was 16. She lived with her mother, but her mother was gone most of the time. One night when Eddie was about two months old, he cried steadily from 11 P.M. to 1 A.M. Joanne tried to feed him, tried to comfort him. Nothing seemed to work. Finally he went to sleep, and she got a few hours rest before school started. That morning she wrote a note to her teacher describing her feelings:

Please help me. I felt like hitting Eddie last night. I'm scared. What can I do?

At her teacher's urging, Joanne shared her feelings with the Infant Center director. She also made an appointment with a social worker from Children's Home Society.

As she talked with Pat, the social worker, Joanne realized she needed some time to consider her feelings, to think through her situation. She agreed to put Eddie in foster care for a short time. Two weeks later she called Pat. "I'm ready to bring Eddie home," she said.

Life didn't suddenly become easy for Joanne. But with continuing support from the Infant Center staff and occasional talks with Pat, she was able to care for Eddie and continue school. She graduated when he was fourteen months old.

Three years later when Joanne, now married and living in another state, heard that her teacher was working on a book for teenage parents, she wrote:

> *I think you should include something about child abuse and neglect. People feel as though it will never happen to them. But you and I know that no matter how good a parent you are, it can still happen. But it can be dealt with if you look for help and can confide in someone as I did.*
>
> *I think that subject is too often avoided, as if it doesn't happen. But people have to realize it does exist. They need to know where they can turn for help. (Joanne, 20 - Eddie, 4 years)*

A teenager's goals and her value system aren't going to change overnight to an adult value system just because she has become a mother. If she is home all day and doesn't have any time to be a teenager, frustration may build up. She needs to do something about it before she risks injuring her child.

> *Girls my age are more likely to abuse because when you're alone and you have to fend for yourself, it's harder. Before Tony was two, I hit him too hard a couple of times. But I'm coping all right now. (Becky, 18 - Antonio, 26 months)*

> *Yes, I get up-tight. When I get really frustrated, I take our dogs and go to the park, and my mom takes care of Todd. That helps a lot, just walking.*
>
> *I think child abuse often happens because the mother is frustrated with her life. (Jill, 18 - Todd, 16 months)*

What do you do if you find yourself constantly upset with your toddler? A young mother, home all day alone with her child in a small apartment, often finds it difficult to cope with a normal toddler. If there are two or more small children, it can get pretty miserable for everyone. Colleen, 18, had too much to do caring for Ruby, seven months old, and Hilda, 21 months. Too typical of her own and her children's lives was the following incident:

> *Hilda was holding a paper cup with a lid. She had a drinking straw she was trying to put through the tiny hole in the lid. It*

wouldn't go in. She kept poking the straw at the top of the cup, getting more and more upset. Soon she was crying in frustration.

Hilda's mother's reaction was, "Shut your mouth right now, shut up. All right, go on in the bedroom and cry, right now." She spanked Hilda, then took her to the bedroom as she screamed, "Wait right there until you calm down." She slapped her, then yelled, "I mean it, Hilda, sit there until you calm down." Then she slapped her again.

Hilda came out of the bedroom and tried again to put the straw in the cup lid. She started sobbing again because it wouldn't work. Mother screamed, "Knock it off, Hilda, or you go back in the bedroom."

This anecdote may seem almost unreal. If Mother had paused just long enough to show Hilda how to stick the straw in that hole, this crisis might never have occurred.

But put yourself in that young mother's place. She has another smaller child. She doesn't like her husband much. Money never lasts until payday. She hates her apartment. Yet she knows no way out.

Some of my friends have told me there have been times when they were so mad at the child they think they could really hurt them. They have to walk away.

People are afraid to talk to somebody about it because they think they are strange because they feel like hitting their kids. They should know there are places they can go that are not going to steal their children from them.

It's kind of like husbands that hit their wives—if you do it once, you probably will do it again. (Yumiko, 16 - Marty, 21 months)

WHO NEEDS HELP?

How does a parent decide if s/he needs help? We know that all of us feel very angry at our children occasionally. It's how we react to those feelings that is important.

Jim Mead, Director, *For Kids Sake, Inc.*, a parent-support group in Brea, California, offers a "National Parenting Test." He asks parents to answer the following questions:

1. Do you sometimes strike your child without thinking?

2. Do you feel better after you spank your child?

3. Do you sometimes spank your child with a belt or switch?

4. Are you the only person who takes care of your child?

5. Do you feel alone and frustrated by your child?

6. Do you sometimes leave bruises or marks on your child when he's bad?

7. Does potty training upset you?

8. Does your husband or wife sometimes hurt the children and you're afraid to say anything?

9. Do you sometimes feel sexually attracted to your child?

10. Do you feel relieved when you yell at your child?

11. Does your child's crying and screaming make you mad?

12. When your child is bad, does it remind you of your childhood?

13. Is your child different from other children?

14. Do you punish your child for toilet accidents?

15. Do you sometimes leave your child alone when you know you shouldn't?

16. If you could give your child away without any questions asked, would you?

17. When you were a child, were you ever abused physically or mentally?

Mead asks parents to take this test, then add up the number of "Yes" answers they have. He thinks most parents will answer "Yes" to at least one question. These parents are probably "normal" loving parents who lose their cool occasionally.

Mead thinks those who answer "Yes" to four or five questions may have a high level of frustration or hostility. He urges these parents to get professional help.

If six or more questions are answered "Yes," Mead recommends professional counseling for the parents. He also strongly suggests the children be given a vacation with Grandma or another loving relative or friend while their parents receive counseling. These aren't necessarily bad parents, but their frustration level has gotten so bad that it has gone beyond their coping skills. They need help.

Help is available almost anywhere in the United States for parents who are abusing their children or think they might be close to doing so. One of the best resources is *Parents Anonymous*. It was started more than ten years ago by a mother who was involved in child abuse. With some help from a professional counselor, she and other parents who were abusing their children started meeting together to talk and offer support to each other.

More than 800 chapters of Parents Anonymous are now in operation in the United States and Canada. You can contact any of these groups at any time of day or night. Either find their listing in your local telephone directory or call their toll-free number: (800) 421-0353; California: (800) 352-0386.

Members of Parents Anonymous meet in small groups with a professional sponsor. They share the confusion and anger with which they are struggling. They support and encourage each other in finding positive ways to cope with the job of childrearing.

Apparently PA works. Independent evaluators have found that physical abuse usually stops within the first month of a parent's involvement in the organization.

Your county or state Mental Health Association can usually refer you to a number of local counseling programs. Get their phone number from the information operator or your phone book.

Your local college or university may be able to direct you toward help. Call their Psychology Department and ask about local counseling programs.

After sharing the above suggestions, Mead added, "If you have tried all of the above ideas and aren't satisfied, call *For Kids Sake,* (714) 990-KIDS, 24 hours a day. We will try to assist you in finding help in your area."

BECKY ATTEMPTED SUICIDE

Some teenage mothers get so desperate they consider suicide. In fact, for each suicide attempt made by a non-parent teenager, seven adolescent mothers try to end their lives.

At one point, Becky decided she could cope no longer. She took an overdose of pills, but the Paramedics were called in time to save her life. She shared her story:

I'm back with my mother now. It's been a rough year, the worst I've ever had. I swore I wouldn't move back, but I had no place else to go.

Antonio was 1½ when we moved in with Betty and her daughter. I didn't know her, but she had a house with two bedrooms, and she needed someone to share the expenses.

It didn't work out for me right from the beginning. My welfare check didn't come that first month, and I had no money. A friend lent me enough for rent and a little food for Tony and me. I got a job working nights at a convalescent hospital. Betty stayed with Tony. I was taking adult school classes during the day.

I enrolled in college in February. To be a doctor is my dream, and I was finally starting. But things were getting worse and worse between Betty and me. Her daughter was three, but she cried all the time. I couldn't stand the constant screaming. The house was a mess. The only time it got cleaned was when I

did it. We just didn't get along, so I left.

Tony and I moved in with some friends for a few days. Then we "visited" someone else for awhile. Floating from place to place was grim.

Everything seemed bad. I was so upset that finally one night I took 30 Darvons. I was staying at another friend's house, a room in the garage where me and Tony slept.

My friend's sister-in-law found me in convulsions, and she called the Paramedics. They rushed me to the hospital, and I was in intensive care for two days. I'm still getting ambulance bills.

They released me to my mother. I'm very glad they found me. Things could have been worse. I just panicked.

I should have gotten counseling. Now I have a list of counselors and hot lines that I can call if I ever feel that desperate again. I carry it with me in case I ever need it.

Me and my mother have fought, and we both are stubborn. I thought for sure she wouldn't let me come back here. But I've been here two months. There have been a couple of rough times, but everything is OK. She's helping me get an apartment now.

I had to add two years to my age—say I was 20—before they would even show me an apartment. You can't tell them you're on welfare either because people won't rent to you if you're on welfare. They're worried about whether they'll get their rent on time. What if your check is late?

My mom is paying for the apartment, paying the first and last month's rent, paying for the stove and refrigerator. If someone only has welfare, they can't make it. I didn't get a check on the 15th—it was lost in the mail. What would I have done if I hadn't been living here?

Living here was really a problem when Tony was small. "Go pick up that baby right now. I don't want to hear him cry," my mom would say. It was pretty bad, which is why I moved out the first time.

But I would advise anyone, "If you argue with your relatives, make up. You've got to swallow your pride." All those months, my mom would have helped me. I just wouldn't ask. I was too proud.

But I learned one thing. Before you move out, you have got to have money. That's why I'm not rushing it this time. I'm taking it slow. People think when you move out, you can live off welfare the rest of your life. But you can't do that. If I hadn't come back here for a couple of months, I couldn't do it. Now I

have my clothes ready and things I need for my apartment.
If I had it to do all over again, though, I would still have had
Tony, no matter what. He's a neat little boy. We'll make it.
(Becky)

HELP FROM COMMUNITY RESOURCES

If you're having more problems than you can handle by yourself, the first step is to accept the fact that you need help. Some people find it very hard to admit that they aren't making it on their own.

You're probably already getting informal help. Families often are a good source of support. So are friends. In fact, other young parents can offer tremendous support simply because they're facing some of the same problems that are bothering you.

You may need help beyond what your family and friends can give. Perhaps they can suggest community resources for you to contact. Inquire about resources from other people with whom you interact—the director of a child-care center, your minister, doctor, or teacher.

Also check your telephone book. As Jim Mead suggested, your county or state Mental Health Association and the Psychology Department at your local college may recommend counseling services.

If you are receiving AFDC (welfare), ask to see a social worker when you need special help. Social workers often have far too heavy caseloads, but some are able to provide extra help to their clients.

If you have a local community center, the social worker there may be able to tell you where to go for help with your problems. Your hospital social service department may be a good resource.

More than 300 agencies in the United States are connected with the Family Service Association of America. These agencies offer individual and family counseling at low cost, as well as a variety of other family services. For the agency in your area, check your telephone directory under the following listings: Family Service Association, Council for Community Services, County Department of Health, Counseling Clinic, Mental Health Clinic, or United Fund.

Generally you can get a list of hot lines from your telephone operator. Dial "O," then say, "I have this type of problem. Can you help me?"

You may find, as you call hot lines and other community services, that phone numbers you have been given are not helping you. Too often the number has been changed, your call is answered by a recording, or the person responding tells you that agency can't help you.

When this happens, don't give up. If a person answers your call but can't help, ask for referrals. Tell him/her you need help, and you don't know where to call next. Explain how much you would appreciate any ideas s/he may give you.

If you're pregnant unexpectedly, your community probably has several agencies specifically organized to help you and others in your situation. Call the Planned Parenthood Association, Florence Crittenton Services, Catholic Charities, or family or children's services. Or talk to your guidance counselor, your doctor, or your pastor.

If you are a single parent, find out if there is a support group for single parents in your community. Check with the above resources for information about such groups. In some areas, Children's Home Society sponsors single-parent support groups.

Marriage and family counselors are usually listed in the telephone yellow pages. Your community may have a cost-free counseling agency, or the cost may be based on your income. If you have very little income, you may not be charged a fee.

Independence and self-sufficiency are wonderful things—if they work. All of us need extra help at some time in our lives. If this is your time of special need, do whatever is necessary to get that help. Both you and your child will be glad you did.

Chapter Fifteen
Your Future— Your Child's Future

A mother who has her first child before she is 18 is apt to be poor during much of her life. Many young mothers find they must rely on welfare or minimum wages for survival. In fact, in about half the families receiving AFDC (Aid to Families with Dependent Children), the mother had her first baby when she was a teenager.

However, it doesn't seem to be the early parenting that causes the poverty. *It's the lack of a good education and job skills.* That lack, of course, often goes hand in hand with early motherhood.

Most young mothers of 15, or even 17, find it difficult to continue their education. An obvious reason is the lack of good child care in many areas. Even if a grandmother is available for baby sitting during the day, a teenage mother will find high school life different and usually harder than it is for her non-parent friends. Often it's too difficult. A large majority of the women in this country who deliver a child before age 18 never finish their high school education.

CONTINUING SCHOOL IS CRUCIAL

Statistics show, however, that *if* a young mother completes her education and doesn't have additional children right away, she may do as well as her friends who delay childbearing until later. But if she becomes pregnant at an early age, gets married, drops out of school, and has more children rather quickly, she's likely to have money problems throughout her life. The point is that these are factors you may be able to control. You start with your own situation. If you are a young mother and you are keeping your child, that's where you start with your life planning.

If you aren't already married, you may decide to postpone your wedding. You may make sure you don't get pregnant again before you think you're ready for another baby. And you can do everything possible to continue your education.

I want to graduate, get a job, and move into a better district. The kids around here don't respect their parents, and I don't want Felipe to grow up here. There are too many troubles, little kids writing on the walls, breaking holes in the fences. I don't want Felipe doing these things. There are too many fights, too many people shooting each other here.

I want to get a job, but I know if I started working now, I wouldn't go back to school. I think I can get a better job if I graduate. (Roseanna, 15 - Felipe, 2 years)

I want to finish school for sure. It will be hard, but I've got to finish. I want some kind of secretarial job, but I'll stay home with the baby for awhile. At first I want a part-time job. Then when Racquelle starts school, I'll work full-time. (Cheryl, 15 - Racquelle, 2 months)

I stayed in school. You got to go to school so you can get the kind of job you want. I'm not on welfare—I never was. But when paycheck time comes around, I'm out of money. But I'm getting there. It's being independent that counts.

I want to be an administrative secretary, so I'll be going to junior college for the next two years. (Ginger, 18 - Sean, 17 months)

It's harder being a single parent although Alice's father has been helping me. But he's too serious—he says within a year we should have this and that, and we'll get married. But I'm not going to marry nobody.

This is what I want to do. I'm going to finish high school in two years, I hope. Then I want to go to nursing school. I don't want to be on welfare all my life. I feel I want to make my own money.

My real reason I'm trying so hard is because my mother's family downed me for having the baby, saying I'm nothing but a tramp. Nobody on that side thinks I'll finish school. They think I'll have two or three more kids before I'm out of school. I want to do it for myself—but also to prove something to them. I want to be somebody.
(Melanie, 15 - Alice, 13 months)

MARRIAGE MAY LIMIT SCHOOLING

High school mothers who get married are far more likely to drop out of school than are their single friends. Of those who are neither wives nor mothers, less than 10 percent drop out before finishing high school. A higher percentage of unmarried teenagers who have a baby never graduate from high school. And even more of those who marry—a whopping 80 percent—quit school before they graduate.

Sometimes a husband insists he doesn't want his wife to continue her education:

My husband doesn't want me to go back to school, but I want to. I keep telling him we need me to work because of inflation and everything. If he insists, I don't know what I'll do. I'll try to convince him. He only went through sixth grade, but his father taught him to drive tractors, and he's a good mechanic. (Deanna, 15 - Paula, 3 weeks)

Even if she's married, the girl should get a job and learn to be independent—especially the way so many are getting divorced today. If she never knew anything, dropped out of school because she got pregnant, and got married, the only thing she's learning is cleaning and cooking. Beyond that, she doesn't know much if she doesn't ever get a job.

A lot of kids think they have to marry because they're pregnant, but that's a bunch of nonsense.

I didn't feel good about myself at first when I knew I was pregnant. Later, I thought of the way I was, and I decided I didn't want Janis to grow up the way I did. I had to change a lot of my attitudes and think what I wanted to do to change myself.

So often the mother is going to support the child. I like to work because it makes me feel more independent. I don't have to rely on anybody else. (Darla, 17 - Janis, 2 years)

Nearly half of all families headed by women live in poverty. Women without a high school education are more likely to head a family than are women who graduated. Yet these women with less education won't be able to earn as much as will their better-educated friends.

It seems ironic—if she doesn't have an education, she can't earn as much money. Yet she is more apt to be the sole wage earner for her family. Life isn't always fair.

FEWER GRADUATES NEED WELFARE

Evidence suggests that women who achieve at least a high school education are only half as likely to live in households receiving AFDC as are women who never graduated.

I'm getting ready to get off welfare although I'll still get MediCal. I don't need welfare. The sooner I get off, the better.

You get lazy. I got lazy. I didn't want to work. I didn't want to go to school. It's better spending money I've earned. I hate it when people just live off welfare.

Now that I'm working and I'm back in school, I feel better about me. People say, "Oh, you have a baby—I guess you dropped out of school." I say, "No, she didn't stop me from going to school. I'm going to graduate with my class." I like school now.

After I graduate, I'm going on to college. My mother said I should be

a lawyer because I like to argue so much. I'd like that. (Candi, 16 - Janet, 18 months)

I was going to stay home until after I had the baby, but when I heard of the special class, I decided to go back to school. I might never have finished high school except my older sister always said I'd be the one who would drop out. I decided to show her.

When Martha was little, we stayed by ourselves for almost a year. I stayed home most of the time, watching TV and being bored. At that time, I wasn't helping myself. I was depending on my parents plus welfare.

But now I'm self-supporting. I feel good about myself because I'm doing it on my own. I've found out I can cope, and I love my job. I'm a nurse's assistant, and I'm taking a medical terminology class.

I think I'm a better mother when I like myself. (Alta, 22 - Howard, 3 years, and Martha, 6 years)

Often it's important not to put off getting your education. If you have graduated from high school, you may decide to go ahead with your training as soon as possible.

After I graduated, I was thinking about not going on to school for a couple of years. Then I thought, if I work for two years, I won't want to go back. So I decided to go on right now. I'll start getting my training to be an R.N. I'd like to work in an emergency room or when they come out of surgery. (Ginny, 17 - Juan, 4 months)

You have to take the chance if you want to get ahead. I used to say, "Well, I'll start school, but if it gets too involved, I'll just quit." Now I'm thinking about the better future I'll have if I get an education.

In September I'm going back to school in the evening. If that doesn't work, I may quit working, get a grant, and go to school full-time. I think I'll put my school first now.

Sometimes I think, "Oh, I have to work," but I want to get ahead. Administration of justice—counseling—something to do with the police force but not out on the street. I always wanted to be a probation officer. (Shirley, 20 - Virginia, 4 years.)

Shirley graduated from high school three years ago when Virginia was fourteen months old. Because she had learned office skills in high school, she started working for the county in the welfare department a few months later. After working directly with people applying for welfare, she has some firm opinions on the subject:

> *You don't get anywhere on welfare. I hear people saying, "I have these two children who are starving . . . " All I can say is if you care for yourself as a person and for those children, you'll go out there and work. I could never get what I want waiting for a check on the first and the fifteenth—I couldn't live off what somebody else gives me just because I have a baby. I want a lot of things for me and my daughter. (Shirley)*

Shirley, who may soon quit her office job to go back to college, points out the advantages of learning basic job skills such as typing:

> *I tried working in a factory and there's nothing there except hard work. If you know a skill like typing, perhaps shorthand, you can get into business jobs where you don't have to work so hard, get so dirty. I think everyone should at least take typing. A lot of people don't like it, but if you can type, you can always find a job. (Shirley)*

Remember, if you complete high school, your chances of being on welfare are half what they are if you drop out before you graduate.

JOB CAN HELP SELF-ESTEEM

Parents who continue their education and hold good jobs obviously are much better off than are parents who quit school and whose only income is their AFDC grant.

Many young mothers also discussed the difference a job can make in the way they feel about themselves. They often mentioned that when a mother thinks well of herself, when she has good self-esteem, she's a better mother than she is when she's unhappy with herself.

> *My being happy has so much to do with mothering. When I was depressed, I couldn't get into mothering Rudy and Joy like I wanted to. I would try to force myself, but I couldn't. Then I would feel guilty.*
>
> *The kids and I had a rough life for about a year after I split. I had realized I didn't love Ellis, that I never did. I didn't love*

him, but I needed him—I don't know why. He was never work-
ing, and I was miserable with him. I was on welfare almost the
entire time. I was so miserable that I hated myself and I hated
him.

Then I started getting stronger. I finally moved into an apart-
ment by myself.

When I went to school to be a medical assistant, I felt so good
because I knew I was doing something for me. I wanted some-
thing in medicine, but I wanted to do it quickly. I have got-
ten into a field I love, that I've wanted to be in ever since I was a
little girl.

That's important. You have got to do things for yourself, you
have got to be happy with yourself before you can be happy with
your kids. (Brigette, 22 - Rudy, 3 years, and Joy, 4 years)

Amy is convinced that staying home with a child is not a healthy
way to live.

I think staying home is a difficult thing for any mother to do. I
think that was the worst three months of my life—staying home
and living on welfare.

It was between college and going to work. The doctor prescrib-
ed Valium because I couldn't handle staying home. I can stay
home one day from work, and I'm dying to go back the very next
day.

Working mothers should remember it's the quality, not the
quantity of mothering. You could be home all day with your kids
and spend no time with them—and you can go to work and come
home and spend one good hour together. (Amy, 23 - Kent, 7
years)

Celia, on the other hand, likes being home with her children and
her husband:

I know the kids are going to grow up, and I don't want to sit
home all the time. I love doing what I'm doing now, but they
won't be this little forever. I want to have something for myself.

So I'm going back to school one night a week this fall. Norm is
pleased that I am.

When I see a young mother sitting home alone with her kids,
doing nothing but waiting on them and her husband, I feel like
saying, "Don't sit home, being bored and getting fat. Your

*husband won't like you any more—and neither will you like your-
self. (Celia, 21 - Lance, 18 months, and Laurel, 4 years)*

Shirley didn't marry her baby's father, but for a long time she
assumed that they "should" marry. But she and Ben changed, and
they finally realized marriage was not a good plan for them. She explained her thinking:

*I'm trying to think more about myself now. I think a lot of
girls get into a situation where they don't think highly of
themselves. For a long time I stuck with Ben because I thought
that was what I deserved. Finally I realized—why should I be taking this when I haven't done anything wrong?*

*We thought our role was me and him and the baby, and even-
tually we were supposed to get married. I think I would have put
myself real low as a person if I had gone on. Neither one of us
was happy. I finally realized we couldn't keep something we had
five years ago. I would think, we used to do this, we used to do
that—but that's what we used to do, not what is happening now.
Now is what is important.*

*We loved each other. I guess we still do because we were each
the first love of the other. It's sad, but I'm happy now. I understand why a lot of girls are on welfare when they're young, but I
think they should try moving on.*

*A woman shouldn't try to stay in the same place. She should
try to make herself a better place. The only way you can be happy is if you have respect for yourself. (Shirley)*

DAY CARE DESPERATELY NEEDED

More than 225,000 babies were born to girls 17 or younger in 1976,
according to the National Center for Health Statistics. Only 8 percent
of these young women released their infants for adoption. The rest are
rearing their children themselves.

Most of these young mothers need day-care services in order to
complete their high school education. Day care isn't available for
teenage parents in most school districts in the country.

Finding day care for her child is a serious problem for many young
mothers. They need to continue their education, acquire job skills,
and work in order to be self-supporting. But to do this, they must
have day care for their children. The lack of day-care services con-
demns many young parents to reliance on welfare income for survival.

Some young parents have a mother who is home at least part of the time. Alison's mother works, but is home by early afternoon. She is willing to take care of Stevie when she gets home, so Alison has planned a work schedule which will permit her to be home with her son during much of his waking time:

GRAND-PARENTS

SCHOOL CHILD CARE

DAY CARE CENTER

FAMILY DAY CARE

HOME VISIT CHILD CARE

I'm going to look for a job soon as a hospital ward clerk. I'll try to get swing shift so I can be here most of the day with Stevie. My mother comes home from work by mid-afternoon. She could take care of Stevie when I go to work.

He stays up late, so I could put him to bed when I get home at 10 or 11 P.M. I'd like to be able to do that. (Alison, 18 - Stevie, 2½ months)

Frank Furstenberg, author of *Unplanned Parenthood: The Social Consequences of Teenage Childbearing,* interviewed 400 pregnant adolescents living in Baltimore in 1966. Many of these young women were interviewed again one, three, and five years after delivery.

Most of the young women (90 percent) lived with a parent or close relative when they were pregnant. Three out of five were living with relatives a year later. Almost half (45 percent) were still with parents or a close relative five years after delivery.

Only one in four of these young women stayed with their families throughout the five-year study. About 10 percent returned home after being married and divorced. Others had moved out on their own, then returned. Only 22 percent, about one in five, were living alone at the end of the five years.

Adolescents who marry often continue living with parents. In Furstenberg's study, one-third of the married mothers were still living with relatives a year after childbirth.

Young mothers who remained with families were likely to be better off economically at the end of this study than were those who left home before or immediately after their child was born. They generally had more education and tended to have better jobs. Apparently the help they received from their families during their early years of parenthood was beneficial.

Many of the young mothers I interviewed spoke of the benefits of living with their families:

> *I've been lucky because my mom watches Art for me. Bill's parents are supportive, too, although he has married and has a little baby now. But his parents have always liked me, and have given me the financial help I need.*
>
> *The hard part has been the mental part of it, realizing I'm only 19 years old and I have a three-year-old son.*
>
> *I have to do something—I can't depend on them for the rest of my life. That's why I'm working and going to school. I want to be independent some day, and I'm not right now. There are times when it's hard, but that's normal. I had a lot of support from my friends, and from his family and mine. (Margie, 19 - Art, 3 years)*
>
> *My mother has been a great help in all this from the beginning. She takes Sharon to school. She also picks her up and takes care of her until I get home.*
>
> *I don't spend as much time with Sharon as I'd like, but I like my job, and it pays good. I'm trying very hard to become somebody important—not fame-wise or anything like that. I just want to make it and survive all of life's problems. And I'm doing fine now. (Marlys, 19 - Sharon, 3½ years)*

IF RELATIVES CAN'T HELP

Many grandparents, of course, are not available for baby-sitting. In the first place, they may not want to care for a child. Perhaps your mother feels she has raised her family and she doesn't want to start over again. You can probably understand her feelings.

Even if she's willing to baby-sit, Grandma may have a job herself. Everyone in your family may already be working. There may be no one at home who will/can take care of your baby for you.

Unless you're one of the lucky few teenage parents in this country whose school offers child care for its students' babies, you have a real problem. You know how important it is to continue your education. Perhaps you've finished high school, but you want to get further job training or go on to college. You may be ready to get a job now, and you don't want to settle for staying home and living on welfare income.

Who will care for your child while you're in school or working?

Most day-care centers are for preschoolers, children who are at least two years old. Many will accept only children who are toilet trained. Your community may not even have a child-care center which accepts babies and toddlers. To find out, check with your school district and with family service agencies.

Family day care may be available. In this arrangement, a person cares for a small number of children in her/his own home. Some day-care homes are licensed, some are not.

In order to provide good day care, one person should be responsible for no more than five children including her/his own. No more than two of these children should be under two years of age.

If you can afford it, you might prefer to find a caregiver who will come to your home to care for your child. Babies and toddlers aren't likely to want the same schedule as you must follow. Being able to let Suzie sleep while you go on to school could be good for both of you.

CHOOSING A CAREGIVER

The decision you make about day care for your child is extremely important. Yet some people appear to put less thought into selecting a caregiver for their child than they do in buying a car! Whether you choose a day-care center, family day care, or a caregiver who comes to your home, be sure you put a lot of thought into your choice.

Ask questions, lots of them. Don't hire the first person you find. Talk to several caregivers, then choose the one you think would be best for your child. One mother described her search for a caregiver for her small son:

I started answering other people's ads in our local paper. Then I ran an ad myself, and that was how I met the best ones.

When people called me, I would ask them a bunch of questions. I could tell from

that first telephone conversation that I didn't want some of them.
I interviewed at least twenty people before I decided.
   I had lots of questions. How many kids did she care for? How
old were they? I'd ask her how she disciplined children. What did
she do when a baby cried? When my son starts crawling, how will
she protect her house? If she said she used a playpen, I usually
marked her off my list.
   If I liked what she said on the phone, I would visit her, preferably
without a lot of advance notice. I wanted to see what her house was
like, how she coped. If she cared for other kids, I would try to visit
while they were there. If her house was too neat, I'd worry.
   Of course I wanted to be sure she had a place for Bryan to eat, to
sleep, to play. What kinds of activities would she have for toddlers?
I asked all sorts of questions. (Tricia, 18 - Bryan, 6 months)

Remember, you're the employer when you hire a caregiver. You're
the one making the decision. You have the right to ask about anything
that might have something to do with your child's welfare. Ideally,
you'll be able to find someone who will care for and love your child
in much the same way as you do when you're with him.

Before you make your selection, be sure to ask if the caregiver takes
care of sick children. If she doesn't, perhaps you have a friend or
someone in your family who is willing to be "on call" for baby sitting
during minor illnesses. Babies and children get sick at inconvenient
times.

Once you find a caregiver, will you continue checking on the kind
of care your child is receiving? If he isn't talking yet, he can't tell you
what is going on when you're gone. Even if he is older, you need to
know as much as possible about his "other home."

You could make excuses to visit your child occasionally at unex-
pected times. This is one way to learn about the kind of care he is
receiving. A good caregiver should welcome your interest and concern.

PAYING FOR CHILD CARE

Finding child care is one thing. Paying for it is another. If you
qualify for AFDC, talk to your social worker. There may be extra
money available for child care while you continue your education or
learn job skills.

If you are on welfare, perhaps you could get into a WIN (Work Incentive) Program. This is a program that provides assistance with on-
the-job training and with enrollment in job-related training programs.

WIN recipients may get extra help with child care, transportation, and other job related expenses while they are in school or in job training.

If you can't afford to pay a caregiver, and you have no one who will take care of your child at no charge, can you trade child-care duties with another young parent? It would be hard to make such an arrangement work if you need to attend high school full-time. If you're interested in attending night school, or if you're a college student, a trade might work.

Schedule your classes so you can care for the other child while her mother is in class. Then she can be responsible for yours while you go to school. It would be hard to care for two children while you're trying to study. It could be a way, however, to get that education you need so badly for your child's sake as well as your own.

WRITING YOUR "LIFE SCRIPT"

Several years ago Arthur Campbell described the effect of an early birth on the life of an adolescent mother (*Journal of Marriage and the Family,* May, 1968). He wrote that a girl who has a child when she is 16 "suddenly has 90 percent of her life script written for her." By "life script" he meant the story of her life, the way she would live throughout her years.

Campbell said the young mother would probably drop out of school and would not be able to find a steady job, a job which would pay enough to provide for herself and her  child. She might feel she had to get married. "Her life choices are few, and many of them are bad," Campbell concluded.

He pointed out, however, that if she could continue her education, improve her vocational skills, find a job, and, when she was ready, marry someone she wanted to marry, her life script would be quite different.

Most of the young women in this book are not settling for a life of hardship because of early childbearing. Instead, many are continuing their education and are acquiring job skills. They are not accepting a life script filled with poverty and unhappiness. But they are finding that "writing" a successful life script is a difficult task.

As Leica points out, single parenting takes a tremendous amount of energy and determination:

> *It's hard to parent on your own. If I had to do it again, I wouldn't. I would do really different because I still want to run around and do my own thing.*
>
> *When I go shopping, Gary goes with me. On the weekends I spend mornings and afternoons with him. Sometimes I go out on Friday and Saturday nights. I spend week nights with him, but soon I'll start a class.*
>
> *When people tell you it's going to be difficult, believe them. It's going to be a lot harder than they say it is. I knew it would be a hassle, but I didn't think it would be as hard as it is being a full-time mother and going to work.*
>
> *I'll start college in the fall, but that will be only for a couple of years. Then it will be easier. But it's going to get harder before it gets easier because I have a lot to do to prepare my life for both of us.*
>
> *I have to be able to support myself and Gary by myself before I go ahead and get married. I don't want to be stuck with no education and no job skills. I want Gary to have the best there is. (Leica, 18 - Gary, 3½ months)*

Even a very young mother can be in charge of her life script . . . *if* she continues her education and acquires vocational skills. For many (most?) young mothers, this will be very difficult.

But you and your child, like Leica and Gary, deserve "the best there is." If you get your education and improve your vocational skills, *you* can be in charge of your life script.

More power to you!

Appendix

Toys to Make
for Children Under Two

The following ideas were compiled by Sally McCullough, head teacher, and the staff of the Tracy Infant Center, Cerritos, California. They generously agreed to have these ideas included here for the benefit of teenagers—parents and non-parents—who read this book.

FIRST AND MOST IMPORTANT: SAFETY NOTES ON TOY MAKING

1. Any pieces you use must be too large for your baby to swallow, or they must be *securely* fastened or enclosed.

2. Thoroughly wash containers, such as plastic bottles, before using them.

3. Always check for rough edges.

4. Paint, embroider, or sew on any facial features for stuffed toys. Be sure all seams are strongly sewn.

5. Don't use staples or any other small fasteners which could come loose.

6. Whenever you use paint, make sure it is *non-toxic.*

7. Don't use masking tape. Babies love patiently to pick it off, chew, and try to swallow it.

8. Loose strings can be dangerous because your baby might try to swallow them or he could become tangled in them. No piece of string should be longer than six inches, and all pieces should be securely tied.

9. Examine toys frequently to make sure they're in good condition.

PICTURE FRAME FOR CRIBS (A First Toy for Infants)

Tie this picture frame to the side of the crib. Simple pictures of faces are particularly enjoyed by young infants.

MATERIALS:
12 by 18 inch rectangle of heavy-weight clear plastic.
Medium-weight yarn in bright colors.
Very simple pictures of faces or shapes.

PROCEDURE:
Overcast edges of plastic with yarn, bringing stitches about ¾ inch in from the edge.
Attach two two-foot lengths of yarn to each corner.
Using clear cellophane tape, attach one or two pictures to the plastic.

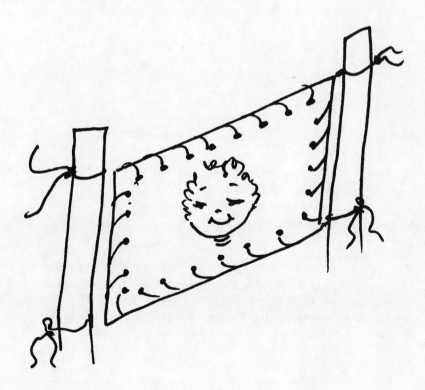

ROLL-A-BELL

MATERIALS:
Two cans of the same size
(soup or 16-ounce).
Three large jingle bells.
These must be too big to
swallow.
Contact paper.

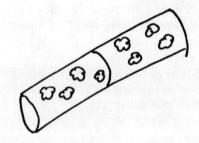

PROCEDURE:
Put the bells in one can.
Tape the open ends of the two cans together.
Cover the two with contact paper on the sides.

NOISE MAKER

MATERIALS:
One 16-ounce vegetable or fruit can.
One 6-ounce tomato paste can.
Six inches of light-weight rope.

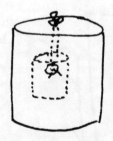

PROCEDURE:
Punch a hole in the bottom of both cans. Check cut edges for any
roughness. Smooth by running a can opener around an extra time.
Tie a knot in the rope. String it from the inside up through the bottom of the tomato paste can, then upward through the hole in the
bottom of the 16-ounce can. Tie another knot in the rope.

PULL-A-CLOTH

This toy may help baby learn to grasp items.

MATERIALS:
One 3-pound coffee can.
Three lids to fit the can.
Eight to twelve large scraps of cloth (voile, velvet, tricot, satin, double knits, burlap, broadcloth, etc.

PROCEDURE:
Be sure top edge of can is smooth. Going around the top of the can with a can opener a second time may smooth the edge.
In one coffee can lid, cut a round hole 2½ inches in diameter. (The child's fist will be able to go through this hole.) In another lid, cut a hole 1½ inches square. (This hole is large enough to encourage the child to grasp the cloth with his palm.)
In the other lid, cut an eliptical hole ¾ by 2½ inches. (This shape will encourage thumb-finger pinching).
Cut the cloth scraps 12 to 18 inches long and just narrow enough to pull through the hole. They should not come through the hole too easily.

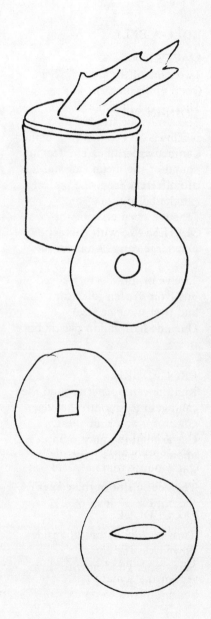

COIN-IN-SLOT

This is an activity your child can manage alone. The feel and sound of the metal can and lids are different from the typical purchased toy.

MATERIALS:
One large can (29-ounce fruit can).
Twelve or more safety edged lids from frozen juice cans (six- and twelve-ounce size).
One one-half gallon plastic bottle.

PROCEDURE:
Run the can opener around the can again to smooth the edge. Check for any roughness.
Cut around the plastic bottle about 3½ inches from the bottom.
Then cut a slot in the center of the bottom ¼ inch by 2¾ inches.
Turn bottom of bottle upside-down over the can.
Show your child how to drop the lids in the can.

VARIATION-SPOOL DROP

MATERIALS:
One 29-ounce tin can.
One half-gallon plastic bottle.
Four to six spools of the same diameter.

PROCEDURE:
Be sure can edge is smooth. Rough edges can often be removed if the
can opener is run around the top a second time.
Cut top part of plastic bottle off—about 3½ inches from the bottom.
Cut a round hole in the bottom slightly larger than the spools.
Turn bottom of bottle upside-down over the can.
Show your child how to drop the spools in the can.

CARTON TUNNEL

Your child will enjoy crawling in and out of the box. Or she may just sit inside for a private quiet time. She would also love to help you paint it if you have wide brushes and tempera paint.

MATERIALS:
A very large carton.
Small carpet pieces.
Pictures.

PROCEDURE:
Lay the carton on its side.
At one end, make a circular hole big enough for your child to crawl through. Cut triangular holes for windows on the sides.
You can make a square hole on the other end. He can crawl through that one, too.
Cut the carpet scraps into squares, triangles, and circles. Pour a thin stream of white glue around the edge of the shapes. When the glue is partially set, press the carpet shapes onto the inside of the box. Hold until it sticks. Also glue magazine pictures inside.

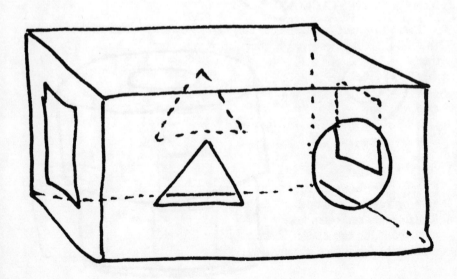

STACKING AND NESTING TOYS

PLASTIC NESTING TOY

This is particularly nice for sand play.

MATERIALS:
One each of three different sizes of plastic bottles (gallon, half-gallon, and quart, each with a round bottom).

PROCEDURE:
Cut each bottle off four inches from the bottom.

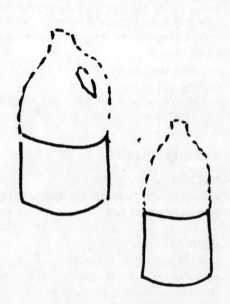

TIN CANS TO STACK AND NEST

These have nice sounds. They can also be used for containers for the child. He'll put objects in them, then take them out again and again.

MATERIALS:
One soup can.
One 16-ounce vegetable or fruit can.
One 29-ounce fruit can.

PROCEDURE:
Check to be sure cans are clean and top edges are smooth. Rough edges can often be removed if the can opener is run around the top a second time.

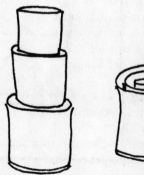

CORNMEAL OR SAND TOYS

Many items normally found in the kitchen will make excellent sand toys. Examples are colanders, cooking spoons, coarse sieves, pots, and metal bowls.

Check the handles of these items. The ends need to be very thick to prevent injuries.

The nesting and stacking toys are good in the sand box also. Here are a few more ideas:

SAND FUNNELS

MATERIALS:
Plastic bottles: one-gallon, half-gallon, or quart size.

PROCEDURE:
Cut the top off at the point where the bottle has reached its full width. These tops make excellent funnels.

SAND PAILS

MATERIALS:
One-gallon plastic bottle. A half-gallon bottle may be used to make a smaller pail.
Thin wire coat hanger.

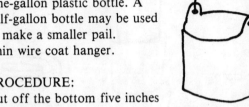

PROCEDURE:
Cut off the bottom five inches of the bottle.
Cut hanger and bend it to make a handle. Insert one end into each side of the top, then bend wire up on the inside so that it is securely fastened.

DRESS-UP CLOTHES

Toddlers enjoy dressing up in bigger clothes. This activity helps promote beginning imaginative play. It also helps them learn self-help skills. Size 4 shirts and sweaters, short petticoats with elastic waists, adult size socks that stretch and will easily pull on over bare feet or shoes are all fun for your child's dressing-up times.

Play hats may also add to the fun.

PLAY HATS

These make durable hats for dress-up time.

MATERIALS:
One-gallon plastic bottle.
Brightly colored yarn.

PROCEDURE:
Cut the bottle off about four inches from the bottom. Contour it into an interesting shape—scallops, duck bill, etc.
Over-cast the edge and decorate with yarn. (A heavy needle will go easily through the plastic.)

TEXTURE BOOK

MATERIALS:
Assorted fabric pieces of different colors and different textures.

PROCEDURE:
Cut the pieces into uniform squares or rectangles, 6'' by 6'' or larger.
Stitch around the edge.
Stitch the fabric pieces together along the left side, forming a book.
These cloth pages can be embroidered or appliqued before you sew
them together to form a book. Choose objects to embroider or appli-
que which your child will recognize.

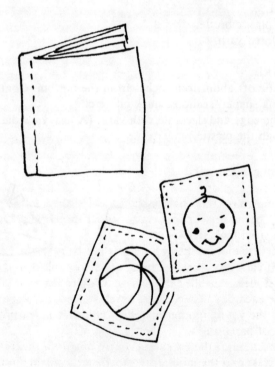

Description of Interview Group

All the young mothers interviewed for this book were enrolled in
the Teen Mother Program at Tracy High School, Cerritos, California,
before, and generally for a short time after, their babies were born.
Started in 1972, the Teen Mother Program is a self-contained class
offered by the ABC Unified School District as an option for pregnant
students.

Academic classes required for high school graduation are an important part of each student's schedule. Equally valuable parts of the program are the special offerings dealing with early pregnancy and
parenthood. Prenatal care, prepared childbirth, and loving, responsible parenting are stressed.

The district also operates a developmental Infant Center on campus.
Students may have their babies and toddlers cared for at the Center
while they attend high school classes either on the Tracy campus or at
another district high school.

Each high school mother who places her baby in the Center spends
one period each day working there, often with her own child. Most
pregnant students enrolled in the Teen Mother Program also work in
the Center each day. The Center, a well-staffed, developmental facil-
ity, offers the young mothers excellent guidance in learning the art
and skills of parenting.

Partly because of the parenting course taught in the Teen Mother
Program class and the laboratory experience available in the Infant
Center, these young parents are certainly not a random sample of

teenage parents.

They are a group of parents who are, by definition, part of the highly publicized "teenage pregnancy epidemic." Most of these young people, however, have very little in common with the stereotype of the 17-year-old mother living alone in the little apartment producing baby after baby, and miserably existing on welfare. Nearly all are working hard at being good parents and productive members of society.

Some of the young women interviewed are relying on welfare for income at this point in their lives. Almost without exception, however, they are eagerly working toward the time when they will be self-sufficient.

Sixty-one young mothers were interviewed. Each delivered a child when she was a teenager.

AGE AT FIRST DELIVERY

Age	13	14	15	16	17	18	Total
Number	1	3	7	25	15	10	61
Percentage	1.6%	4.9%	11.5%	41.0%	24.6%	16.4%	100%

Forty of these babies were less than two years old when their mothers were interviewed. The remaining 21 mothers have first-born children aged two to seven. Eleven have had a second child, nine of them within the past two years. Only six (10 percent) of the total sample had a second baby within two years after delivery of their first-born.

When they were interviewed, twelve mothers had no children younger than two years of age. Interviews with these "older" mothers did not center on caring for babies and toddlers. Rather, they shared their feelings about their personal lives as very young mothers. Most of their "stories" are in Chapters 13, 14, and 15.

Slightly more than half (27) of the students enrolled in the Teen Mother Program during the 1979-1980 school year were interviewed. Those enrolled but not interviewed included those who had moved away or for some other reason were not available for interviews. Several others who did not return to school after a late spring or summer delivery were not interviewed.

In addition to the 1979-1980 students, the interview group included eleven young mothers enrolled in the Teen Mother Program 1978-1979; eleven from the 1977-1978 class; and twelve enrolled some time between 1972 and 1977. The young women from the 1972-1979 classes were selected for interviewing either because they had responded to an earlier letter describing the proposed book, or simply because they were available and willing.

Ethnic make-up of the interview group closely follows that of the school district:

	Anglo	Hispanic	Black	Asian or Pacific Islander	Other	Total
Research Sample						
Number	37	18	5	1	0	61
Percentage	60%	30%	8%	2%	0	100%
School District						
Number	12,332	5,773	1,324	2,812	709	22,950
Percentage	54%	25.1%	5.7%	12.2%	3%	100%

About half of all students enrolled in the Teen Mother Program either marry the baby's father or are living with him by the time their baby is born. The interview sample tended to follow this pattern, with twenty-seven having been married to, or having lived with, the baby's father at some time.

At the time of the interviews, the following relationships were in effect:

Number	Percentages	Relationship with Baby's Father at Time of Interview
11	18%	Married to him.
6	9.8%	Married, then divorced.
8	13.1%	Living with him.
6	9.8%	"With" him but not living together.
2	3.3%	Baby's father is deceased.
28	45.9%	Not involved with him.

The interview sample is weighted toward single mothers because of a special circumstance: single mothers are more apt to stay in school than are married teenagers. Mothers who have stayed/are staying in school at least until high school graduation were preferred candidates for interviewing.

A very high percentage (about 80 percent) of women in the United States who become mothers before age 18 never finish high school. However, slightly more than half (32) of the women in this sample have graduated from high school. Nineteen were still in school at time of interview. Ten had dropped out of school before earning a high school diploma. They had attended school during pregnancy and usually for a time after delivery, but stopped before they graduated.

Nineteen of the 61 women interviewed had dropped out of school *before* enrolling in the Teen Mother Program, nine because of pregnancy, and ten *before* they became pregnant. All nineteen returned to school via the Teen Mother Program. Eight of these former dropouts have graduated from high school, and four are still in school. Perhaps pregnancy was the incentive they needed to continue their education.

Most (51) of the young mothers were living with their parents or another close relative when their babies were born. Five others moved back with parents/relatives sometime later. Only five young women, all of them married at time of delivery, had not lived with their parents or other close relatives after childbirth. The support most of these young women received from their families no doubt played an important role in their positive acceptance of early motherhood.

All quotes in this book are "real." Very little editing has been done except for occasional cutting of repetitious words and statements. Mothers' and children's ages are accurate. Names, of course, have been changed, and often the sex of the child. Occasionally, other identifying data has been altered, but the young women's comments are always their own, not the author's.

For more information about the Tracy Infant Center and Teen Mother Program, contact Jeanne Lindsay, 6595 San Haroldo Way, Buena Park, California 90620.

References

The following resources are mentioned and/or quoted in *Teens Parenting*. For an extensive annotated bibliography of books dealing with adolescent pregnancy, school age parents, and parenting in general, see the separately available Teacher's Guide for *Teens Parenting*.

Barr, Linda, and Catherine Monserrat. *Teenage Pregnancy: A New Beginning*. 1978. New Futures, Inc., 2120 Louisiana NE, Albuquerque, NM 87110.

Furstenberg, Frank F., Jr. *Unplanned Parenthood: The Social Consequences of Teenage Childbearing*. 1976. New York: Free Press.

Gordon, Ira J. *Baby to Parent, Parent to Baby*. 1977. New York: St. Martin's Press.

Gribben, Trish. *Pajamas Don't Matter*. 1979. Sacramento, CA: Jalmar Press.

Hildebrand, Verna. *Parenting and Teaching Young Children*. 1981. New York: Webster Division, McGraw-Hill Book Company.

Koschnick, Kay (ed.). *Having a Baby*. 1975. Syracuse, NY: New Readers Press, Laubach Literacy, Inc.

Lansky, Vicki. *Feed Me-I'm Yours*. 1974. Minnetonka, MN: Meadowbrook Press. Also 1977. Des Plaines, IL: Bantam Books

Leach, Penelope. *Your Baby and Child from Birth to Age Five*. 1978. New York: Alfred A Knopf.

Lindsay, Jeanne Warren. *Pregnant Too Soon: Adoption Is an Option*. 1980. Buena Park, CA: Morning Glory Press.

March of Dimes Birth Defects Foundation. *Preparenthood Education Program*. 1978. White Plains, NY: Supply Division, MOD.

Pizzo, Peggy Daly. *How Babies Learn to Talk*. 1974. Washington, D.C.: Georgia Appalacian Outreach Project of the Day Care and Child Development Council of America.

Thevenin, Tina. *The Family Bed*. 1976. Minneapolis: Thevenin.

U.S. Department of Health, Education, and Welfare, Office of Child Development, Children's Bureau. *Prenatal Care*. 1973. Washington, D.C.

White, Burton L. *The First Three Years of Life*. 1975. Englewood Cliffs, NJ: Prentice-Hall, Inc.

Index

309

ABOUT THE AUTHOR

Jeanne Warren Lindsay has worked closely with several hundred pregnant teenagers and school age parents during the past nine years. She is the teacher/coordinator for the ABC Unified School District Teen Mother Program at Tracy High School, Cerritos, California. Most pregnant students in the district choose to attend this class rather than continue at their regular school during pregnancy.

Ms. Lindsay has an M.A. in Anthropology and an M.A. in Home Economics from California State University, Long Beach. She specialized in child development and the socialization of the child while in graduate school. Her teaching credentials include General Secondary Life, Pupil Personnel Services, and Administrative. She is a member of the California Alliance Concerned with School Age Parents, and she edits the *CACSAP Newsletter*.

Previous books by Ms. Lindsay include *Pregnant Too Soon: Adoption Is an Option; They'll Read If It Matters: Study Guides for Books About Pregnancy and Parenting; You'll Read If It Matters, A Student Manual; Parenting Preschoolers: Curriculum Help and Study Guides* (for teachers); and *Parenting Preschoolers: Study Guides for Child Care Books* (for students).

Ms. Lindsay and her husband, Bob, have five children.

Pam Patterson Morford has illustrated all of Ms. Lindsay's books. Ms. Morford teaches biology at West Lane Junior High School, Indianapolis, Indiana. She and her husband, Norm, have three children.

MAIL ORDER FORM

Teens Parenting—The Challenge of Babies and Toddlers

Quality Softcover - $9.95; Hardcover - $14.95
96 page Teacher's Guide - $5.95.
48 page Student Study Guide - $2.50.
(Quantity Discounts on Book and Study Guides)

Other Books by Jeanne Lindsay

Pregnant Too Soon: Adoption Is an Option - Latest information on adoption together with personal stories of young birth mothers who released their babies for adoption.
Paper (EMC Publ.), ISBN 0-88436-778-9, 204 pp., illus. $5.95.
Hardcover (MGP), ISBN 0-930934-05-9, 208 pp., illus. $13.95.

Two sets of study guide books to be used *with* already-in-print and easily obtainable books about pregnancy and parenting:
They'll Read If It Matters: Study Guides for Books About Pregnancy and Parenting
ISBN 0-930934-00-8, 243 pp., illus., spiral binding. $7.95.
You'll Read If It Matters, A Student Manual
ISBN 0-930934-01-6, 144 pp., illus. $4.95, 10/$45.00.
Classroom Set: one copy, *They'll Read*; and 30 copies, *You'll Read*. $125.00.

Parenting Preschoolers: Curriculum Help and Study Guides (for teachers)
ISBN 0-930934-03-2, 192 pp., illus. $7.95.
Parenting Preschoolers: Study Guides for Child Care Books (for students)
ISBN 0-930934-02-4, 96 pp., illus. $3.95, 10/$35.00.
Classroom Set: one copy, Teacher's Guide; and 30 copies, Student Manual. $100.00.

- -

Morning Glory Press
6595 San Haroldo Way
Buena Park, CA 90620

Quantity		Price	Total
	Teens Parenting: The Challenge of Babies and Toddlers		
_____	Quality Softcover, ISBN 0-930934-06-7	$9.95	_____
_____	Hardcover, ISBN 0-930934-07-5	$14.95	_____
_____	Teacher's Guide, ISBN 0-930934-09-1	$5.95	_____
_____	Student Study Guide, ISBN 0-930934-08-3	$2.50, 10/$20.00	_____
	Pregnant Too Soon: Adoption Is an Option		
_____	Paper, ISBN 0-88436-778-9	$5.95	_____
_____	Hardcover, ISBN 0-930934-05-9	$13.95	_____
	Parenting Preschoolers: Curriculum Help and Study Guides		
_____	Teacher's Guide	$7.95	_____
	Parenting Preschoolers: Study Guides for Child Care Books		
_____	Student Manual	$3.95, 10/$35.00	_____
_____	Classroom Set (*Parenting Preschoolers*)	$100.00	_____
_____	*They'll Read If It Matters* (Teacher's Guide)	$7.95	_____
_____	*You'll Read If It Matters* (Student Manual)	$4.95, 10/$45.00	_____
_____	Classroom Set (*They'll Read, You'll Read*)	$125.00	_____
		TOTAL	_____
	Please add 10% postage/handling (min.-$1.50, max.-$10.00)		_____
	California residents add 6% sales tax		_____
		TOTAL ENCLOSED	_____

NAME _____

ADDRESS _____

_____

MAIL ORDER FORM

Teens Parenting—The Challenge of Babies and Toddlers

Quality Softcover - $9.95; Hardcover - $14.95
96 page Teacher's Guide - $5.95.
48 page Student Study Guide - $2.50.
(Quantity Discounts on Book and Study Guides)

Other Books by Jeanne Lindsay

Pregnant Too Soon: Adoption Is an Option - Latest information on adoption together with personal stories of young birth mothers who released their babies for adoption.
Paper (EMC Publ.), ISBN 0-88436-778-9, 204 pp., illus. $5.95.
Hardcover (MGP), ISBN 0-930934-05-9, 208 pp., illus. $13.95.

Two sets of study guide books to be used *with* already-in-print and easily obtainable books about pregnancy and parenting:
They'll Read If It Matters: Study Guides for Books About Pregnancy and Parenting
ISBN 0-930934-00-8, 243 pp., illus., spiral binding. $7.95.
You'll Read If It Matters, A Student Manual
ISBN 0-930934-01-6, 144 pp., illus. $4.95, 10/$45.00.
Classroom Set: one copy, *They'll Read*; and 30 copies, *You'll Read*. $125.00.

Parenting Preschoolers: Curriculum Help and Study Guides (for teachers)
ISBN 0-930934-03-2, 192 pp., illus. $7.95.
Parenting Preschoolers: Study Guides for Child Care Books (for students)
ISBN 0-930934-02-4, 96 pp., illus. $3.95, 10/$35.00.
Classroom Set: one copy, Teacher's Guide; and 30 copies, Student Manual. $100.00.

- -

Morning Glory Press
6595 San Haroldo Way
Buena Park, CA 90620

Quantity		Price	Total
	Teens Parenting: The Challenge of Babies and Toddlers		
_____	Quality Softcover, ISBN 0-930934-06-7	$9.95	_____
_____	Hardcover, ISBN 0-930934-07-5	$14.95	_____
_____	Teacher's Guide, ISBN 0-930934-09-1	$5.95	_____
_____	Student Study Guide, ISBN 0-930934-08-3	$2.50, 10/$20.00	_____
	Pregnant Too Soon: Adoption Is an Option		
_____	Paper, ISBN 0-88436-778-9	$5.95	_____
_____	Hardcover, ISBN 0-930934-05-9	$13.95	_____
	Parenting Preschoolers: Curriculum Help and Study Guides		
_____	Teacher's Guide	$7.95	_____
	Parenting Preschoolers: Study Guides for Child Care Books		
	Student Manual	$3.95, 10/$35.00	_____
_____	Classroom Set (*Parenting Preschoolers*)	$100.00	_____
_____	*They'll Read If It Matters* (Teacher's Guide)	$7.95	_____
_____	*You'll Read If It Matters* (Student Manual)	$4.95, 10/$45.00	_____
_____	Classroom Set (*They'll Read, You'll Read*)	$125.00	_____
		TOTAL	_____
	Please add 10% postage/handling (min.-$1.50, max.-$10.00)		_____
	California residents add 6% sales tax		_____
		TOTAL ENCLOSED	_____

NAME _____

ADDRESS_____

_____